ENGAGING PUBLIC RELATIONS

A Creative Planning Approach

Third Edition

Bruce L. Smith
Charles O. Kaufman
Gilbert D. Martinez
Texas State University—San Marcos

Kendall Hunt
publishing company

Kendall Hunt
publishing company

www.kendallhunt.com
Send all inquiries to:
4050 Westmark Drive
Dubuque, IA 52004-1840

Printed in the United States of America
10 9 8 7 6 5 4 3 2

CONTENTS

ABOUT THE AUTHORS

Bruce Smith is a professor of mass communication at Texas State University-San Marcos. He worked in radio and television for more than 20 years and is the former chair of mass communication programs in Texas, South Dakota and, Alaska. Smith holds a doctorate from Boston University, an MBA from Murray State University (Kentucky), and an M.S. in Radio/TV/Film from Miami University (Ohio.) His research focuses on advertising creativity.

Charles O. Kaufman is a senior lecturer and internship coordinator at Texas State University-San Marcos. A former business editor and assistant marketing services director at the Austin American-Statesman, Kaufman also worked at The Fort Worth Star-Telegram and the Arkansas Gazette. After a 16-year newspaper career, he started Kaufman Communications, a public relations and corporate communications firm. Kaufman holds an MSJ from Northwestern University's Medill School of Journalism and a BJ from The University of Texas at Austin.

Gilbert D. Martinez is a senior lecturer and assistant director in the School of Journalism and Mass Communication at Texas State University-San Marcos. A former reporter with The Jersey Journal in Jersey City, N.J., he received his JD from Fordham University School of Law in New York. He has written about teaching journalism classes in interactive television classrooms, co-authored an article in *Journalism and Mass Communication Educator* about how journalism instructors learn how to teach, and co-authored a chapter on sampling in research methods in communications.

PREFACE

Why write a public relations textbook? There are plenty in print already. What could we contribute that was sufficiently different to justify putting another one into print?

We wrote this book as a response to years of teaching large sections of introductory PR courses using various textbooks. They were generally well written and thorough in their coverage of public relations history, terminology, and practice. But some important things were missing to make the class more engaging and experiential.

We have observed that most students have little or no prior experience with formal planning of any kind. They also have had no creative problem solving training. Both are important life skills that are useful in many contexts besides public relations. We included chap-

ters in the book on those subjects to prepare students for the planning and creative challenges they may face in their careers.

The heart of the book is Chapter 6: Creating a Public Relations Plan. It is a lengthy chapter because it takes students through the process of creating each section of a plan, including worksheets to guide them through the creation of a 10-part PR plan as a class project. Our hope is that this book can introduce students to the important facts of PR history, theory, vocabulary, and professional practice by engaging them in the creation of a public relations plan that brings the concepts to life. Rather than only reading about other people's public relations strategies and tactics, we want to prepare students to create their own.

OVERVIEW OF PUBLIC RELATIONS

What is public relations? ▼

For many people the image of public relations is blurry. One stereotype is the P. T. Barnum type of press agent who hypes or exaggerates events. Another image is of Washington lobbyists and power brokers such as Jack Abramoff, accused in 2006 of routing illegal contributions to legislators in Congress in exchange for favors for his clients. Another familiar public relations figure is the presidential press secretary who responds to aggressive questioning from the Washington press corps. And of course there is the image of the partying PR professional who mixes with celebrities and organizes social events—the character Samantha Jones from the HBO television series "Sex and the City." All of these images contain elements of truth about public relations, but they do not tell the whole story.

Public relations plays an important role in all sorts of institutions, including education, government, the military, corporations, nonprofits, religious groups, entertainment, sports, travel, fashion, and even agriculture. Today, most large and many small institutions employ public relations professionals.

The U.S. Bureau of Labor Statistics publishes an Occupational Outlook Handbook that estimates job prospects for many different jobs and professions. The 2011 Handbook estimated faster than average creation of jobs in public relations through at least 2018, the last year for which they had projections. The Handbook notes that

> "Employment of public relations specialists is expected to grow 24 percent from 2008 to 2018, much faster than the average for all occupations. The need for good public relations in an increasingly competitive and global business environment should spur demand for these workers, especially those with specialized knowledge or international experience. Employees who possess additional language capabilities also are in great demand."

More than 300,000 people in the United States work full-time in public relations. By 2018, the U.S. Department of Labor estimates that number will rise to 350,000. Moreover, that reflects full-time PR employment only. Many people do public relations as a part of jobs that include other duties. The pastor of a church has public relations responsibilities, for example, as does the owner of a small business. Coaches, artists, musicians, doctors, and lawyers all do some public relations work. Their titles do not indicate that PR is part of the job, but the duties they perform are familiar public relations functions.

The Public Relations Society of America (PRSA) adopted the following definition of public relations in 1988 (prsa.org):

> "Public relations helps an organization and its publics adapt mutually to each other."

The word "organization" is used rather than "company" or "business," because today public relations is used by businesses, charities and other nonprofits, trade unions, schools, religious groups and individual celebrities. The word "publics" recognizes that all organizations have multiple publics or stakeholder groups from which they must earn consent and support. For example, a corporation must be concerned about its relationships with consumers, employees, suppliers, retailers, government regulators, local communities, stockholders and other groups. Finally, the definition of public relations also makes clear the two-way nature of the relationship between an organization and its publics. Effective public relations cannot be based just on outward directed communication targeting publics. PR professionals spend much of their time doing research, listening to feedback from stakeholder groups and communicating what they hear back to decision makers in the organization. This two-way aspect of public relations requires research, planning, communications dialogue and evaluation of message outcomes.

Two-way exchange

Publicists or press agents who handle publicity for celebrities or publicize events have as their goal to attract as much media attention as possible. They use news releases and other tactics to promote a client or event. This is largely one-way communication. The emphasis is on getting messages out to media and getting those messages published or broadcast.

> **The most effective long-term public relations encourages a two-way exchange.**

The most effective long-term public relations, however, is a two-way exchange. Two-way communication in public relations means telling an organiza-

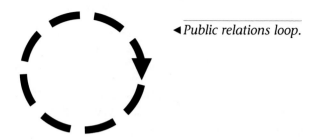

◄ *Public relations loop.*

tion's story effectively. At the same time, it also involves listening carefully to publics to understand their needs and their response to the organization's statements and actions. The feedback from audiences enables an organization to adapt both its actions and its communication. This process is a loop, an endless cycle of communicating with important publics, listening to feedback from them, adapting actions and messages and then repeating the process.

Public relations requires a continuous cycle of communication, listening, adaptation, and communication. **Feedback**—getting information back from key publics—is vital in this process because it closes the loop.

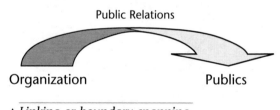

Public Relations

Organization   Publics

▲ *Linking or boundary spanning.*

Public relations **links** or connects an organization and its publics. Another term for this is **boundary spanning.**

Mutually beneficial relationship

Effective public relations should promote win-win relationships with an organization's stakeholder groups. Both the organization and its publics should feel they benefit from the relationship. If public relations tactics deceive or exploit a public, the public will likely become resentful and the reputation of the organization will suffer.

Management function

Public relations executives are generally part of the inner circle or **dominant coalition** of large organiza-

tions. The dominant coalition is the group of people who have the most influence on policymaking and strategy formation at the top of an organization. They provide advice to the organization's leadership. Often, the head of public relations has an office in the executive suite not far from a chief executive officer. The reason? Many actions of organizations have an impact on relationships with employees, customers, regulators, voters, stockholders, and communities. Public relations professionals provide counsel about the likely impact of actions on those relationships. It is a voice that helps organizations to avoid damaging mistakes.

Presidential press secretaries such as the late Tony Snow, Ari Fleischer, and Scott McClellan in the George W. Bush administration were public relations professionals who were part of the inner circle. Their job was to explain administration policies to the media in a timely and accurate manner. Many press secretaries have extensive experience as journalists and understand how journalists gather and report information. Their advice is useful to top policymakers who want to anticipate the reaction of the media and the public.

Deliberate and planned

Proactive public relations encourages deliberate and planned strategic behavior. It constantly monitors the environment of organizations and the feedback coming from various audiences. Public relations professionals set goals and develop strategies and tactics as part of a plan to manage proactively an organization's communication with its publics and perceptions of the organization and its activities. This does not mean that unexpected events and crises do not happen to organizations with strong public relations programs, but they should be less common and more easily managed. When public relations provides proper counsel, and clients listen to that counsel, organizations may avoid crises.

Focus on all publics

Advertising and marketing communication are concerned mainly with communicating with consumers about products and services. Their focus is on external publics, primarily consuming publics. Public relations, on the other hand, is concerned about relationships with all of the publics of an organization, both internal and external. For a corporation, the key publics will include employees, media, consumers, suppliers, stockholders, regulators, legislators or other public officials, and residents of communities where it has operations. Nonprofit groups are concerned about their members, audiences, funding agencies, media, clients, boards of directors, regulators and staff. Universities communicate with current and prospective students, parents, alumni, donors, media, staff, faculty, legislators, regents, state coordinating boards, and accreditors. Managing multiple relationships at the same time is the challenge of public relations.

Reputation management

Reputation is the general (or collective) opinion of an institution or individual. It takes shape over time. Direct and indirect experiences influence reputations. Direct experience occurs when someone works for an organization, buys its products or services, or invests in the company. Indirect experience comes from news coverage, advertising, and word of mouth. The reputation of most organizations is a product of indirect experience through media. Comparatively few people have direct experience with organizations. Media shape our perceptions, good and bad.

Public relations helps organizations build and maintain good reputations. The public relations firm Hill and Knowlton published "Return on Reputation: Corporate Reputation Watch 2006" (hillandknowlton.com). One conclusion it drew is, "Clearing the aftermath of a series of high-profile scandals that have irreversibly changed the corporate landscape, we now live in a business world where perception is valued as much as performance and profit." The report notes that more than "90 percent of analysts agree that if a company fails to look after reputational aspects of its performance it will ultimately suffer financially too.

> People have seen the giant-killing power of failures in corporate reputation and the need to maintain public trust and confidence. However, corporate reputation is a multifaceted concept that constitutes far more than just avoiding scandals. External image has a direct impact on bottom line shareholder value. A positive reputation has commercial benefits. Consumers like to support companies that do good and behave ethically.

> For any company, promoting a positive image to the outside world helps recruit and retain the best staff, increase sales and build successful strategic relationships. But for listed companies reputation

has an even more direct impact on performance through the financial community that grades, rates and invests in them (*hillandknowlton.com*)."

A number of organizations track reputation. Harris Interactive (harrisinteractive.com) tracks corporate reputations and publishes rankings each spring. The 2011 ranking listed the following companies as having the best reputations in the U.S.: (1) Google; (2) Johnson & Johnson; (3) 3M Company; (4) Berkshire Hathaway; (5) Apple; (6) Intel Corporation; (7) Kraft Foods; (8) Amazon.com; (9) General Mills; (10) The Walt Disney Company.

During the same time, Forbes magazine (forbes.com) published a list of the most reputable companies, based on a survey conducted by Reputation Institute (reputationinstitute.com). Their top 10 list had many of the same names: (1) Amazon.com; (2) Kraft; (3) Johnson & Johnson; (4) 3M; (5) Kellogg's; (6) UPS; (7) Fed Ex; (8) Sara Lee; (9) Google; (10) Walt Disney Company. Differences between the two lists probably reflect differences in sampling methodologies and the wording of questions.

Crisis management ▼

Reputations take a beating when highly publicized crises occur. The reputation of Exxon (now Exxon-Mobil) crumbled when the Exxon Valdez hit Bligh Reef in Alaska's Prince William Sound, spilling 30 million gallons of oil and killing an estimated 250,000 birds and thousands of other creatures. Crises involving BP, Toyota, Enron, Ford, and Firestone did similar damage to corporate reputations. Negative news reports can damage the reputations of individuals as well. Rep. Mark Foley of Florida, Sen. Trent Lott of Mississippi, and Rep. Gary Condit of Colorado exited powerful positions in Congress after news accounts questioned their behavior. Even governments are not immune from damage to their reputations. Events in Iraq turned public and media opinion against the United States in much of the world, and public opinion in the United States eventually turned against President George W. Bush, at least partly because of the war.

The goal of public relations is to cultivate a positive reputation for clients and to help them restore their reputations after a crisis. Some organizations do an extraordinary job of responding to crisis and avoiding lasting damage to their reputations. Examples include

Cison Corporate Media Reputation Index
Top Ten Companies (January–March, 2008)

1.	Microsoft
2.	JP Morgan Chase
3.	Apple
4.	Walt Disney
5.	IBM
6.	Verizon
7.	Wal-Mart
8.	Bank of America
9.	AT&T
10	Cisco Systems

SOURCE: *cision.com*

Johnson & Johnson's handling of the famous Tylenol poisoning incident in the 1980s and Odwalla's recall of fruit juice contaminated by E. coli in the 1990s. Both corporations were able to bounce back quickly from the incidents because they responded effectively. Both also had excellent reputations before the crises that gave them credibility with the public and media.

Celebrities experience scandals and missteps that may require PR crisis management. Three examples in recent years include actor Mel Gibson, former Vice President Dick Cheney, and former President Bill Clinton. Gibson's headline-making arrest for drinking and driving became even more scandalous when media reported that he made racist comments to the arresting police officer. Cheney accidentally shot his hunting partner and then waited many hours to visit the shooting victim or to report the incident to the media. President Clinton's conduct in the Oval Office with a White House intern still chases his reputation. Missteps like these can generate a firestorm of negative publicity and badly damage reputations. Public relations professionals develop strategies for responding to unexpected situations and then handle the process of communicating accurate information to the media and public.

Proactive public relations is deliberate and planned.

Crises place organizations on the defensive and force them to respond to events as they occur by explaining their actions to the public. This is *reactive* public relations. The organization must react to events. Whereas proactive public relations maps out a strategy for positively managing public opinion, reactive public relations focuses on damage control.

Large organizations generally have crisis response plans. Crises can and do happen to most organizations—eventually. Safety issues force the recall of products. Environmental disasters happen. The economy goes into recession and personnel layoffs and plant closings become necessary. Sometimes executives engage in unethical or illegal behavior. Bad things happen that no one can predict.

A crisis management plan tries to anticipate the problems most likely to occur in an industry and the steps needed to handle a situation. For example, oil tankers occasionally run aground and spill oil into the ocean. Pharmaceutical companies must recall drugs that prove unsafe after widely reported injuries and deaths. Software makers are the victims of viral attacks on their products. Labor unions initiate strikes against a company or industry and bring operations to a halt. Certain events have a likelihood of happening to organizations, eventually. Crisis plans should anticipate those likelihoods.

No one can know exactly what the specific circumstances of a crisis will be in advance; therefore, crisis management plans should focus on identifying an organization's crisis management team. Which key players in the organization will mobilize to deal with the problem? Who will be in charge? Who will be the spokesperson for the organization and answer questions from the media? A public relations person is usually on a crisis management team. The PR person handles media relations and information generation and distribution. Sometimes a PR professional will serve as the spokesperson during the crisis and answer questions from the media. At other times, the spokesperson may be the head of the organization or a high-ranking executive, and the PR professional's role is to counsel that individual, preparing him or her for press conferences and interviews.

Functions of public relations ▼

What do public relations professionals do? Here is a list of just some of the services that public relations people provide:

▶ Counseling to management
▶ Public opinion research
▶ Media relations
▶ Publicity
▶ Crisis management
▶ Employee/member relations
▶ Community relations
▶ Speech writing
▶ Government relations
▶ Lobbying
▶ Issues management
▶ Investor relations
▶ Industry relations
▶ Development/fund raising
▶ Multicultural relations
▶ Special events
▶ Social media management
▶ Publication writing and editing

Public relations tactics

Public relations professionals use many different tactics to achieve objectives for clients. The process of creating a public relations plan and choosing appropriate objectives for the plan receives greater depth in later chapters. The decision to use particular objectives depends on the objectives, the target audience(s) and the resources of the client. The most common tactics, traditionally, were the following:

▶ News releases
▶ Media kits
▶ News conferences
▶ Interviews

▶ Feature articles
▶ Special events
▶ In-house publications

The traditional tactics were print focused and emphasized getting stories into newspapers and magazines. Electronic media such as television and radio required public relations practitioners to develop variations of traditional tactics for those media. Today, most clients want an online presence in the interactive new media, requiring very different tactics such as the following:

▶ Web site
▶ YouTube videos
▶ E-mail
▶ Facebook, LinkedIn, Twitter and other social media sites

Job titles ▼

For a variety of reasons public relations professionals may not have the words "public relations" in their job titles. The military refers to public relations as "public affairs." Corporations often use the title "corporate relations." Universities and other nonprofits prefer "public information" or "media relations." PR professionals may have such other titles as:

▶ Corporate communications
▶ Corporate relations
▶ Marketing communication (often shortened to Marcom)
▶ Community relations
▶ Publicist
▶ Press agent
▶ Media relations
▶ Public information
▶ Communications coordinator
▶ Communications specialist
▶ Publicity manager
▶ Marketing public relations
▶ Customer relations
▶ Consumer affairs
▶ Community affairs
▶ Promotions director
▶ Constituent relations

It is wise to assume that most organizations have one or more people responsible for public relations. Depending on the nature of the organization, however, titles may obscure the function and make it less than obvious as to who is doing the organization's PR work. This may occur because "public relations" has some negative baggage. Ironically, a profession that is about reputation building and management, itself has a poor reputation in many circles. Some organizations avoid the phrase for that reason. Others blend PR functions with other responsibilities and choose a job title that may not reflect the PR responsibilities associated with it.

Flack and spin ▼

Some negative terms used to disparage public relations professionals are **flack** (sometimes spelled flak) and **spin doctor**. Journalists use the term flack as a pejorative (expression of contempt) for PR people. It has existed since the 1930s. While there is debate about the origin of the term in reference to public relations, its military meaning refers to artillery aimed upward to target aircraft. PR professionals have the image of slick spokespersons that deflect criticism directed at their clients much like artillery flack shoots down or diverts incoming aircraft.

A spin doctor originally referred to a politician or campaign that used unethical or misleading tactics. One of the earliest uses of the term appeared in a New York Times article in 1984 following the Reagan/Mondale presidential debate. Spin now refers more generally to any effort by PR people to find a positive side to a story. The spin doctor attempts to minimize negative news coverage by getting ahead of a story and redirecting the story's focus, much like applying spin to a baseball or a golf ball to control its direction. Putting a positive "spin" on a story is an attempt to redirect the story's focus from negative to positive, or at least to counterbalance negative information with a positive perspective.

William Safire was a political columnist for The New York Times and also an etymologist, or a historian of words. In his book, "New Political Dictionary," he defined spin as the "deliberate shading of news perception; attempted control of political reaction." Eric Dezenhall, in his book "Damage Control" (2007), says there are limits to spin. He asserts, "You can only spin a public that wants to be spun—reinforcing existing sentiments and prejudices, rather than reversing fundamental positions." In a sense, spin only works if the

IMAGE © DUNDANIM, 2009. USED UNDER LICENSE FROM SHUTTERSTOCK, INC.

▲ *Before the term became associated with public relations, flak referred to a type of German anti-aircraft cannon used in World War II.*

public wants to believe the story you are trying to tell. If the story is too contrary to the prior opinions and beliefs of the public, they will not buy it.

Is spin ethical? David Guth and Charles Marsh (2006) argue that if PR people use "accurate information within an appropriate context—there is no problem. . . . it is only when one attempts to distort, hide or mislead those ethical concerns arise. Of course, everyone operates within his or her own frame of frame of reference. For that reason, one person's 'facts' may be another's 'spin.' "

The focus of publicists is narrow while the focus of public relations is expansive.

PR and publicists ▼

People often confuse the broad profession of public relations and the job of the publicist. They are not the same thing. Journalists tend to think of all PR people as publicists, but there are important differences. Publicists focus on one PR task: They seek media coverage of stories about their clients. Their job is to get publicity. Public relations, on the other hand, is a management function. Seeking publicity is part of the job, but public relations professionals have a broad concern with reputation and with relationships with many different publics. The focus of publicists is narrow while the focus of public relations is expansive.

PR and journalism ▼

The primary skill of journalists is writing and storytelling. Journalists focus on the presentation of fair and balanced information. They communicate to mass audiences often through a single mass medium. A newspaper reporter, for example, usually writes exclusively for a newspaper. TV journalists do stories for television. That is changing to some degree because of the Internet, where print and video journalism have converged on many Internet sites. Still, most journalists concentrate on storytelling in one medium or another, whether written, videographic or photographic.

Public relations professionals perform a wide variety of tasks. Writing is part of the job, but so are management counseling, organizing special events, planning, budgeting, and speechwriting. PR people solve problems and communicate with different publics using print, electronic and other media. A PR person is an advocate for a client and has no compulsion to take the balanced and objective perspective of a journalist.

PR and advertising ▼

Advertising involves buying space and time in mass media generally to sell products and services. The focus of advertising is on external audiences, particularly consumers. It is part of the **marketing mix** of an organization. The mix, called the **4-Ps**, includes product, price, placement, and promotion. Advertising and public relations are both part of the promotion component of the marketing mix.

In advertising, **gatekeepers** are not much of an issue. Gatekeepers are the editors and reporters who choose which news stories to cover, what angle to take, which facts to include, and where a story will appear in a publication or on air. Since advertisers purchase space and time, they have guaranteed placement of their messages. They have substantial control over when and where messages appear.

Public relations focuses on both internal and external audiences. PR is also part of the promotion component of the marketing mix, but its concern is with more than marketing. Public relations professionals communicate with many publics to build relationships and improve awareness and understanding of everything from institutions to ideas. PR uses interpersonal communication and mass media to reach publics. Public relations seeks free media coverage of newsworthy events. The downside of free media placement is that gatekeepers become more influential. Reporters and editors decide which stories are newsworthy and how to report on them. PR professionals have little control over how media use a story.

Reach and **frequency** are advertising terms. Reach refers to the number of different people reached with a message. Frequency refers to the number of times the average audience member is exposed to a message. Advertising has considerable control over reach and frequency because advertisers buy the time or space in the media to place their messages. Advertising can largely guarantee reach and frequency. Many public relations messages are subject to gatekeepers like editors and reporters who make reach and frequency less predictable. A news release, for example, may go out to many publications, but not get used by any of them. The result: zero reach and frequency. Another news release might be published widely and even picked up by a national news service or network. The audience in that case might be huge. A more contemporary example is YouTube. Only 10 or 20 people might watch a video posted on YouTube, or it could go viral and reach millions at virtually no cost to the client. Such a viral success would be a home run, but outcomes are unpredictable.

The process that public relations people use to create PR plans, strategies and tactics are intended to make reaching out to audiences with messages on behalf of clients as effective as possible. PR can deliver credible messages to large audiences, in spite of the frustrating barrier that gatekeepers can present, but it requires a deliberate process that is organized and strategic.

Marketing public relations focuses specifically on PR that supports the marketing and advertising programs of an organization. The targeted audience consists usually of consumers, and advertising and public relations messages integrate to reach them more effectively. Public relations professionals are generally uncomfortable reporting to marketing executives because of the narrow focus of marketing public relations on selling products and services. PR professionals often feel that such a narrow focus ignores other important stakeholder groups. A separate, more independent public relations department is, they feel, better able to communicate with the community, regulators, employees, stockholders and other important audiences.

Integrated marketing communication (IMC) ▼

A trend during the past 20 years is to integrate advertising, public relations, and other marketing activities such as sales promotion into a single strategy. **Integrated marketing communication**, or **IMC**, is an effort to coordinate messages from different parts of an organization to provide a consistent view of the organization that can achieve maximum impact. In the past there was little coordination between the people who handled advertising, sales promotion, and public relations. Consumers sometimes received mixed messages about products and institutions. Today, most advertising campaigns have a public relations component just as public relations plans often include some advertising. The goal is to integrate all messages seamlessly so they tell the same story. In practice, only a degree of integration usually occurs because of turf battles between the different advertising, public relations, and marketing specialists.

Looking at integration from the point of view of audiences is important. Every communication from and about a client affects the reputation of the client. Some messages are planned. An advertisement or news release sent to the news media serve as planned messages. However, audiences also notice unplanned messages resulting from a PR crisis. So are positive and negative mentions on social media. A viral YouTube video that holds a client up to ridicule can be very damaging. A poor performance by a corporate executive at a news conference or while testifying in front of a Congressional committee can also do mischief to a client's image. Integration, or IMC, means trying, to the extent possible, to coordinate and manage all forms of communication about a client, with the goal being to minimize the number or dissonant or conflicting messages. In other words, it is an effort to tell the same, consistent story about a client's products, priorities and values. Since unplanned events and crises occur, all communication cannot be managed and integrated, but consistent messaging remains the goal.

Role of PR in organizations ▼

The status and role of public relations in organizations varies considerably. Some PR departments concentrate on journalistic and technical duties such as writing news releases and speeches and responding to media inquiries. In other situations, public relations has a visible role at the highest levels of organizations, providing counsel to top management and participating in the development of corporate plans and strategies.

The role of public relations in a particular organization is a product of many factors. Large, complex organizations are likely to incorporate PR into the policymaking process because experience has led them to understand that public policy issues, public attitudes, and corporate identity all affect the bottom line. They know that success is more difficult if an organization is at odds with its many publics or has developed a poor reputation because of a highly publicized crisis or simple neglect of institutional identity. If top management sees public relations as part of the dominant coalition, then PR people usually have considerable authority and autonomy.

In a small company, a few people in a single department typically handle advertising and public relations. Smaller institutions may relegate public relations to a technical role. A single individual or a small staff working with limited resources and many responsibilities may perform PR functions. Management may not look for advice and expect only that staff execute strategies.

PR people themselves play a role in determining the importance of public relations in an organization. Traditional practitioners who come out of newspaper journalism may feel most comfortable writing news releases, editing publications, and performing other technical tasks consistent with their training and experience. Individuals trained more broadly in the management functions of public relations are also comfortable doing research, engaging in problem solving, and providing counsel to management. The skills and interests of practitioners can affect the role they play in organizations.

Outsourcing of public relations ▼

Increasingly, organizations are **outsourcing** some or all of the functions of public relations to public relations firms. Outsourcing is the delegation of non-core operations from internal staff to an external entity. Organizations do it to save money and to focus energy on critical competencies. A company that makes bicycles, for example, may decide that what they know best is how to make bicycles. They contract public relations work to an outside company that specializes in PR, so that they can focus on their core business.

Public relations firms do everything from provide specialized services such as writing and distributing news releases or drafting speeches to the full planning and execution of complete PR plans. Using a PR firm may be a more cost effective way of obtaining professional services. Many companies outsource at least some of their public relations activities.

An organization might need many or just a few services from a PR firm. Among the services that PR firms provide are the following:

- ▶ Executive speech writing
- ▶ Marketing communication (Marcom)
- ▶ Research and evaluation
- ▶ Writing and distribution of news releases
- ▶ Production of video news releases
- ▶ Writing and production of annual corporate reports
- ▶ Planning of annual corporate stockholder meetings
- ▶ Crisis communication
- ▶ Media analysis
- ▶ Community relations
- ▶ Events management
- ▶ Public affairs
- ▶ Employee communications
- ▶ Branding and corporate reputation
- ▶ Investor relations
- ▶ Analyst relations
- ▶ Executive media training
- ▶ Integrated marketing communication
- ▶ Lobbying

Advantages of PR firms

PR firms offer many advantages over trying to do all public relations **in-house**. In-house refers to a department within an organization. PR firms typically have access to a broad range of skills and expertise, including specialty areas that few in-house departments can provide. Many PR firms are part of corporate conglomerates that also operate advertising agencies, which facilitates the integration of all marketing communications. The largest public relations firms have global operations with offices around the world, making it easier for organizations to communicate effectively everywhere they have operations. Perhaps most importantly, PR firms can approach the problems or challenges of an organization with objectivity. Outsiders see situations from a fresh point of view, developing strategies with less reverence for how things happened in the past. This objectivity can become an asset to an organization that may want to energize its public relations program with new strategies and tactics. PR programs can become stale and tired, and an infusion of new thinking can become invigorating.

Disadvantages of PR firms

Outsourcing public relations has some risks and disadvantages. A new relationship with a PR firm involves start-up time for the outsiders to learn about the client and its issues. The PR firm may never have more than a superficial grasp of the client's problems. Most PR firms work with many clients and do not make the full-time commitment to a client's needs that an in-house staff of PR professionals can.

Use of a PR firm can generate resentment from the client's in-house public relations staff who may regard the employment of outsiders as a put-down, feeling that they could have handled the job internally. Using a PR firm may also cost more than using an in-house PR department, especially if the organization requires many services.

Compensation of PR firms

Large PR firms charge retainer fees that guarantee the firm's availability to handle a client's needs. The retainer fee includes a defined amount of monthly services based on an estimate of the client's needs. Charges for additional services use hourly billing rates for staff plus reimbursement for out-of-pocket expenses. This system is similar to the way attorneys use retainer fees.

If a client's annual budget for public relations is $120,000, for example, the client will pay the public relations firm $10,000 per month. This relatively small budget would buy perhaps 70 hours of service per month from a PR firm, supporting several team members who work on the account.

Employees of the PR firm who work on a client's account charge their time at individual hourly rates against the monthly fee. If services exceed the monthly retainer fee, the PR firm may add the additional cost to the next month's billing. This system of compensation guarantees the client the support of a public relations firm to meet its needs. The PR firm knows that its client will compensate it for the services it provides.

Sometimes firms quote a fixed fee for doing a project. Firms that specialize in doing news releases charge a set fee for writing and distributing releases. Speech writing specialists charge at a set rate as well. Firms that specialize in designing and constructing exhibits for conferences or planning grand opening ceremonies may also work on a fixed fee basis. This compensation system involves more risk for a PR firm because inaccurate estimates of time and expenses may result in costs that exceed income, and it may not be able to recover the added expenses from the client. Project fees must accurately estimate expenses to avoid unprofitable contracts.

Staffing of PR firms

While titles can vary, PR firms generally employ vice presidents or general managers to oversee the operation of regional offices. These managers spend much of their time selling a firm's services to prospective clients to win new business for the firm. Account supervisors are in charge of one or more account teams. **Account executives** report to supervisors, have direct contact with clients, and handle most day-to-day activities. They are the primary link between the firm and its clients. Assistant account executives (sometimes called account coordinators) do routine work such as compiling lists and writing rough drafts of news releases. The assistant account executive is the usual entry-level position for new employees, including recent college graduates. Many firms hire outside contractors to handle specialized tasks such as photography, specialty writing, video production, and publication design.

Global PR firms

The largest public relations firms have global reach. Most are part of conglomerates that also own advertising agencies. Here are brief profiles for six of the best-known PR firms.

Burson-Marsteller

Burson-Marsteller, founded in 1953 has more than 50 wholly owned and 46 affiliate offices around the world. It is part of the WPP Group, one of the world's largest communication companies with 91,000 employees in 106 countries. Based in New York City, Burson-Marsteller represents such clients as McDonald's, The Coca Cola Company, and Merrill Lynch & Company. Harold Burson, one of the founders of the firm, is still involved. Web site: burson-marsteller.com

Edelman

Edelman has more than 3,000 employees in 51 offices worldwide and is the world's largest independent PR firm (not part of a conglomerate). Based in New York City, it began operation in 1952 and has represents General Electric, Microsoft, Pfizer, Samsung, Wal-Mart and other major corporate clients. Web site: edelman.com

Fleischman-Hillard

Fleischman-Hillard was founded in 1946 and is based in St. Louis. It is part of the Omnicom Group of New York (NYSE: OMC), which also owns three of the 10 largest advertising agencies in the world. Fleischman-Hillard has more than 2,000 employees in 80 offices worldwide. Its clients include Proctor & Gamble, AT&T, UPS, Visa, and Yahoo! Web site: fleischman.com

Ketchum

Omnicom Group also owns Ketchum. Founded in 1923, Ketchum has its corporate headquarters in New York City. It has 24 owned offices and 41 affiliates. Its clients include FedEx, IBM, and Kodak. Web site: ketchum.com

Weber Shandwick

Weber Shandwick also has more than 3,000 employees working at it 119 offices in 72 markets. Based in New York City, it was founded in 2001 from the merger of The Weber Group and Shandwick International. The Interpublic Group of Companies owns it. Its clients include American Airlines, ExxonMobil, GM, MasterCard, and the Milk Processor's Education Program (got milk?). Web site: webershandwick.com

Hill & Knowlton

Hill & Knowlton is one of the oldest PR firms, founded in Cleveland in 1927. Like Burson-Marsteller, it is part of the world's largest global marketing communication conglomerate, WPP Group. Based in New York City, H&K has 73 offices in 41 countries, including 19 in the United States, and it employs 3,000 people. Its clients include Hewlett-Packard, McDonalds, Motorola, and Proctor & Gamble. It has represented such countries as China, Australia, Botswana, Japan, India, Uganda, and Vietnam. Web site: hillandknowlton.com

Public relations skills ▼

Successful public relations practitioners need both communication and creative problem-solving skills. Also helpful are an instinct for persuasion and an ability to make compelling presentations to sell ideas. Some skills are technical, such as writing and editing news releases and other publications. Other useful skills relate to the management function of public relations: analyzing problems, developing creative strategies for solving problems, and making convincing presentations that sell ideas.

The Web site of the Public Relations Student Society of America (prssa.org) lists the necessary skills for success in public relations:

- ▶ Effective written communication
- ▶ Persuasive speaking/ presentational skills
- ▶ Problem solving
- ▶ Decision making
- ▶ Coordination and organizing
- ▶ Conceptualizing
- ▶ Objective thinking
- ▶ Active listening
- ▶ Editing
- ▶ Research/information gathering
- ▶ Production skills (desktop publishing, layout, graphics)
- ▶ Computer skills (basic plus desktop publishing and Internet)
- ▶ Networking/people skills
- ▶ Time management
- ▶ Stress management
- ▶ Multi-tasking

The weekly magazine "PR Week" publishes an annual "Career Guide" for students considering careers in public relations. Their advice is to learn traditional media relations skills but also to become familiar with word-of-mouth marketing, blogging, New Media, and other evolving ways of communicating. Also of value are an international perspective and understanding of financial practices and legislative and regulatory issues.

The U.S. Department of Labor, in its Occupational Outlook Handbook, suggests the following skills for PR professionals:

"In addition to the ability to communicate thoughts clearly and simply, public relations specialists must show creativity, initiative, and good judgment. Decision-making, problem-solving, and research skills also are important. People who choose public relations as a career should have an outgoing personality, self-confidence, an understanding of human psychology, and an enthusiasm for motivating people. They should be assertive but able to participate as part of a team and be open to new ideas."

Learn traditional media relations skills but also become familiar with word-of-mouth marketing, blogging, New Media, and other evolving ways of communicating.

The Public Relations Society of America describes a typical workday for a PR professional on its Web site (prsa.org), illustrating why a diverse set of skills is so important.

"Public relations offices are busy places; work schedules are irregular and frequently interrupted. The junior employee may answer calls for information from the press and public, work on invitation lists and details for a press conference, escort visitors and clients, help with research, write brochures, deliver releases to editorial offices, and compile media distribution lists.

Employees will brief their management on upcoming meetings, help write reports, speeches, presentations and letters, research case histories, help produce displays and other audiovisual materials, proofread copy, select photographs for publication, arrange for holiday and other remembrances, conduct surveys and tabulate questionnaires, and work with letter shops and printers.

Public relations programs operate against deadlines. Under such high-pressure conditions, nine-to-five schedules go out the window. Public relations executives do not sit at their desks for long periods. Meetings, community functions, business lunches, travel assignments, special speaking and writing commitments and unscheduled work on 'crisis' situations often mean long hours."

Traditionally, most public relations people trained as journalists, especially print journalists. That background assured that they had the writing and media experience that PR values. While writing and media knowledge are still important, there is an increased emphasis on management, planning, and logistical skills. Aspiring public relations professionals are encouraged to learn technical skills such as photography, writing, graphic design, and new skills for communicating on the Internet. They are also encouraged to study economics, finance, marketing, political science, organizational communication and other subjects that will contribute to their understanding of how businesses and other organizations operate. Businesses must be profitable to continue to exist and public relations professionals should understand the forces that influence the success of organizations both from inside (employees, stockholders) and outside (consumers, regulators, legislators, and communities). Broad training is the best preparation for success in this environment.

Review questions

1. What are the key parts of the definition of public relations?
2. How do advertising and public relations differ?
3. How do public relations and publicity differ? Stated differently, are PR practitioners and publicists the same thing?
4. What are the advantages of outsourcing PR to a public relations firm?
5. What role do PR people play in anticipating and responding to crises?

6. What is integrated marketing communication (IMC)?
7. Why would PR people resent working primarily on marketing public relations?
8. What do the terms spin and flack mean?
9. What are the important skills that a PR practitioner should have?

Supplemental resources online

http://fleishmanhillard.com/	Fleishman-Hillard Communication
http://www.frankwbaker.com/	Media Literacy Clearinghouse
http://www.hkstrategies.com/	Hill and Knowlton Communication
http://www.holmesreport.com/	PR agenda news, rankings
http://www.medialit.org/	Center for Media Literacy
http://www.prfirms.org	Council of Public Relations Firms
http://www.prsa.org	Public Relations Society of America
http://www.prssa.org	Public Relations Student Society of America
http://www.prwatch.org	Center for Media & Democracy: PR Watch
http://www.webershandwick.com/	Weber Shandwick Public Relations

Chapter references

Bureau of Labor Statistics, U.S. Department of Labor, *Occupational Outlook Handbook, 2010–11 Edition*, Public Relations Specialists, on the Internet at http://www.bls.gov/oco/ocos086.htm (visited January 03, 2012).

Dezenhall, Eric & Weber, John. (2007). *Damage control: Why everything you know about crisis management is wrong*. New York: Penguin Books.

Ewen, Stuart. (1996). *PR! A social history of spin*. New York: Basic Books.

Guth, David W. & Marsh, Charles. (2006). *Public relations: A values-driven approach*. Boston: Allyn & Bacon.

Lattimore, Dan, Baskin, Otis, Heiman, Suzette T., Toth, Elizabeth L, & Van Leuven, James K. (2004). *Public relations: The profession and the practice*. New York: McGraw-Hill.

Newsom, Doug, Turk, Judy Van Slyke, & Kruckeberg, Dean. (2004). *This is PR: The realities of public relations*. Belmont, CA: Wadsworth.

Pratkanis, Anthony, & Aronson, Elliot. (2001). *Age of propaganda: The everyday use and abuse of persuasion*. New York: W. H. Freeman and Company.

PRWeek Career Guide. (2006). New York: Haymarket Media.

Seitel, Fraser P. (2007). *The practice of public relations*. Upper Saddle River, NJ: Pearson Education, Inc.

Wilcox, Dennis L., Cameron, Glen T., Ault, Phillip H., & Agee, Warren K. (2003). *Public relations: Strategies and tactics*. Boston: Allyn and Bacon.

HISTORY OF PUBLIC RELATIONS

Early history ▼

Public relations is not new. People have been trying to influence one another throughout history. More than 2,000 years ago, the Romans coined the phrase, *Vox populi, vox Dei,* the voice of the people is the voice of God. This does not mean that the voice of the people is either wise or good, only that it is powerful and difficult to resist. The Romans recognized that public opinion matters.

Propaganda is an old concept, too. The word comes from the Latin verb *propagare,* which means to reproduce, propagate, or enlarge. Pope Gregory XV created the *Congregatio de Propaganda Fide* or "Congregation for Propagating the Faith", a committee of cardinals established in 1622 to counter the global spread of Protestantism. The term originally referred to the missionary efforts of the Catholic Church, but it came to be associated with the spread of all sorts of opinion, information, and political causes. The negative connotations of the word stem particularly from its use during wars in the 20th century.

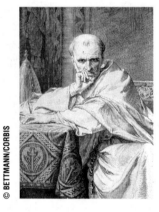

◄ *Pope Gregory XV is credited with an early use of the word propaganda.*

© BETTMANN/CORBIS

Colonial America practiced public relations. American colonies sent pamphlets to Europe promoting the ideal conditions in the colonies. The colony of Georgia, for example, actively recruited Scottish Highlanders to settle and farm. Virginia, in the 1620s, sent a pamphlet to England encouraging settlement. The pamphlet boasted of large brick houses, fertile land for farming, clean water, and air. The pamphlet failed to mention harassment by Indians and the illnesses and harsh weather that frequently plagued the colonists.

During the American Revolution, revolutionaries used public relations tactics to generate support for American independence. The Boston Tea Party was a dramatic protest against the unpopular English Tea Tax of 1773. Fifty men masquerading as Mohawk Indians boarded three ships and dumped their cargo of tea into Boston Harbor. Other seaports copied this act of resistance, which was, in today's PR parlance, a superbly *staged PR event.*

Another example of a dramatic event during the revolutionary period that converted effectively to propaganda was the Boston Massacre. On March 5, 1770, British soldiers on the Boston Common shot five men to death. The word massacre implies the savage killing of a large number of people. Referring to the death of the five men as a "massacre" transformed the dead into martyrs and gave the event a symbolic importance that may have transcended the actual historical events. One definition of massacre is "the act or an instance of killing a large number of humans indiscriminately and cruelly." By that definition, the Boston Massacre probably was not a "massacre." Referring to the Boston event as a massacre gave it greater importance as a rallying focus for disaffected American colonials.

After the Revolutionary War, much debate ensued about how to structure the government of the new Republic. A constitutional convention in 1787 drafted a constitution for the new nation. Adoption of the constitution required the ratification of all 13 states. Support for the Constitution and the system of government it envisioned was not universal. Half the states ratified it quickly, but the other half were less sure and the process was hard-fought.

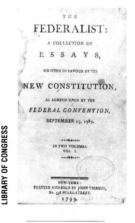

LIBRARY OF CONGRESS

▲ *The Federalist Papers*

The "Federalist Papers," a series of 85 pamphlets published in 1787 and 1788, helped to generate support for the formal creation of the United States and the passage of its Constitution. Some have called the collection of essays one of the best public relations campaigns in history. Written by Alexander Hamilton, John Jay and James Madison under the pen name "Publius," they first appeared in New York newspapers. Later bound together in a book, the essays collectively became known as the "Federalist Papers." Their purpose was to convince New York voters to ratify the proposed constitution.

◄ *Amos Kendall*

Andrew Jackson was the first president of the United States to employ a full-time public relations person in the White House. Jackson hired Amos Kendall, a Kentucky newspaper editor, as the first presidential press secretary in the 1820s. Kendall later became Postmaster General of the United States.

Public relations also helped move people west to settle the frontier of North America. Stephen F. Austin widely publicized the availability of land in Texas and invited colonists to settlements along the Brazos and Colorado Rivers. He published details of a land grant that offered 640 acres to the head of a family, 320 acres for his wife, 160 acres for each child and 80 acres for each slave. Hundreds of families came to Texas attracted by Austin's promotional efforts.

◄ *Stephen F. Austin*

Industrial revolution ▼

In the late 1800s, the world began to change. Industrialization, mechanization, and urbanization changed the character of the United States, especially its cities. People moved from farms to the cities in search of jobs in factories. Millions of immigrants flocked to the United States, especially from Europe, seeking opportunity. They, too, settled in the already crowded and polluted cities.

Conditions were ripe for social unrest. Investigative journalists began to write stories that exposed the appalling conditions of the working class and the extravagant lives of the industrialist families and corporate trusts that controlled much of the nation's wealth. Ida Tarbell wrote articles about John D. Rockefeller and his oil interests for the national magazine "McClure's." A compilation of the articles became a book titled "The History of the Standard Oil Company" (1904). She receives the credit for triggering an investigation that eventually led to the breakup of Rockefeller's Standard Oil Company under the 1911 Sherman Anti-Trust Act.

Nellie Bly was a newspaper reporter who wrote investigative stories about child labor, unfair working conditions, and low wages. She is most famous for an exposé of a New York insane asylum. She had herself admitted as a patient to observe conditions from the inside. Her stories about spoiled meat, beatings from the staff, and hours spent sitting on hard wooden benches from which staff would not allow patients to move led to a grand jury investigation and improvements in funding and care at such institutions. The newspaper articles eventually became a book, "Ten Days in a Mad-House" (1887).

▲ *Nellie Bly*

Upton Sinclair examined the lives of immigrant workers and meat handling practices in the Chicago

◄ *Upton Sinclair*

meat packing plants. His novel, "The Jungle" (1906), influenced President Teddy Roosevelt to order an investigation of the meat packing industry, which led to the passage of the Pure Food and Drug Act in 1906. Sinclair was more of a social crusader than a journalist. Some would say he was a propagandist for the popular socialist movement in the early 20th century, writing about social class struggles and inequities.

◀ *Teddy Roosevelt*

President Teddy Roosevelt was a political reformer and was concerned about some of the extreme industrial practices of his day, but he also railed against the investigative press, calling them **muckrakers** in 1906. He intended it as a slam, but it became a badge of honor among journalists. Muckraking refers, literally, to cleaning a horse stall. To muck a stall is to remove manure. Roosevelt's use of the term referred to a character in John Bunyan's book, "Pilgrim's Progress," published in 1675. The muckraker in the book worked in a stable and only looked downward to rake the filth. Roosevelt thought investigative journalists' reports about corruption, child labor, slums, crime, and unsanitary conditions in the food industry were excessively strident and negative. Roosevelt believed that journalists were mired in the muck like the character in "Pilgrim's Progress." Like the muckraker in Bunyan's story, Roosevelt thought journalists focused so much on misconduct that they could not or would not see the many positive things that were going on around them at the same time. In a speech on April 14, 1906, Roosevelt said:

> "Now, it is very necessary that we should not flinch from seeing what is vile and debasing. There is filth on the floor, and it must be scraped up with the muck rake; and there are times and places where this service is the most needed of all the services that can be performed. But the man who never does

anything else, who never thinks or speaks or writes, save of his feats with the muck rake, speedily becomes, not a help but one of the most potent forces for evil."

By the early 1900s, wealth in the United States had become concentrated. A few industrialists such as Jim Fisk, Jay Gould and Andrew Carnegie, and families such as the Rockefellers and Vanderbilts, had accumulated astonishing wealth. The popular press began to refer to the wealthy as **robber barons**. Both the wealthy and the corporate trusts they controlled became social villains. Pressure mounted for social change.

Revolutionary fervor and socialist political movements were sweeping Europe and becoming popular in the United States as well. Families such as the Rockefellers realized that negative public opinion was a force that they could no longer ignore. It was in this climate of conflict and social unrest in the early 20th century that the birth of modern public relations took place.

Three pioneers of public relations
▼

Many people contributed to the creation and development of the public relations profession. Three individuals made particularly distinct contributions:

▶ Phineas T. Barnum
▶ Ivy Ledbetter Lee
▶ Edward L. Bernays

P. T. Barnum

P. T. Barnum is famous for having said, "There's a sucker born every minute." Some Barnum historians say that it was actually Barnum's competitor who said it, but somehow the statement became attached to Barnum and stayed with him ever since.

◀ *P. T. Barnum, 1810–1881*

Barnum was the master showman. "Life" magazine named him as one of the 100 most important people of the millennium, dubbing him "the patron saint of promoters." He is associated with **hype**—the aggressive promotion of people or events making shrewd use of media and other techniques. Barnum mastered the use of the **staged event**—events created just to give reporters something to report.

Barnum created the largest circus of his time, and eventually collaborated with others to create the Ringling Brothers Barnum and Bailey Circus. A tradition of the circus was to parade down Main Street in towns across the country to generate interest and publicity for the circus. That is an example of a staged promotional event.

Puffery refers to advertising claims that no one takes seriously. No one believes, for example, that polar bears drink Coca Cola. We permit advertisers to use some exaggeration to enliven their messages. P. T. Barnum, however, developed a reputation for going beyond puffery to outright lies to promote his events. He gets credit for being partially responsible for the negative image of public relations.

One example of a Barnum fraud was his promotion of former slave Joice Heth. Barnum claimed that Heth was 161 years old and had been nanny to George Washington. An autopsy conducted after Heth's death proved that she was only about 80. Barnum's association with such outrageous claims secured his image as press agent, huckster, and promoter. He influenced the evolution of the public relations profession with his imaginative approach to promotion.

Ivy Lee

Sometimes known as the first PR practitioner, Ivy Lee created a "Declaration of Principles" that called for honest communication with the public on behalf of a client. He helped to evolve the job of the public relations practitioner from promoter and press agent to counselor. He advised the Rockefellers, the Vanderbilts, and other major industrialists as they dealt with their image problems in the early 20th century.

Lee became famous for helping the Rockefeller family respond to a nationally publicized event in 1914, the death of dozens of men, women and children in Ludlow, Colorado. Coal miners in western states had been trying for years to join the United Mine Workers of America labor union. The coal operators

◀ *Ivy Ledbetter Lee, 1877–1934*

PRINCETON UNIVERSITY LIBRARY

IVY LEDBETTER LEE PAPERS.
PUBLIC POLICY PAPERS.
DEPARTMENT OF RARE BOOKS
AND SPECIAL COLLECTIONS.

led by the Rockefeller-owned Colorado Fuel and Iron Company bitterly opposed them. The mineworkers were on strike in Ludlow, living in tents. On April 20, 1914, the tents were sprayed with machine gun fire and set ablaze. Newspaper accounts portrayed the events in compelling terms. The Rocky Mountain News, in Denver, wrote:

> "The blood of women and children, burned and shot like rats, cries aloud from the ground. The great state of Colorado has failed them. It has betrayed them. Her militia, which should have been impartial protectors of the peace, have acted as murderous gunmen."

John D. Rockefeller, Jr. hired Ivy Lee to rehabilitate the image of the Rockefeller family after Ludlow. Lee advised Rockefeller to go to Colorado, where he met with miners, went into the mines, and even danced with the miners' wives. Lee's strategy was to humanize Rockefeller through personal contact with the miners and to show concern for their conditions.

PHOTO COURTESY ROCKEFELLER ARCHIVE CENTER

▲ *John D. Rockefeller, Jr., visiting with coal miners in Ludlow after the massacre.*

In the past, many companies tried to conceal problems and to resist sharing information with the press. Lee advised them to come clean. He said that eventually the public would find out the facts and it was better for companies to manage how the information came out. Unfortunately, for Lee, his association with Rockefeller and the Ludlow Massacre earned him the nickname "Poison Ivy," a negative moniker that he carried for the rest of his life. Lee earned the nickname, in part, by unknowingly distributing to the media information that later proved false and misleading.

Lee articulated a set of principles that professionals still follow today:

▶ Business should align itself with the public interest and not fight it.

▶ PR people should deal with top executives and carry out only programs supported by management.

▶ Companies should be open and honest with media. Tell the truth. Give only facts.

▶ Companies and owners should be humanized to make them understandable to employees, customers, and the public.

Edward Bernays

Edward Bernays named and literally wrote the book on public relations. Activities that we now call public relations were termed propaganda until almost the mid 20th century. German use of the word propaganda in both World Wars made that word unpopular. Bernays coined the phrase public relations counselor as an alternative name for the profession. He viewed PR professionals as comparable to attorneys, counseling clients.

Bernays wrote several books about public relations, including "Crystallizing Public Opinion" in 1923 and "The Engineering of Consent" in 1955. He also taught the first university course about public relations, at New York University in 1923. He lived to be 103 years old and had a profound influence on the evolution of the profession. He was still active giving speeches and offering professional advice after he was 100 years old.

> *Bernays believed that the consent of the people could be "engineered" through a persuasive program of public relations.*

Bernays expanded the profession of public relations into the more ambitious and controversial realm of seeking to influence and change public opinion and behavior. He founded "modern" public relations. He coined the phrase "the engineering of consent," based on Thomas Jefferson's statement that "in a democracy everything depends on the consent of the people." Bernays believed that a persuasive program of public relations could "engineer" the consent of the people.

To understand how Bernays approached the practice of public relations it is important to know that his uncle was Dr. Sigmund Freud, a pioneer in the field of psychoanalysis. Bernays communicated often with Freud and took the innovative approach of applying modern social science methods to the practice of public relations. He believed that by using psychology one could better understand public opinion and design communication programs that achieved the desired public responses. Some of his critics said that "engineer" really meant manipulate and accused Bernays of manipulating public opinion.

Bernays believed in what communication theorists now call the **two-step flow** of public opinion. He felt it was most important to target and persuade opinion leaders who, in turn, would influence the opinions of the masses. Information would flow first to opinion leaders and then down to the masses. Bernays had a negative opinion of the public. The masses, Bernays

◀ *Edward L. Bernays, 1891–1995*

Two Step Flow

| Opinion Leaders |
| Public Opinion |

▼ ▼ ▼

Ludlow Massacre
SONG BY WOODY GUTHRIE

It was early springtime when the strike was on,
They drove us miners out of doors,
Out from the houses that the Company owned,
We moved into tents up at old Ludlow.

I was worried bad about my children,
Soldiers guarding the railroad bridge,
Every once in a while a bullet would fly,
Kick up gravel under my feet.

We were so afraid you would kill our children,
We dug us a cave that was seven foot deep,
Carried our young ones and pregnant women
Down inside the cave to sleep.

That very night your soldiers waited,
Until all us miners were asleep,
You snuck around our little tent town,
Soaked our tents with your kerosene.

You struck a match and in the blaze that started,
You pulled the triggers of your gatling guns,
I made a run for the children but the fire wall
    stopped me.
Thirteen children died from your guns.

I carried my blanket to a wire fence corner,
Watched the fire till the blaze died down,
I helped some people drag their belongings,
While your bullets killed us all around.

I never will forget the look on the faces
Of the men and women that awful day,
When we stood around to preach their funerals,
And lay the corpses of the dead away.

We told the Colorado Governor to call the
    President,
Tell him to call off his National Guard,
But the National Guard belonged to the
    Governor,
So he didn't try so very hard.

Our women from Trinidad they hauled some
    potatoes,
Up to Walsenburg in a little cart,
They sold their potatoes and brought some guns
    back,
And they put a gun in every hand.

The state soldiers jumped us in a wire fence
    corners,
They did not know we had these guns,
And the Red-neck Miners mowed down these
    troopers,
You should have seen those poor boys run.

We took some cement and walled that cave up,
Where you killed these thirteen children inside,
I said, "God bless the Mine Workers' Union,"
And then I hung my head and cried.

Words and Music by Woody Guthrie
© 1958 (renewed) by Sanga Music, Inc.
Copyright 2000–2006,
The Woody Guthrie Foundation and Archives

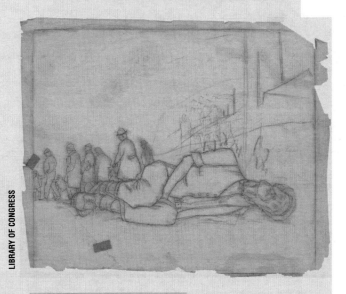

LIBRARY OF CONGRESS

▲ *Ruins of the Ludlow tent camp,
after the massacre.*

▲ ▲ ▲

said, did not want to think for themselves and were ready to accept opinions from better-informed opinion leaders. The challenge of public relations was to communicate effectively with those leaders, then let their opinions filter down and shape the views of the masses.

One example of the use of psychology to change public opinion was a campaign Bernays created for the American Tobacco Company in 1928. American Tobacco was frustrated that society regarded it as improper for women to smoke, especially in public. To expand its market the tobacco company hoped that Bernays could change the negative perception of cigarette smoking by women. Bernays realized that it was not sufficient to advertise to women or to show women in ads with cigarettes. A social stigma required change, and society's ideas about cigarettes and women had to change before a marketing campaign could become effective.

On Easter Sunday, 1928, Bernays convinced a group of New York socialites to walk down Fifth Avenue in the Easter parade. In front of press cameras the women lit up and declared that the cigarettes were "torches of freedom." This act transformed cigarettes into symbols of woman's suffrage and liberation. Even years later the cigarette brand Virginia Slims continued to use that strategy, promoting its cigarettes with slogans like, "You've come a long way baby." Almost overnight, because of Bernays' staged event, women smoked in places where they had not been permitted to smoke before, and cigarette sales increased by 300 percent in the next several years.

For Bernays it was important to understand first why women did not smoke and then to make it socially acceptable for them to smoke. He felt that it was pointless to advertise cigarettes to women until the stigma against smoking ended. Applying psychology helped Bernays to understand the problem and to develop a creative strategy for solving it.

An important figure in the life and career of Bernays was his wife Doris Fleischman. She worked closely with him on many public relations campaigns, although she was invisible to clients. Corporate clients at the time were uncomfortable working with women in business. Bernays did much of the direct contact work with clients, while Fleischman handled details of the campaigns in the background. They were an unusual couple for the time because both worked, they never had children, and Fleischman chose to keep her own name. She is sometimes called the "mother" of

public relations, just as her husband gets credit for being one of the fathers of the profession.

Bernays envisioned full professional status for public relations practitioners, similar to lawyers and doctors. He wanted states to license PR professionals and require rigorous training and screening tests. He was disappointed that it never happened and frequently complained that anyone could set up shop and call him or herself a public relations counselor.

World wars ▼

Public relations played a key role in both World Wars. The first problem public relations (or propaganda as it was called at the time) faced was to break down resistance to military involvement. Americans did not want to become entangled in World War I. They viewed it as a European conflict and had to be convinced that American interests were at stake. Once embroiled in the war, the public needed persuasion to conserve vital materials and to buy Liberty Bonds used to finance the war effort. Public relations helped to sell both acceptance of the war and support for sacrifices on the home front that were necessary to sustain the war effort.

A journalist named George Creel headed the Committee on Public Information, known as the Creel Committee, during World War I. The Creel Committee created propaganda directed at the American public. Edward Bernays worked with Creel and became impressed by the effect that a well-orchestrated information campaign could have on public opinion. When the war ended, Bernays decided to use the promotional skills he had learned

▲ *Posters were widely used during both World Wars to promote the war effort.*

during the war for peacetime purposes, such as helping businesses to promote themselves.

Elmer Davis, another former journalist, played a similar role during World War II, heading the Office of War Information. Besides handling war news for the home front, the OWI launched an information and propaganda campaign overseas. One of the legacies of Davis' work was the creation of the Voice of America in 1942, a system of broadcasting to foreign countries that still exists today.

Corporate public relations ▼

One of the earliest examples of corporate public relations occurred in the 1890s. The companies of Thomas Edison and George Westinghouse competed fiercely with each other over the adoption of a standard for electric systems in the United States. Edison General Electric Company controlled patents and promoted a direct current system, or DC. The Westinghouse Company developed and acquired patents for an alternating current or AC system. Only one system would prevail to become the national standard because the systems were incompatible. Both companies tried to persuade legislators, investors, community leaders, and the public that their system was preferable.

One strategy used by Edison was a fascinating example of public relations. In 1888, the State of New York decided to switch from hanging to using the electric chair for executing condemned criminals. Electrocution seemed faster and more humane. The state chose the AC system of Westinghouse to power the first electric chair. Edison used scare tactics to try to persuade the public that AC power was so dangerous, even lethal, that it was the "executioner's current."

Westinghouse took legal action to try to prevent the use of his AC system for electrocutions. In the end, AC current technology was adopted for both electrifying cities and powering the electric chair. The decision was based on the inherent technical merits of AC over DC technology for large-scale electrification. The public relations campaigns of the two competitors probably factored little in the outcome.

Another important figure in the history of corporate public relations was Arthur W. Page, vice president of public relations at AT&T from 1927 to 1946. Page advanced the acceptance of public relations as a management function. He insisted that he would only take the job at the telephone company if he were involved in policymaking at the highest level of the company. He helped PR to gain acceptance as part of the dominant coalition in the executive suite of large corporations.

Like Ivy Lee, Arthur Page espoused a philosophy of public relations that included these guidelines (prmuseum.org):

▶ Tell the truth.
▶ Prove it with action. Listen to the customer.
▶ Manage for tomorrow—anticipate the future.
▶ Conduct PR as if the whole company depends on it. Consider PR impact of all actions in advance.
▶ Convince employees that public relations is everybody's job in the corporation.
▶ Remain calm, patient, good-humored.

Public relations has evolved over the years from a focus on generating publicity to a sophisticated application of the social sciences. Rather than just writing press releases and staging publicity events, public relations professionals today provide counsel to management at the highest level of many organizations.

Review questions

1. Who were the key figures in the history of public relations and why was each important?
2. How is the term propaganda connected to the Catholic Church?
3. What is muckraking and how did it influence the creation of the new profession of public relations?
4. Who coined the phrase, "the engineering of consent?" What does it mean?
5. Who outlined a Declaration of Principles for public relations, and what were they?
6. What were the PR guidelines espoused by Arthur W. Page and Ivy Lee?

Supplemental resources online

http://faculty.camdencc.edu/abreve/prhistory/home/home.htm	PR History
http://www.prmuseum.com	PR Museum
http://www.ptbarnum.org	P. T. Barnum
http://www.prmuseum.com/awpage/awpage_1.html	Arthur Page
http://www.teacheroz.com/WWIIpropaganda.htm	Propaganda
http://www.voanews.com	VOA

Chapter references

Ewen, Stuart. (1996). *PR! A social history of spin.* New York: Basic Books.

Lattimore, Dan, Baskin, Otis, Heiman, Suzette T., Toth, Elizabeth L., & Van Leuven, James K. (2004). *Public relations: The profession and the practice.* New York: McGraw-Hill.

Pratkanis, Anthony, & Aronson, Elliot. (2001). *Age of propaganda: The everyday use and abuse of persuasion.* New York: W. H. Freeman and Company.

Serrin, Judith, & William, Serrin (Eds.) (2002). *Muckraking! The journalism that changed America.* New York: The New Press.

Sloan, William David, & Startt, James D. (1996). *The media in America: A history.* Northport, AL: Vision Press.

Stauber, John, & Rampton, Sheldon. (1995). *Toxic sludge is good for you! Lies, damn lies and the public relations industry.* Monroe, Maine: Common Courage Press.

Tye, Larry. (1998). *The father of spin: Edward L. Bernays & the birth of public relations.* New York: Crown Publishers.

Wilcox, Dennis L., Cameron, Glen T., Ault, Phillip H., & Agee, Warren K. (2003). *Public relations: Strategies and tactics.* Boston: Allyn and Bacon.

COMMUNICATION THEORY

Definitions ▼

Some understanding of communication theory is useful for public relations practitioners. It provides perspective on how communication happens and why people behave the way they do. The application of theories can help PR people create public relations programs and messages that are more effective.

A **theory** is a generalization about some facts or phenomenon or a way of explaining why something happens. Theories bring together rules, ideas, principles, and observations and try to make sense of them. In addition to providing an explanation, theories are useful because they make it possible to predict or speculate about future events.

A **model** uses theory to create a representation of a system or a process. Models try to explain relationships between the parts of a system. Models often have diagrams that illustrate relationships and the sequence of events in a system.

Goals of communication ▼

People communicate with one another for a variety of reasons. Some of the common goals of human communication include

- ▶ To inform
- ▶ To persuade
- ▶ To motivate
- ▶ To achieve mutual understanding

In an interpersonal setting an individual might teach someone to use a new electronic device (inform). Two people may argue about which political candidate will do the best job (persuade). A mother may coax a child to finish eating the vegetables by promising a cookie as a reward (motivate). Intimate friends may discuss a conflict they had and seek resolution (mutual understanding). Public relations pursues the same goals: A corporation may inform consumers about a new product, persuade people to try the product, motivate them to call an 800 number to order the product immediately, or work with a community to achieve some mutual understanding when the company needs community support to get zoning variances and other approvals before expanding its facilities.

SMCR model ▼

One of the oldest models of communication is the **SMCR model**. It illustrates the key components of the communication process:

> **S** ource
> **M** essage
> **C** hannel
> **R** eceiver

The **source** is the originator of communication. The source can be an individual, a small group, a corporation, or an agency of government. In interpersonal communication, the source is one individual or a small group. In mass communication, including public relations, the source is often an entity or an institution.

The **message** is the content that the source seeks to communicate. Examples of messages in mass communication include news, advertisements, product announcements, corporate earnings reports, and political positions. In interpersonal communication, one person conceives a message. In mass communication, many people may become involved in the creation of a message. A corporation may hire an ad agency to create a television commercial. The ad may require input and approval from dozens of people at both the client organization and the ad agency. Mass media messages are usually the product of groups of people.

Channels are the media through which transmission of communication messages occurs. In interpersonal communication, the channel could be nonverbal (gestures, written) or verbal. People may be in close proximity or communicating at a distance via some

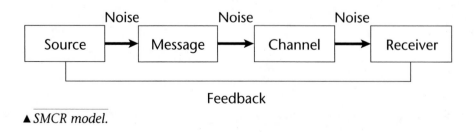

▲ *SMCR model.*

electronic medium such as telephone, e-mail, or text message. In mass communication, the channels are mass media, such as newspapers, television, radio, magazines, the Internet, and books. Public relations makes use of both interpersonal and mass communication channels.

There are five types of communication channels:

1. Mainstream media (newspapers, radio, television, magazines, etc.)
2. Interactive media (Internet, video games, cell phones, interactive television, etc.)
3. Controlled media (media owned by an institution, such as a corporate magazine)
4. Events/groups (speaking to a club, rally, convention, etc.)
5. One-on-one (interpersonal)

Receivers are the recipients of messages. In interpersonal communication, receivers are an individual or a small group. In mass communication, the receivers are usually mass media audiences. Public relations communicates to individuals, small groups, and mass audiences.

Other components of the communication model include **noise** and **feedback**. Noise is anything that interferes with the effective transmission of a message from the source to the receiver. Noise could be physical, such as a poor telephone connection, or it could be semantic, such as a poorly worded message that the receiver cannot understand. Semantic noise occurs when a message is poorly conceived or developed, badly worded, or uses words that receivers do not understand. Noise can occur anywhere in the communication process: source, message, channel or receiver.

Feedback is return communication from receivers to the source of a message. In interpersonal communication, feedback could be a head nod, a yawn, a question, or laughter. Feedback helps message sources to determine whether message transmission, understanding, and acceptance occurred. It gives the source the opportunity to modify future communication to make the connection between source and receiver more effective.

Some feedback in public relations is immediate, such as one-on-one discussions and speeches to small groups. Politicians in a live debate get immediate feedback from a studio audience. If it is a televised debate, however, the candidates cannot see the television audience to gauge understanding and acceptance of messages. This delays the feedback in mass communication, and it could take hours or days to measure—political polls published the day after a debate are an example of delayed feedback.

Barriers to communication ▼

Problems proliferate in the communication process as the number of receivers increases. The most effective two-way communication is two people talking to one another. Feedback is immediate, and it is easy to adapt to feedback. Small groups are more complicated. The feedback is still immediate but a bit more difficult to interpret. Big groups are more complicated still. Giving a speech to thousands of people in an auditorium can be a daunting task. In theory, feedback is immediate. In practice, it is impossible to see or hear most of the audience.

Communication via mass media involves the most barriers to effective communication. The process involves groups of people in institutions constructing messages. These people transmit the messages to mass audiences via mass media technologies. The opportunities for physical and semantic noise are huge when the process involves so many people.

To be successful PR messages must . . .

▶ be received (exposure)
▶ get attention (attention)
▶ be understood (perception)
▶ be believed
▶ be remembered (retention)
▶ be acted upon

Exposure

The first barrier to overcome is message exposure. Public relations must choose channels of communication that will reach the targeted receivers. This means choosing the right media. For example, fewer young people read newspapers and watch TV news, while older audiences are less involved with blogs and the Internet. Message exposure depends on making the right choices about which media to use.

Selective exposure is the tendency of people to expose themselves to messages with which they agree or which are relevant to their needs at a particular moment. Political liberals may avoid the radio program of Rush Limbaugh while conservatives might avoid programs on the MSNBC cable network. We avoid messages that are contrary to our opinions. There are so many media messages bombarding us that we avoid exposure to those we do not like or do not need. The challenge in public relations is to get the right audiences exposed to a client's messages—audiences for whom the messages are relevant.

Once professionals select the media, they must choose the particular media *vehicles*. If magazines are the medium of choice, for example, the next question is, "Which magazines?" Should they place messages in Business Week, Seventeen, Sports Illustrated, or People? The audiences for each publication are quite different. Making the wrong choices could waste a lot of money by putting a message in front of an uninterested audience.

Another challenge is to disseminate messages accurately through the filtering process of the media gatekeepers who control distribution of information or messages. Many public relations messages serve as the basis for news stories. A news release is sent to a newspaper. The newspaper decides whether to report on the event and write a story. If a story receives coverage, it will give considerable free publicity to an organization. However, what will the story say? Is the story accurate? Is the story the one that the organization wanted to tell or did the media pursue a different angle and make the focus of the story something different?

Reporters and editors are the gatekeepers who decide which stories are covered, what the stories will say, and where the stories will appear in the media. The goal of public relations is to see that stories are both covered and covered accurately. There are no guarantees, however, because PR people cannot control the editorial process of the news media.

Attention

Messages must also get attention. Each day thousands of media messages bombard us. It is impossible to digest all of them. There would be no time to do anything else. Most messages to which we are exposed do not get our attention. Filtering occurs through a process called **selective attention**. There are, for example, countless billboards along any Interstate highway vying for our attention, but we notice only a small percentage of them. Most billboards are irrelevant to our needs as we pass them. For a person driving cross-country who is becoming hungry and tired, however,

billboards for restaurants and hotels become relevant and get noticed.

The challenge for public relations is to create messages that break through the clutter of competing messages and get attention. It helps if the messages, like billboards advertising hotels and restaurants, are in the right place at the right time to meet the needs of motivated audiences.

> *For public relations, the challenge of selective perception is to transmit a message accurately from source to receiver without too many changes in the meaning.*

Perception

Everyone has attitudes, opinions, and beliefs through which we interpret incoming messages. **Selective perception** involves the interpretation of a message, which can differ from person to person. Sometimes receivers interpret messages differently from what the message source intended. It is likely that any large group of people will interpret or perceive a particular message somewhat differently from one another. Each individual applies his or her experience, knowledge and attitudes to the process of interpreting of the message. Some people will perceive the message much as the source of the message intended. Others might take away a completely different meaning from the same message. For public relations, the challenge of selective perception is to transmit a message accurately from source to receiver without too many changes in the meaning. The construction and delivery of messages must enable target audiences to understand them accurately.

If a message contains information that conflicts with our behavior or beliefs, a state of **cognitive dissonance** or discomfort exists. Until the resolution of this dissonance, we feel uneasy. There are several ways to deal with information that makes us uncomfortable. We can discount the credibility of the source of information or the accuracy of the information itself. We can rationalize that the problem does not apply to us or we can change our beliefs to fit the new information.

If a new car buyer reads in a newspaper that a leading product safety group found the model just purchased unsafe, the consumer experiences discomfort or dissonance about the purchase. He or she can resolve the dissonance in several ways. The consumer might say that the testing methods used were unrealistic and unfair. Automobile manufacturers often use this strategy when confronting a challenge to one of their products. Some consumers will believe it. A consumer might also rationalize that he does not drive in the manner that would trigger the product defect, again rendering the information irrelevant. Finally, the consumer might accept the information as true and regard the purchase as a mistake. He might try to sell the vehicle or get his money back. All of these strategies would enable the consumer in this example to resolve the state of cognitive dissonance.

Retention

The final filter that message receivers apply to incoming messages is that of **selective retention**. No one can remember every message he or she reads or hears. It is not possible. An individual is more likely to recall important and relevant messages than those that are not. The challenge of public relations is to construct messages in memorable ways and to persuade audiences that the messages are important enough to remember.

Acceptance, attitude change, action

If messages successfully jump over all the other hurdles, the hope is they can then gain acceptance (belief that they are true), change attitudes when necessary, and motivate audiences to take some action. A politician, for example, hopes that voters will believe his messages, respond favorably to them, and vote for him on Election Day. In practice, few messages are so effective that they can overcome all the barriers and motivate receivers to take action. Most falter along the way.

Hypodermic needle theory ▼

The **hypodermic needle** theory suggests that media have an immediate and powerful effect on audiences. Paul Lazarsfeld and other scholars articulated the theory in the 1950s. It addressed a contemporary concern of the era about propaganda campaigns in World War II and the Cold War. Media seemed to have the power to overwhelm audiences and command cognitive and behavioral change. The theory conceived of media as

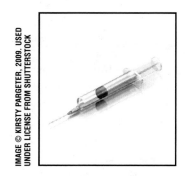

◄ *The hypodermic needle theory suggests that communicators can almost inject an idea into an audience and the audience will accept it. Stimulus-response.*

so powerful that they could inject ideas into the minds of audiences, who would be powerless to resist the messages. Another name for this idea is the "magic bullet" theory. People saw messages as bullets that professionals could fire into the heads of audiences. This is a cause-and-effect type of theory. They thought media messages were so powerful that they could cause immediate changes in thinking.

The problem with this theory is that it assumes that audiences have little ability to resist media messages. Message receivers in this model appear as passive receptors who will believe whatever the media tell them. Subsequent research has found that the stimulus-response model is a poor predictor of behavior in the real world. The communication process and individual behaviors are too complicated to explain with such a simplistic model. The emphasis today is on understanding the many factors that influence attitudes, beliefs, and behavior. In fact, for public relations practitioners, audience resistance to accepting messages is one of the big challenges of the job.

Uses and gratifications theory ▼

Audiences come to media for different reasons and play an active and goal-driven role in choosing media. The same person might watch television with a variety of different goals in mind. She might want to see a weather forecast for the next Saturday as she plans her weekend. She watches an old movie for entertainment. She might tune into a cable news channel to hear a discussion on a subject that interests her. She might even watch a cable TV shopping channel to make a holiday purchase. In the same way, she has a variety of reasons for reading newspapers or magazines, listening to the radio, and surfing the Internet. **Uses and gratifications theory** tries to explain why people use media.

This is relevant in public relations because professionals must tailor messages to the needs of audiences to whom they direct them. It is important to understand why people use a particular **medium** and a particular **vehicle** within a medium. Medium is the singular word for *media*. Television is a medium. Radio, newspapers, magazines, books, and the Internet are each a type of medium. More than one medium becomes the plural—media. A media vehicle is the particular magazine, radio station, television program, book title, or Internet site. If someone watches "South Park" on television, for example, then television is the medium and "South Park" is the vehicle.

There should be a match between messages and media. If a particular media vehicle, like "South Park," is light entertainment for people seeking to relax, the audience might not welcome a serious commercial and could ignore it, leave the room, or change the channel. An amusing commercial for a popular consumer product would be a better fit and more appropriate to the tone and content of the media vehicle in which the ad appears. The commercial with a more serious message would likely work better if placed in a news or other informative program.

Media perform four functions according to uses and gratification theory:

▶ **Surveillance.** Media allow us to monitor our environment and events around us. News and weather are classic examples of the surveillance uses of media. Media also help consumers learn about products and services to inform their purchase decision making.
▶ **Entertainment/diversion.** Much media serves the purpose of enabling us to relax and escape from our routines and problems.
▶ **Personal identity.** Media can be a source of messages that reinforce opinions and values and guide individuals to greater self-understanding.
▶ **Personal relationships.** Sometimes media serve as companions and substitutes for interpersonal relationships. Radio provides a background accompaniment. It fills the silence. Television characters and personalities become virtual or simulated friends. People regularly talk back to their televisions and become emotionally involved in story lines.

When media consumers are seeking entertainment and diversion, they are very passive. Passive audiences are not a good target for messages that contain detailed content, because passive audiences engage less intellectually with the messages and media. Creative messages that get attention are the best way to reach passive audiences. Visuals, drama, emotion, and celebrities work well. Talking heads delivering serious messages do not work well.

A person seeking information for a consumer purchasing decision is a more active user of media. He will be receptive to detailed information about the comparative merits of products. A person thinking of buying a new flat screen LCD television, for example, is likely to notice advertisements for such TVs or may read about them in Consumer Reports and other publications and will seek out information from sources such as the Internet. This individual is open to more specific and detailed information that will help inform a purchasing decision.

*M*aking messages understandable ▼

Even when messages reach the right audience using appropriate media and media vehicles, they will fail to communicate because of poor execution of the message. One must write messages carefully for targeted publics or audiences. The writing must take into account such factors as education, social class, language, regional differences, and cultural background. Communication requires a shared understanding of words, gestures, icons, dress codes, cultural rules, and other symbolic messages. If the message source creates a poorly written message, the receiver will not understand it—or perhaps not understand it in the way intended.

One way to improve communication is to write simply so that most people can understand the message. The **Flesch-Kincaid** Grade Level formula measures the ease of reading a document. By analyzing the complexity of vocabulary, sentence structure, and use of punctuation, Flesch-Kincaid can estimate the school grade level necessary to comprehend a document. Most computer users have ready access to Flesch-Kincaid in Microsoft Office Word's spelling and grammar check tools.

One can achieve better readability scores by writing short sentences. Convert long sentences into two or more shorter sentences. Avoid unnecessary commas. Use everyday words.

Flesch-Kincaid Grade Level

Score	School Level
90 to 100	5th grade
80 to 90	6th grade
70 to 80	7th grade
60 to 70	8th and 9th grade
50 to 60	10th to 12th grade
30 to 50	some college
0 to 30	college graduate

Sample Readability Scores	
Comics	92 (highly readable)
Consumer ads in magazines	82
Movie Screen	75
Seventeen	67
Reader's Digest	65
Sports Illustrated	63
The New York Daily News	60
Atlantic Monthly	57
Time Magazine	52
Newsweek	50
The Wall Street Journal	43
Harvard Business Review	43
The New York Times	39
The New York Review of Books	35
Harvard Law Review	32
Standard auto insurance policy	10
Internal Revenue Code	–6 (impossible to understand)

Understandable communication is even more difficult when target audiences speak a different language as a native language or when there are significant cultural differences. In multilingual and multicultural settings, translation of messages must take place using culturally relevant references and images. Larger public relations firms today have multilingual staffs and overseas offices to help them create messages that are understandable and appropriate to diverse audiences.

*A*cronyms and jargon ▼

Symbols, acronyms, slogans, and other devices can provide useful shortcuts that simplify messages and make them more memorable, but they can also confuse. An important question is this: Will everyone who reads or sees the message understand its meaning?

Acronyms use the first letter of words. People sometimes pronounce the words using the abbreviated written form. Acronyms are everywhere: Mothers Against Drunk Driving becomes MADD, the United Nations is simply the UN, and the American Medical Association is the AMA. Other familiar acronyms include UNESCO, USA, NATO, NCAA, ABA, and YMCA. Many acronyms are a mystery to most people: OSL (open source lab), WFM (workflow management), TRANSEX (training system exerciser), G8 (group of eight), NUDIS (nuclear detonation information summary.) People in government, the military, and technology industries make extensive use of acronyms that are difficult for outsiders to understand. Most organizations adopt some acronyms that become widely accepted as communication shortcuts. It is only when used with outside audiences that there is a problem.

Jargon presents a similar communication problem. Jargon is a terminology, slang, or "lingo" commonly used by a particular group or profession. It is a vocabulary known to those inside a group. Often the terms are technical and knowing the jargon signals that a person is an insider.

> *The challenge with jargon is that words are used so commonly in one setting that it is easy to forget that their meaning is not clear to outsiders*

Examples of jargon include buy-in, benchmarking, branding, modality, paradigm, synergy, value added, ramp up, annuitants, intranet, marginal-cost pricing, f-stop, 404, Bambi, bio-break, greenmail, debenture, twisted cable, and cyberpork. An article or speech for a technical audience is an appropriate use of technical jargon. A press release about a new product is not a good use of jargon because many readers will not understand the words. The challenge with jargon is that words are used so commonly in one setting that it is easy to forget that their meaning is not clear to outsiders. Public relations professionals should play an editing role and try to catch confusing acronyms and jargon before they appear in documents that an organization will use.

Jargon and acronyms can be useful as communication shortcuts. Rather than saying Mothers Against Drunk Drivers over and over again, the acronym MADD can be substituted. Jargon similarly enables people who work in the same field to share a vocabulary that relates to the technology, concepts, procedures, and professionals in the field. One of the definitions of jargon, in fact, is "the vocabulary peculiar to a particular trade, profession or group. Another definition of jargon, however, is "unintelligible or meaningless talk or writing; gibberish." When jargon and acronyms are misused they cease to be useful short-cuts and become gibberish , and are barriers to effective communication. The trick is to know when it is appropriate to use particular acronyms or jargon. It should be asked, "Will everyone who receives this message understand what this means?" If the answer is no, avoid taking the shortcut.

Branding

Another useful communication shortcut is **branding**. The American Marketing Association defines a brand as a "Name, term, design, symbol, or any other feature that identifies one seller's good or service as distinct from those of other sellers." When a consumer encounters Apple, Mercedes, Starbucks, Coca Cola or McDonald's, he or she visualizes a particular set of products or services and certain characteristics associated with those products and services.

A brand calls to mind a whole bundle of meaning that surrounds a company, product or service including the brand's personality and distinguishing characteristics. The brands Mercedes and Toyota, for example, call to mind distinctly different types of cars. Similarly, McDonald's and KFC communicate a lot of information in their brands. Brands are powerful communication shortcuts.

Interbrand (interbrand.com), a global brand management company, named the following brands as the best worldwide in 2011:

1. Coca Cola
2. IBM
3. Microsoft
4. Google
5. GE
6. McDonald's
7. Intel
8. Apple
9. Disney
10. HP
11. Toyota
12. Mercedes
13. Cisco
14. Nokia
15. BMW
16. Gillette
17. Samsung
18. Louis Vuitton
19. Honda
20. Oracle

The value of brands is that they change a product or service from a commodity to a noncommodity. Commodities are products that are indistinguishable from one another. One is as good as another. Consumers should logically choose the least expensive. Milk is milk is milk. In fact, the basic ingredients of a particular product are usually much the same, if not identical. Shampoos contain mostly the same ingredients, except perhaps for fragrance. The basic ingredients of laundry detergents, bottled water, butter or deodorant do not differ much. So why pay more for one product than another? What consumers are paying for is the psychological value that brands add to products. Some call this the symbolic value of brands.

Advertising legend, David Ogilvy, said that products like people have personalities. The brand is the expression of that personality and it not only distinguishes like products from one another, it justifies paying more for a product whose basic functional utility is much like cheaper versions of the product. This explains why people pay $200 for designer jeans rather than $25 for a more generic label at a discount store.

The image and reputation of brands is valuable. David Ogilvy said, "Every advertisement should be thought of as a contribution to the complex symbol which is the brand image." Marketing departments and advertising agencies define and promote brands. Public relations also contributes to brand development, and can be especially important when crises occur and brand images suffer damage from product recalls or other events. When the Tylenol fell victim to product tampering that resulted in the death of six consumers in the early 1980s, many pundits predicted that the brand Tylenol was dead. Tylenol and its corporate parent, Johnson & Johnson, did such an extraordinary job of handling that crisis that the brand not only survived but prospered.

Persuasion ▼

Persuasion is an activity or process in which a communicator attempts to induce a change in the belief, attitude, or behavior of another person or group. Persuasion is a key task of public relations. Edward Bernays referred to persuasion by PR practitioners as the "engineering of consent." He believed that by applying an understanding of the psychology of persuasion public relations could move public sentiment in a desired direction.

◀ *Aristotle*

© BETTMANN/CORBIS

Aristotle ▼

Almost 2,500 years ago, the Greek philosopher Aristotle outlined three critical components of persuasion. They are still important today.

1. Ethos
2. Logos
3. Pathos

Ethos

Ethos is an appeal based on the credibility of an information source. Does the speaker have expertise? Is there evidence of sincerity, wisdom, virtue, and good will? Is the source trustworthy? If the source is not believable or credible, then the recipient regards the message with suspicion.

How does public relations establish ethos? The use of testimonials and spokespeople is a common strategy. Physicians, engineers, and experts of all sorts lend credibility to a message. Public relations will often suggest experts for the media to use as information sources for stories. A political campaign that focuses on the style, experience, and character of a candidate is another appeal to ethos.

Logos

Logos is an appeal to logic or reason. Why, rationally, should someone believe a message? What facts or evidence exists to support a claim? Organizations often supply research data to support claims. Election brochures that outline the positions of candidates on major issues are using appeals to logos. Logic works best with active audiences.

Gary Orren, a professor of public policy at the Kennedy School of Government at Harvard University, reflected on the 2000 campaign for president of the United States. Orren's analysis of campaign messages found that George W. Bush's messages appealed heavily to ethos. The messages of Bush's opponent, Al Gore, appealed more to logos. In that campaign messages about credibility resonated more effectively with voters than appeals to logic. What works best changes with the times. One cannot assume that a campaign strategy that works well once will do so again, because of complicated changes in the larger political and economic environment. Voters are looking for one thing today and something else tomorrow.

Pathos

Pathos is an appeal to emotion. Fear, pity, love, hate, anger, patriotism, and loneliness are emotions that resonate strongly with people. Pathos plays on those emotions to arouse an audience. Advertisements often use emotion combined with drama and visuals to reach consumers rather than explaining the detailed specifications of a product. Consumers see the product used by young, happy consumers. A candidate who tries to manipulate emotions by playing on the fears of voters is using pathos. Propaganda is often pathos-driven.

Many people thought President Ronald Reagan was a master of pathos. He told stories to illustrate points that registered emotionally with audiences. Properly done, pathos can make an argument more vivid and memorable. Audiences may not remember the exact details of a logical argument, but they may remember a compelling story that illustrates the point.

Aristotle believed that persuasive rhetoric should contain all three appeals—ethos, logos, and pathos. A politician speaking in a debate, for example, would attempt to establish credibility based on his experience (ethos), suggest some specific positions or reasons why he is the preferable candidate (logos), and tell stories or give examples that would illustrate points in a memorable way (pathos).

Elaboration Likelihood Model ▼

The **Elaboration Likelihood Model** describes two paths to persuasion. Understanding the two options enables the public relations practitioner to devise appropriate strategies and tactics.

1. Central route
2. Peripheral route

Suggestions for effective persuasion

► Celebrities work best with passive publics (ethos).
► Testimonials and endorsements add credibility (ethos).
► Logic works better with sophisticated audiences than emotion (logos).
► Statistics lend credibility (logos).
► Emotion and fear work best with passive publics (pathos).
► Examples can make situations real or put a face on an issue (pathos).
► Drama can get attention (pathos).
► Radio and television messages can be more persuasive than print but do not work well with complicated messages (pathos).
► Positive appeals are better remembered than negative.
► High fear works best when people can take immediate action. Do not arouse fear when people cannot act on the emotion.
► Understand the audience. Play to an audience's self-interest. Reinforce favorable opinions. Try to make messages compatible with prior attitudes.
► Keep messages simple. Do not make every argument possible.

Central route

The **central route** to persuasion presumes that an audience is in a thoughtful state, willing to engage the message actively with an open mind. Communication is direct and to the point. Messages can be logical. A message that focuses on the safety, engineering, and performance of an automobile takes the central route to persuasion.

Messages using the central route to persuasion include more facts and logic. Print messages such as brochures, trade journal articles, and news reports all take the central route. The underlying assumption is that the audience can and will process rational information.

Peripheral route

The **peripheral route** is useful when audiences are in a passive state. Passive audiences devote relatively little attention or effort to processing communication. Such audiences become targets of less direct messages. There is more emphasis on emotion, imagery, and symbolism. Messages are likely to be entertaining. An automobile ad takes the peripheral route to persuasion when it shows a motorist speeding along an ocean side highway. The ad portrays the product as a part of a lifestyle and says little or nothing about its features or benefits.

The peripheral route assumes that audiences are likely to tune out a serious message containing a lot of details and logical arguments. Public relations professionals must construct peripheral messages to overcome the audience's passivity and disinterest by grabbing their attention in an entertaining manner while presenting a small amount of information.

> *Target messages to specific audiences. If an audience is active, messages can be straightforward, direct, logical, and factual. If the audience is passive, then a more indirect and entertaining approach is usually advisable.*

The usefulness of the elaboration likelihood model in public relations lies in knowing how important choices are about when, where, and how to communicate with audiences. PR people must construct messages in a manner suitable for the targeted audiences. If an audience is active, then messages can be straightforward, direct, logical, and factual. If the audience is passive, then a more indirect and entertaining approach is usually advisable. At every stage in the communication process public relations practitioners must think about the audiences that they are trying to reach and create appropriate messages. To do otherwise would be to waste a client's money.

Agenda setting theory ▼

Agenda setting theory says that media do not tell people what to think. They do influence what people think about. The stories that appear in the newspaper and on television newscasts are the stories that people believe are most important. Journalists set the agenda by deciding which stories to cover and how to cover them. If the media ignore a story, it likely will be invisible to most of the public. The Internet and blogs are democratizing the storytelling process to a degree, but most people still rely on traditional media for news.

Agenda setting theory proposes that media are influential in two ways:

1. Media influence issue or product *awareness*. If the media cover a story, it generates considerable publicity, and awareness of the issue or product increases.
2. Media influence issue *salience*. Salience is the prominence or importance of something. An issue gains status or prominence if the media cover it. Journalists cover only a small number of stories each day because of the limitations of print space and broadcast time. If a story is important enough to cover, it gains prominence.

Agenda setting theory is important in public relations because PR people spend a lot of time trying to manage the awareness and salience of stories. Getting the media to cover a story can result in substantial free publicity for a client. Achieving the same coverage through paid advertising could be outrageously expensive if it is possible at all. If a story about a client is positive, public relations will try to persuade the media that the story is important enough to cover. If a story is negative, PR people may try to downplay the importance of the story to minimize its salience and the awareness that would come from negative press coverage.

> *Agenda setting theory says that media do not tell people what to think. They do influence what people think about.*

Media dependency theory ▼

Most people depend on media sources for their information. It is difficult if not impossible for each individual to research and verify all of the information we receive or need. When a major story happens, for example, most people will read newspapers, watch television, or search the Internet for information. Many people also come to depend on particular sources of information for commentary and analysis about the news. A conservative individual, for example, may seek out Fox News and Bill O'Reilly to get facts and insights about an event. Liberal viewers may gravitate to MSNBC and Rachel Maddow, Chris Matthews or Al Sharpton for their take on news events. Politics, then, becomes a convenient way for news organizations to market themselves to the public.

Media dependency theory has a close connection with agenda setting theory. If people depend on media for information, then that empowers the media to set the agenda. Media decisions about which stories to cover and how to cover them determine what most people know about a story. Most people do not have the time, skills, or inclination to research stories themselves. They accept the media's coverage as a reasonably reliable source upon which to base their knowledge and opinions about events around the world.

Framing theory ▼

Not all facts associated with an event can fit into a story because of limitations of space and time. The facts included in a story represent a "frame" or view of the events and are never the entire story. Inevitably, some facts, opinions and points of are omitted. Journalists make choices about which facts to include and what point of view to emphasize.

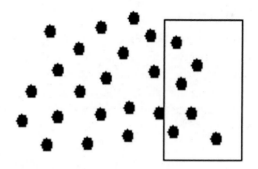

▲ *A story can include only some facts about an event. They represent a "frame."*

Chapter 1 discussed the concept of spin and the spin doctor. Spin is a pejorative term that suggests an attempt to manipulate perceptions of an event. It is the attempt to refocus attention from the negative aspects of a story to something more positive. Sometimes it refers to promotion of a counter argument that takes attention away from negative portrayals in the media.

Spin can involve such techniques as choosing facts in a selective way that emphasizes the positive—what some call "cherry picking" the facts. Another technique is to use **euphemisms** that obscure meaning and make the facts seem less unpleasant. An example of a euphemism is calling civilian casualties in a war "collateral damage." Still another way to minimize coverage of a story is to release the information on a day when many competing stories will exist, and the story may fall through the cracks and get little notice.

Spin relates to framing theory. Every story involves many facts and perspectives. Reporters never have the airtime or print space to report everything. They have to make choices about which facts to include and what point of view to take on the story. The point of view taken is a frame—a single way of seeing the event. They could report most stories with a different mix of facts and opinions that would frame the story in another way. There is no such thing as "a" story. Journalists must make choices about which facts to include and whom to quote. Two reporters covering the same event can tell different stories.

This is not a criticism of journalism. Journalists never have the space in print or the time on air to include all information about a story. Reporters and editors make choices about what is most important and most interesting. Those choices represent a single frame on the event. Another journalist might choose a different combination of facts, opinions and images that reflects a distinctly different frame.

13 Common story frames

The Project for Excellence in Journalism lists 13 frames that journalists commonly use. They include:

► **Straight News Account:** No dominant narrative frame other than outlining the basic who, what, when, where, why, and how

► **Conflict Story:** A focus on conflict inherent to the situation or brewing among the players

► **Consensus Story:** An emphasis on the points of agreement around an issue or event

► **Conjecture Story:** A focus around conjecture or speculation of what is to come

► **Story:** An explanation of the process of something or how something works

► **Outlook:** How the current news fits into history

► **Horse Race:** Who is winning and who is losing

► **Trend Story:** The news as an ongoing trend

► **Policy Explored:** A focus on exploring policy and its impact

► **Reaction Story:** A response or reaction from one of the major players

► **Reality Check:** A close look into the veracity of a statement made or information given

► **Wrongdoing Exposed:** The uncovering of wrongdoing or injustice

► **Personality Profile:** A profile of the newsmaker

SOURCE: www.journalism.org

On cable TV, Fox News and MSNBC frequently look at the same news events in different ways, drawing very different conclusions about an event. A speech given by a major political figure could be micro analyzed and interpreted differently, often from a distinctly political perspective of liberals and conservatives.

Public relations professionals hope to influence the **framing** of stories. They seek to focus attention on facts and opinions that represent clients most favorably. PR people are advocates for clients, much as attorneys are advocates for their clients. The effort to focus attention on the favorable aspects of a story is ethical so long as the techniques used to accomplish it do not involve lies and deception. Ultimately, journalists still choose the frame used to construct stories based on the facts and opinions they feel are most important to their audience. Efforts to spin a story may succeed in balancing the facts in a story. If an organization commits a major blunder, however, it is unlikely that pub-

lic relations will be able to make the story go away or spin it from bad news to good.

A reporter could write a story about a presidential candidate who makes an embarrassing statement in many different ways. The story could focus on the simple facts of what the candidate said. Another frame might focus on the personality of the candidate as a means of understanding the misstatement. One approach could place the gaffe into historical perspective, with discussion about prior misstatements by the candidate and what the errors collectively say about the candidate. Reaction to the comment is another frame, including reactions from the public and opinion leaders. Given the limitations of time and space, a journalist unable to report every conceivable aspect of the story will focus on only one or a few of the possible frames. The choice of frame is a journalistic decision, but public relations advisers will likely promote a point of view that is less damning to their client.

Failing that, the PR challenge is to engage in damage control to mitigate the negative publicity. A public apology and an explanation of the comment would provide a new frame on the story.

Models of public relations ▼

James A. Grunig developed four public relations models to explain key concepts of public relations:

1. Press agentry model
2. Public information model
3. One-way asymmetric model
4. Two-way symmetric model

Press agentry or publicity model

The practitioner engages in one-way communication from the organization to its publics. It is the oldest form of public relations and reflects the P. T. Barnum approach to persuasion, which can become manipulative and deceiving. Because it is a one-way model, there is little or no feedback from audiences. The emphasis is on getting messages out into the media.

Public information model

Like press agentry, the public information model relies on one-way movement of information. The intent is to inform. Often used by government, educational institutions, and not-for-profit organizations, the focus is on creating awareness and educating audiences. There is little or no feedback from the audiences. Information flows one way.

One-way asymmetric model

Some organizations use social science research methods to persuade audiences. They use research instruments such as surveys, interviews, and focus groups to understand audiences and then create messages to influence and persuade the audiences. This focus is on influencing publics about an organization. Modern political campaigns sometimes may use research to ascertain public opinion about issues, so that politicians can tell audiences what they want to hear. Public relations pioneer Edward Bernays received criticism for using social science research methods to manipulate publics rather than to engage in genuine dialogue with them.

Two-way symmetric model

The modern view of public relations is the two-way symmetric model that seeks mutually beneficial relationships and win-win outcomes. To understand publics better, organizations engage in research. The organization and its publics react to one another. This model reflects the boundary spanning and linking functions that Chapter 1 discussed.

Theories and models can help public relations professionals better understand audiences and audience behavior. Strategies and tactics grounded in a solid understanding of human behavior are more likely to achieve client goals. Modern PR practitioners focus on two-way communication that values the participation of the publics as much as the persuasive power of organizations.

Review questions

1. What is the SMCR model? What are the parts of that model?
2. Why is it difficult to persuade audiences to change their attitudes, beliefs, and behaviors?
3. Why is the hypodermic needle theory too simplistic?
4. How can we make messages more readily understandable to audiences?
5. How can we make messages more persuasive?
6. When would one take a central route to persuasion? When would the peripheral route be preferable?
7. Do media tell audiences what to think?
8. Is there such a thing as "a" story? How can PR people influence the framing of a story?
9. Why is the two-way symmetric model of public relations the most accepted model today?

Supplemental resources online

http://www.sourcewatch.org/index.php?title=Doublespeak	Doublespeak
http://www.wordspy.com/words/smartsizing.asp	Doublespeak
http://pages.stern.nyu.edu/~wstarbuc/Writing/Flesch.htm	Readability

Chapter references

Chesebro, James W., & Bertelsen, Dale A. (1996). *Analyzing media: Communication technologies as symbolic and cognitive systems.*

Dewey, John. (1927). *The public and its problems.* New York: Holt.

Frey, L. W., Botan, C. H., Friedman, P. G., Kreps, G. L. (1992). *Interpreting communication research: A case study approach.* Englewood Cliffs, NJ: Prentice Hall.

Lattimore, Dan; Baskin, Otis; Heiman, Suzette T.; Toth, Elizabeth L & Van Leuven, James K. (2004). *Public relations: The profession and the practice.* New York: McGraw-Hill.

Lutz, William. (1996). *The new doublespeak.* New York: HarperCollins.

Patterson, Philip, & Wilkins, Lee (Eds.). (1998). *Media ethics: Issues & cases.* Boston: McGraw-Hill.

Pratkanis, Anthony, & Aronson, Elliot. (2001). *Age of propaganda: The everyday use and abuse of persuasion.* New York: W. H. Freeman and Company.

Wilcox, Dennis L., Cameron, Glen T., Ault, Phillip H., & Agee, Warren K. (2003). *Public relations: Strategies and tactics.* Boston: Allyn and Bacon.

Notes

chapter

4

RESEARCH

The Institute for Public Relations (instituteforpr.org) calls research "the science beneath the art of public relations."

Research is crucial to producing effective public relations. It enables public relations professionals to understand the problems of clients, identifies important audiences with whom the client should be communicating, tests messages to improve their effectiveness, and measure the outcomes of public relations campaigns. Many would call this "applied" research, or research that seeks to solve practical problems.

Definition of research ▼

One simple definition of research calls it the organized and systematic process of finding answers to questions. Another says that researchers should search for knowledge with an open mind for the purpose of solving problems. These definitions lead to these insights about beneficial public relations research:

► It should be conducted in an orderly, systematic manner.
► It should be free of bias, done with an open mind.
► It should answer questions that help to solve practical problems.

Some organizations rely on their experiences and hunches to make decisions. They assume that past behavior is a good indicator of future behavior. The basis of good public relations programs, however, is facts rather than hunches. Facts are necessary about the competition, target audiences, and public opinion. Research enables an organization to obtain better answers to important questions. Better information results in better plans and better results for the client.

Consider the questions that researchers might ask during an election campaign:

► Do people favor Candidate A or Candidate B for the election?
► Why do people like one candidate or the other?
► What is it about each candidate that voters dislike?
► What are the demographic characteristics of supporters of Candidate A and B?
  ■ Age
  ■ Gender
  ■ Race/ethnicity
  ■ Income
  ■ Urban or rural

  ■ Political party preference
  ■ Religious convictions
► How strongly held are their opinions?
► What issues are of greatest concern to voters?
► How many people actually plan to vote?

Answers to these questions would enable a candidate's campaign to have an informed understanding of how the candidate compares with competitors and what issues resonate with the electorate. Strategies and tactics based on good research can counter misunderstandings, emphasize issues and positions that interest voters, and focus energy on groups of undecided voters. Research yields information that enables public relations professionals to recommend actions that produce change.

If a political campaign commissions a poll at the start of a campaign and asks questions like those above, the results serve as **benchmark** or **baseline**. This data is necessary for comparison purposes. It is a starting point. A future evaluation of a public relations plan can use a baseline to measure change. If the campaign asks the same questions a month or a year later, it can judge how attitudes and opinions have changed and what effect the program of public relations may have had on influencing voters.

In another example, suppose that on January 1 the awareness of an organization is 10 percent. That is the baseline. On December 31 of the same year, awareness is 20 percent. The baseline statistic enables us to know that awareness has doubled from 10 to 20 percent in one year. The baseline provides a basis for comparison, a means of measuring change over a period of time.

Data vs. information ▼

What is the difference between **data** and information? Data are a series of observations, measurements, statistics, and facts. Data become **information** when we analyze, describe, and understand the data. When we make meaning of data, we have information.

Organizations have a lot of data. Computers produce endless tables of numbers. However, what do the numbers mean and how can they be applied to a problem? The availability of data offers the possibility of analysis. The availability of information empowers the creation of strategy and change. Transforming data into information is the key.

Public relations practitioners should ask the following questions before conducting research. Answering these questions helps to focus the research, saving both time and money.

▶ What is the problem?
▶ What kind of information is needed?
▶ How will the results be used?
▶ What specific public(s) should be researched?
▶ Can the organization do the research itself or should it hire an outside consultant?
▶ How will research data be analyzed, reported, and used?
▶ When are results needed?
▶ What will research cost and what can the organization afford?

Primary and secondary research ▼

Research is crucial to understanding the situation of a client and to developing messages that communicate effectively with publics. The first research a group usually does is called **secondary** research, sometimes also called preliminary research. Secondary research involves searching through existing information. If secondary research does not answer all of the questions, then the group may commission **primary** or original research, which is sometimes called formal research. Many small clients can only afford to do secondary research. Deadlines or budget may limit their ability to conduct primary research for a campaign.

▲ *Libraries are an excellent source of secondary research information, both published and online.*

Secondary research

Secondary research examines information, typically publications, that already exist. The process often begins with a review of an organization's own records, commonly called "archival" information. The researchers examine Web sites, sales data, letters from consumers, annual reports, and other internal documents. Some people refer to this as "mining" preexisting information.

Information about competitors or an entire industry is available from trade publications or the Internet. Library reference rooms contain published U.S. census reports, the Statistical Abstract of the United States, Simmons' Media and Markets, and countless trade and academic journals. Online sources of background information include the Web sites for the U.S. Bureau of Labor Statistics, the U.S. Bureau of the Census, the Center for Media Research, the American Consumer Satisfaction Index, and the Advertising Media Internet Center. Factiva.com is a joint service of Dow Jones and Reuters. It provides extensive business information online. The Gartner Group and other companies provide industry-specific information. Gartner, for example, provides analysis and research for technology industries. Some secondary information is free and provides a good starting point for understanding a product, company, and industry. Other secondary sources require a subscription or fee. Many libraries permit free access to online databases.

Primary research

Primary research is new or original research undertaken to answer specific questions. Researchers use surveys or focus groups, for example, to gain insights about how various publics feel about a client, product, or problem. After reading the available secondary research information, what questions remain? Getting answers to specific questions may require some kind of original research.

If the objective, for example, is to improve the image of a client, it is necessary to have a baseline or starting point. What do various publics think about the organization right now? How strongly held are the opinions? Why do people feel the way they do? How do they feel about competitors? Primary research is the tool for answering such questions and measuring opinion change over time.

Some public relations organizations have the capacity to do primary research themselves. Most do not. Many groups commonly outsource research to organizations such as the Harris Poll or the Gallup Organization. Badly done research is not helpful and may yield reckless conclusions that lead an organization astray. Good primary research meets demanding standards. Many organizations recognize that they do not have the training and experience to do this kind of research themselves and contract out the work to specialists who can do it properly.

In general, primary research helps to:

▶ identify and categorize stakeholder groups,
▶ analyze and assess attitudes, opinions, and behaviors,
▶ test ideas for communicating with key groups.

Public opinion research ▼

Much public relations research measures public opinion. **Publics** are a group of people who share a common problem or goal and recognize their common interests. Demographics or psychographics help identify or define a public. Public opinion is not necessarily mass opinion.

John Dewey, in his 1927 book, "The Public and Its Problems," categorized publics as groups that

▶ face similar indeterminate situations,
▶ recognize what is indeterminate about their situations,
▶ organize to do something about the problem.

According to this definition, to be considered part of a "public," individuals must recognize that there is a situation that affects them in a significant way, that they are part of a group of people who are similarly affected by the situation, and that the group organizes itself in some manner to voice their opinions and concerns.

Public opinion research measures such things as attitudes, opinions, awareness, knowledge, intentions, motivation, and actual behavior. A company that makes a consumer product will eagerly pursue answers to the following questions:

▶ What do consumers in a product category think about a client?
▶ How aware of the client are they?
▶ How much knowledge do they have?
▶ Is the information they have accurate?
▶ Do they intend to buy the client's product?

▶ What motivates consumers' buying decisions?
▶ Have they bought the product in the past?
▶ If so, how often and how recently?
▶ Were they satisfied?
▶ In what ways were they dissatisfied?
▶ How does their experience with the client's product compare with those of competitors?

Informal research

One can do some public opinion research inexpensively using **informal** research methods. For example, a PR person could interview a modest number of community leaders for their opinions. A special committee might convene to investigate a topic and to invite public opinion. Researchers can monitor media to identify community issues that are generating substantial discussion and debate.

Formal research

Formal research involves contacting a larger sampling of the public. It seeks a broader picture of opinion than informal research can provide. Those who conduct formal public opinion research use various methods. They include:

▶ Mail surveys
▶ Telephone surveys
▶ Web and e-mail surveys
▶ Piggyback surveys
▶ In-person interviews
▶ Intercept interviews
▶ Focus groups

The most common type of formal public opinion research is surveying, using a questionnaire to solicit responses, usually via mail, telephone or e-mail/Web. Researchers use statistical computer software to tabulate and analyze the results. Mail surveys are relatively inexpensive to conduct, but the response rate is usually quite low. Telephone surveys are more expensive and have the disadvantage of aggravating people who regard them as intrusive, much like telemarketing. Web and e-mail surveys are now common, extremely inexpensive, and use software that automatically tabulates the results. This saves both time and money. On the downside, the e-mail/Web respondents may not represent a public as a whole, because the self-selected respondents who complete e-mail surveys tend to be more motivated and technologically savvy. There is also no centralized database of e-mail addresses, making it impossible to draw a true random sample.

Piggyback surveys are a variation of the telephone survey. Some survey research companies routinely conduct surveys that ask 20 or 30 questions of a random sample. An organization can "buy" as many of the questions as it might need and share the cost of the survey with several other organizations who also only need to ask a few questions. This makes reliable research affordable for small organizations that otherwise would be unable to afford the high cost of an entire survey. Another name for this type of survey is "omnibus" research.

One research company, lpsos (lpsos.com) describes a piggyback or omnibus survey this way:

> "Think of an Omnibus survey as your research car pool. You save money by sharing a vehicle, (the survey), by going to a common destination, (the respondents). Although the vehicle is shared, the results from your questions are confidential and only available to you. Omnibus surveys are a quick and cost-effective way to get answers for smaller surveys. . . ."

In-person interviews are expensive because of the time and individual attention involved. Interviewers question each respondent separately. If they conduct many interviews, the task becomes costly. In addition, the interviewers themselves can bias results. The appearance or speech accents of interviewers can bias subjects.

Intercept interviews are a variation of the in-person interview. They typically occur in a mall or other public place where interviewers intercept shoppers and ask them to spend a few minutes answering questions. Research aides with clipboards are a common sight in malls for conducting such intercept interviews. Because of the way they chose the sample, the results are not statistically reliable but can provide valid and interesting insights.

Focus groups involve organizing groups of eight to 12 people and leading the groups in open-ended discussions of a topic. They need a trained moderator to keep discussions focused. Researchers videotape the groups and later carefully analyze the discussions to identify themes and issues and possible messages that might resonate with a particular public. While the results are neither statistically reliable nor scientifically gathered, they do provide useful insights about people's attitudes. Follow-up surveys may be useful to explore further some of the insights gathered from focus groups.

An important caveat or warning about focus groups is that it is risky to conduct only one. It is advisable to conduct at least several group discussions. Why? What if a focus group gathers together 10 people with outrageously peculiar opinions? The oddness of the results might not be apparent if there was only one focus group conducted. It would become apparent that the first group produced outlying or odd opinions if there were other groups to which the results could be compared. Participation in focus groups is seldom based on random sampling methods, so there is a greater possibility that participants will not be representative of an entire public. Further, focus groups involve relatively small numbers of people. One group member with strong opinions has more power to skew the results of a focus group than a large random sample survey involving hundreds of participants. Focus groups are a relatively inexpensive and useful research method, but the results should be approached with an understanding of the limitations.

Qualitative and quantitative research ▼

There are two types of primary research:

1. qualitative,
2. quantitative.

Qualitative research

Qualitative research usually involves unstructured open-ended questions using nonrandom samples. It is not intended for statistical analysis. Focus groups are an example. The goal of qualitative research is to explore a topic broadly, looking for clues as to what is going on and why. Here are some descriptors of qualitative research:

► Subjective
► Likely to be biased
► Soft data (not mathematical)
► Open-ended questions
► Exploratory, like a "fishing expedition"
► Valid but not reliable
► Not projectable to larger populations (cannot be generalized)
► Nonrandom samples

Quantitative research

Quantitative research seeks statistically reliable hard data. It is numbers-oriented. The goal of quantitative research is to produce insights that use a random sample of respondents to produce results that PR people can project onto the wider public. For example, political polls use samples to estimate how the entire electorate feels about a candidate or issue. Descriptors of quantitative research include:

▶ Objective
▶ Hard data (mathematical—think numbers)
▶ Closed-ended questions (forces a choice and is more structured)
▶ Descriptive or explanatory
▶ Valid and reliable
▶ Projectable to larger populations (results can be used to generalize about a population
▶ Random samples

Experimental research and content analysis ▼

Public relations also employs **experimental research**. Researchers conduct experiments most often to pretest messages to measure their effectiveness in communicating and the response they evoke from audiences. Controlled environments minimize external factors and distractions while gauging the response to messages. Media campaigns cost too much money to leave results to chance. Message testing reduces the risk of failure.

Another type of research is called **content analysis**. Public relations uses content analysis to analyze text, audio and video content systematically. It codes, quantifies, and analyzes words and concepts. In public relations, the texts could be articles that appear in newspapers and magazines, blog references on the Internet, or references in television and radio newscasts and talk programs. The goal is to make some sense of what the media are saying.

Researchers can use content analysis to analyze media stories to record positive and negative references to a company. The tally can include which stories get covered and the key messages in each story. This analysis gives the client useful feedback on how media are covering stories about them.

Content analysis may involve searching major newspapers for references to a particular issue, individual, or organization. References are then coded in various ways for analysis. For example, public relations could analyze media coverage of a political candidate. How often is the candidate mentioned in media? What issues in the campaign get mentioned? Are editorials about the candidate favorable or unfavorable?

PR professionals could, for example, analyze stories about the Iraq War to determine what percentages of references to the war are positive and negative. What issues about the war are being discussed and by whom? What editorial position are newspapers taking? Is media coverage consistent or have there been changes in the amount of coverage, type of coverage, or tone of coverage over time?

Populations and samples ▼

Quantitative research often involves the use of **samples**. It is too expensive to question an entire population. Using probability theory, researchers can query a subset of the population and generalize those results to the entire population. Depending on the purpose of the survey, and the survey methodology, sample sizes may range from 300 to 2,000 people. Low cost surveys involving e-mail or the Internet may generate participation by thousands of people, but that does not

Qualitative Research	Quantitative Research
Soft data	Hard data
Open-ended questions	Closed-ended questions
Exploratory	Descriptive, explanatory
Valid but not reliable	Valid and reliable
Not generalizable	Generalizable
Nonrandom samples	Random samples

necessarily mean the results are accurate, because the samples are not random.

Three types of samples ▼

Random sampling

Random sampling requires that each member of a population have an equal chance of selection for inclusion in the sample. Random sampling yields the most reliable results.

Getting a random sample is not easy. If a researcher stops every tenth person walking down a street, is that a random sample? No, because everyone does not walk down that street. Can you call every tenth number in the phone book? No, because not everyone is listed in the phone book.

How might a university administration get a random sample of its students? Since universities know who is registered for classes in a semester, it would be possible to choose every tenth or twentieth student in the registration database. Every student would have an equal chance of being in the survey. The survey would be, therefore, truly random. Similarly, one might use a list of all members of a club or a professional association as the basis for sampling. Such a list should be reasonably complete and up to date.

For telephone sampling, computers can randomly generate numbers in a calling area. They could generate numbers that include both listed and unlisted numbers. The problem with this system is that a large percentage of the numbers generated and called would not be in service. There would be many wasted calls.

Systematic sampling

Systematic sampling uses a list or directory from which to select a random sample. It can be reliable if the list or directory is highly inclusive of the population surveyed. Telephone books, for example, were once highly inclusive. Today, however, many people have discontinued landline phone service and are using only mobile phones. Many phone subscribers opt for unlisted numbers and do not appear in directories. Phone books are not perfectly inclusive as a result.

The student or faculty directory of a university may be sufficiently inclusive to be suitable for systematic sampling of those populations. A membership directory, such as that for the Public Relations Society of America, is another example of a list that one could use to draw a random sample of PRSA members.

Systematic sampling using some sort of directory or list offers a practical means of accessing a population in a random manner. Directories are out of date the moment the moment of publication. People move. Change phone numbers. Adopt new last names. Therefore, no directory is completely accurate. For many research purposes, this approach is adequate and cost effective.

Quota sampling

Quota sampling (also called proportional sampling) strives to obtain a sample that includes people from important subgroups. The researcher may want some reasonable proportion of the sample from different genders and ethnic and age groups. Using a quota compromises the reliability of the survey but assures the researcher that the results represent important publics.

An example of quota sampling is intercept interviewing in a shopping mall. At first, an interviewer might approach every third or fifth shopper to solicit his or her participation. Selecting shoppers at this point is random. Later, however, interviewers may become more selective and approach mostly males. Fewer males go into shopping malls than females, and males are more inclined to avoid researchers with clipboards. The researcher eventually may need to target males to get a sufficient number of male respondents in the sample.

In another example, a student group might want to survey student opinion on an issue. They may only plan to question 100 students and want the respondents to mirror closely the demographics of students on the campus. They will try to question a proportionate number of males, females, and minority group members. The results of the survey will not be statistically reliable, but they will reflect the opinions of a diverse group of students.

Convenience sampling

Another type of sample is the convenience sample, also sometimes called a grab, an opportunity, or even a haphazard sample. Convenience samples, as the name implies, involve choosing subjects for research based on their convenient availability to the researcher. An example on a college campus would be to hand out a questionnaire in several classes. Clearly, the sample is not random. It is neither a systematic nor a quota sample. In a report of the results, the researcher should confess to using a convenience sample and qualify the results of the research by saying that the results are not likely to be a statistically reliable reflection of the opinions of a larger population.

Despite their limitations, graduate students and others whose purpose is to learn research methods, to test a theory, or to gather some preliminary information about a subject often use convenience samples. E-mail and Internet-based surveys are in common use today to acquire convenience samples.

One caveat with regard to e-mail and Internet surveys is that respondents are what researchers call "self-selected samples." That means that respondents take the initiative to respond and participate. Studies suggest that the people who readily respond to such surveys may not be typical of a general population. They are likely to feel stronger in one direction or another and want to participate for that reason. They might be angry or very happy and want to share those feelings. Other individuals with more moderate and less emotional attitudes have less motivation to take the time to participate in a survey. The caveat, therefore, is to be careful about interpreting information that comes from self-selected samples. It could be quite uncharacteristic of a larger population.

Margin of error ▼

No research can deliver perfectly reliable results. Some error is always present, reported as the margin of error.

Results are accurate plus or minus this margin of error. If results say that 49 percent of voters favor one candidate and 51 percent favor the other, with a margin of error of 5 percent, the results are too close to call. Here is why:

▶ Candidate A polls 49 percent. With a 5 percent margin of error the actual percentage favoring Candidate A could be anywhere from 44 to 54 percent (49, plus or minus 5 percent).

▶ Candidate B polls 51 percent. With a 5 percent margin of error the actual percentage favoring Candidate B could be anywhere from 46 to 56 percent (51, plus or minus 5 percent).

The margin of error varies with the size of the sample. Larger samples yield a smaller margin of error and less uncertainty. When results are within the margin of error the group commissioning the research should proceed with caution because the results are less predictive.

Is sampling accurate? Can 1,500 people accurately represent the opinions of a large population? Consider this anecdotal question: When you need your blood tested will you insist that they take *all* your blood or will a sample be sufficient? Most of us would say that we trust a sample of blood.

The principle is the same with survey sampling. Properly done sampling yields reliable results. In public relations a margin of error of 5 or 6 percent, requiring samples of 300 to 400, is often adequate. The results do not usually need to be as precise as, for example, national election polls. A bit more error can be tol-

Sample Size	Approximate margin of error (95 percent confidence)
300	6 percent (plus or minus)
400	5 percent
600	4 percent
1,100	3 percent
2,000	2 percent
9,500	1 percent

EXAMPLE: A survey sample of about 1,100, a common sampling for national surveys, yields a margin of error of approximately three percentage points.

A margin of error calculator is available online, compliments of the American Research Group (http://www.americanresearch group.com/moe.html)

erated because the client seeks only a sense of public opinion and that does not require a large sample with a small margin of error. Knowing in advance how researchers will use their results makes it easier to make sample size decisions that minimize costs for the client.

Reliability and validity ▼

▶ What is meant by the "reliability" of research?

▶ What is meant by the "validity" of research?

Reliability

Reliability refers to the consistency of results. If repeated research, using the same size sample and questionnaire, gets the same results, say it is said to be reliable. For example, if a survey conducted of students in two different classes yields wildly different results from one class to the other, the results would be considered unreliable. The probable cause of the reliability problem is that there was not random selection of the individual students surveyed in each class from the entire population of students. Reliability is a function of the quality of samples. If the sample is drawn randomly from a population, the results should be reliable within the margin of error of the sample size. When the sample is not random, the results are not reliable.

Validity

Validity is concerned with whether the research measures what it is supposed to measure. The wording of questions and the manner in which they are asked affects validity. If there is bias to the wording of questions, the survey results are not valid. Sometimes researchers deliberately biased questions because they want a particular response. Questions are worded in a way that increases the likelihood that respondents will answer in the desired manner. The results may serve the purposes of the researcher, but they do not reflect the real opinions of a public. They are not a valid (or accurate) measure of opinion.

Suppose the clock in the classroom consistently runs one hour late. Is the clock a valid and reliable measure of time? The clock is not valid because it incorrectly measures the time (validity is measuring accurately what is supposed to be measured). However, it is reliable because it does what it does consistently. It always runs late (reliability is getting the same results consistently).

Suppose that researchers surveyed a random sample of students at a university and asked them the fol-

---

Sample questionnaire

▶ **Open-ended question** How do you feel about welfare reform?

▶ **Closed-ended question #1** (multiple choice) Which of the following best represents your opinion about the success of welfare reform?
1. It was a big success
2. It was a modest success
3. It was mostly unsuccessful
4. It was very unsuccessful

▶ **Closed-ended question #2** (semantic differential) Using a 7-point scale indicate how successful you think welfare reform was:

Very Successful						*Very Unsuccessful*
7	6	5	4	3	2	1

▶ **Closed-ended question #3** (simple dichotomous) Welfare reform was successful.
1. agree
2. disagree

▲ *If the clock in a classroom consistently runs one hour late, is the clock a valid and reliable measure of time?*

lowing question: Are students paying too much for tuition and fees, and should costs be lowered to make education more affordable?

The question would yield reliable results because the sample is random. However, the results would likely not be valid because the design of the wording will prejudice the response. A different wording of the question might yield a different response.

Results are only as valid as the questions. Badly worded questions bias the results. Take these two questions:

▶ Should government provide adequate food for the needy?
▶ Should funding for welfare be increased?

Different wording can result in different responses. Most Americans believe that the needy should be provided with adequate food. At the same time, the majority resists increasing funding for welfare.

Another problem with surveys is **courtesy bias**. Respondents tend to be accommodating. They may provide the answer they think the researcher wants. If it is clear that Pepsi is conducting a survey and interviewers ask respondents if they prefer Pepsi or Coke, a larger percentage will respond that they prefer Pepsi than might be the case if it was unclear who was asking the questions. For that reason, the group sponsoring the research often conceals its identity.

Here are some simple guidelines for asking questions in a survey:

▶ Use **closed-ended** (multiple-choice) questions. They are easier for respondents to answer, and the results are objective, hence, easier to analyze. *Open-ended* (essay) questions require more thinking on the part of respondents and take longer to answer. They also cannot receive statistical analysis as readily as closed-ended questions. They do have the advantage of allowing respondents to answer a question in their own way, which could offer interesting insights.
▶ Keep surveys short. Long surveys fatigue the respondents. Many people resist participating in a survey if they think it may take too long. Others will quit before they are finished if they become tired of answering questions.
▶ Keep sensitive demographic questions in categories. Rather than asking for someone's exact income, provide several income ranges and ask the respondent to select a range.
▶ Use simple, familiar words. Respondents must accurately understand the questions.
▶ Avoid leading questions that will bias responses in one direction or another.

Review questions

1. What is the difference between research reliability and validity?
2. What is the difference between quantitative and qualitative research?
3. What is the difference between primary and secondary research?
4. What is the difference between formal and informal research?
5. What is the difference between open- and closed-ended questions?
6. How do you go about getting a random sample?
7. How does courtesy bias affect research results?
8. What is a baseline (or benchmark)? Why is it important?
9. What type of research is most commonly used in public relations?
10. How large a sample is needed to get a 3 percent margin of error?

Supplemental resources online

http://us.cision.com/media-analysis/media-analysis-overview.asp	Research company
http://www.aboutpublicrelations.net/research.htm	Research resources
http://www.aapor.org/	Public opinion research
http://www.pewinternet.org	Research about the Internet
http://www.pollingreport.com/	Political polls
http://www.ropercenter.uconn.edu/	Roper Center
http://www.harrispollonline.com	Harris Poll
http://www.nielsenmedia.com	Nielsen Media Research

Chapter references

Creswell, John W. (1994). *Research design: Qualitative & quantitative approaches.* Thousand Oaks, California: Sage Publications Inc.

Fink, Arlene. (1995). *How to ask survey questions.* Thousand Oaks, CA: Sage.

Fowler, Floyd J. (1993). *Survey research methods.* Newbury Park, CA: Sage Publications Inc.

Frey, L. W., Botan, C. H., Friedman, P. G., & Kreps, G. L. 1992. *Interpreting communication research: A case study approach.* Englewood Cliffs, NJ: Prentice Hall.

Lattimore, Dan, Baskin, Otis, Heiman, Suzette T., Toth, Elizabeth L., & Van Leuven, James K. (2004). *Public relations: The profession and the practice.* New York: McGraw-Hill.

Weiner, Mark. (2006). *Unleashing the power of PR: A contrarian's guide to marketing and communication.* San Francisco: Jossey-Bass.

Wilcox, Dennis L., Cameron, Glen T., Ault, Phillip H., & Agee, Warren K. (2003). *Public relations: Strategies and tactics.* Boston: Allyn and Bacon.

Notes

CREATIVITY AND CHANGE

Much of what public relations people do is routine: writing press releases, drafting speeches for executives, answering questions from the media. While these activities require some creativity, they fall under the heading of technical execution. The professionals who routinely do these tasks may be thought of as public relations technicians.

Creativity in public relations becomes more evident in the planning process. The best public relations plans anticipate and solve problems, nurture relationships with stakeholder groups, and create memorable tactics that change attitudes and behaviors. Having a major impact on important publics requires more than sending news releases to editors. It requires an ability to think through a client's problems and to invent strategy and tactics that respond effectively to the identified needs.

Edward deBono is one of the leading scholars on the psychology of creativity. DeBono says that humans favor routine ways of doing things. Our brains, he says, seek patterns or routines. Instead of spending a lot of time engaging in original thinking about mundane tasks, we develop automatic responses to everyday problems. In other words, we have habitual responses to routine tasks.

These routines or patterns are **heuristics**—rules for solving problems. Based on experience we create rules or guidelines that enable us to make decisions with less thought. Such shortcuts liberate us from having to ponder seriously every decision we make. Heuristics guide many of the purchasing decisions that consumers make. Consumers simplify the shopping process by basing decisions on prior experiences with brands, products, and stores. People will typically buy the same brand of toothpaste, shampoo, cereal, and other disposable items. They engage in more deliberate comparison-shopping for less routine and more expensive items. .

Heuristics are necessary or else the number of decisions we would have to make each day would overwhelm us. If every decision required complete analysis, we would be immobilized. It might take hours to buy a small number of items in a grocery store. Heuristics enable us to deal with repetitive problems quickly so that we can devote more time to solving important problems.

The drawback to habitual responses is that our reliance on rules, systems, and ideas that worked well in the past may outlive their usefulness when it comes to new problems. Clinging to past ways of doing things can be a disaster in a world of accelerating change in which old solutions may not fit new problems.

Kurt Lewin, a psychologist, developed a theory in the 1950s that described change as a three-step process:

1. Unfreeze behavior
2. Change
3. Refreeze behavior

The first step is to unfreeze behaviors. Before people will change a behavior, they must abandon the mindset that causes them to do things in the same way. Breaking a habit requires more effort than repeating a familiar behavior. People need convincing that a change is required and that the discomfort associated with change is preferable to the consequences of failing to change. In other words, people must recognize that in the long run change will be less painful than failure to change.

How do you unfreeze a behavior? Unfortunately, many times change occurs because of forces outside the control of an organization or individual. The environment imposes the need for change. For example, video rental stores such as Blockbuster were very comfortable with a business model that involved renting videos for a day or two at a cost comparable to tickets to the cinema. Videos returned late were subject to a late return fee. Netflix introduced a competitive service that allowed consumers to order DVDs from home, to receive them by mail, to keep them as long as they wish, and to pay a standard monthly fee that translated to lower cost per video rental. Blockbuster eventually refashioned its services and prices as a response to sharply declining video rental sales that occurred because of the new competition, but their response was too late. Today, Blockbuster is largely irrelevant in the video rental marketplace

Once behaviors become unfrozen, change occurs. People who resist a change often find that the new behavior is not so terrible after all. It may not be the change itself that was so painful, but rather the resistance to the change. The fear and anxiety associated with anticipating change can be more painful than change itself.

Sometimes individuals and organizations fail to change even when it is obvious that change is happening with or without their consent. Change-resistant institutions eventually face only two options: change or death. American automakers were heavily dependent on large SUV and pickup trucks with high profit margins. When gasoline prices went over $4 a gallon consumers began to choose lighter, more fuel-efficient vehicles. Sales and profits for U.S. automakers plummeted. Automakers had to confront changing consumer preferences and restructure their operations and product lines to reflect new realities.

After behaviors are unfrozen and change occurs the new behaviors become frozen again. As before, behaviors become habitual and resistant to change. Having surrendered to change and learned to do things in a new way, the new behaviors become rigidly frozen as well. The cycle repeats itself as behaviors unfreeze, change, and refreeze.

Why is this relevant to public relations? First, because public relations practitioners are counselors to the leaders of organizations. Public relations helps organizations to monitor their environments and to listen to important publics. Public relations professionals may be the first to sense an important change in the environment and must inform management about the forces at work and the need for change.

Second, public relations people get into habits, too. They get comfortable doing things in a familiar way and may need reminders of the value of reexamining what is being done, how it is being done, and why. Innovation in a program of public relations is as necessary as innovation in other parts of an organization. Sometimes public relations firms and advertising agencies lose accounts because their efforts become predictable. Clients feel the only way to get a fresh perspective on their needs is to hire new people to oversee the effort. Public relations needs creativity to gain and keep clients, and to serve client needs.

Social media are challenging public relations old-timers who were comfortable with traditional PR tactics and strategies. The new media landscape was unfamiliar to both PR practitioners and their clients. Public relations firms had to hire new employees with a new set of skills to handle Internet and social media tactics. Many small entrepreneurial PR firms have emerged that specialize in creating Web sites and generating messages for Facebook, YouTube, LinkedIn, Twitter and other social media sites. Established PR firms often acquire these start-ups companies to gain instant access to the new skills they need to serve clients.

What is creativity?
▼

There are three ways of seeing creativity. We can look at the characteristics of the creative person, the creative product, and the creative process. All three are important.

> *Every child is an artist. The problem is how to remain an artist after he grows up.*
>
> **—Pablo Picasso**

© 2009 JUPITERIMAGES CORPORATION

Creative people
▼

When asked to brainstorm the characteristics of creative people certain words typically come to mind:

- ▶ Capable
- ▶ Clever
- ▶ Confident
- ▶ Egotistical
- ▶ Humorous
- ▶ Individualistic
- ▶ Informal
- ▶ Insightful
- ▶ Intelligent
- ▶ Wide interests
- ▶ Inventive
- ▶ Original
- ▶ Reflective
- ▶ Self confident
- ▶ Unconventional
- ▶ Resourceful

We see creative people as special. They seem to have a style, a way of thinking and openness to new experience that many of us lack. Interestingly, research suggests that all people are creative, at least when we are young. Over time, the authorities in our lives, at home and in institutions such as school, may nurture and reward adherence to rules and conforming behaviors. Creative people resist this pressure to keep "thinking inside the box."

At a conference in Glasgow, Scotland, in 2005, sponsored by the Scottish Book Trust, there was considerable discussion about the effect of education on creativity. Creative thinkers wither with age, according to Sir Ken Robinson, chair of the British government's report on creativity, education, and the economy. It was time, he said, to unchain teachers and students so that there is less emphasis on training students to focus on one right answer, which stifles creative thinking.

Robinson described research that showed that "young people lost their ability to think in 'divergent or non-linear ways,' a key component of creativity. Of 1,600 children aged three to five who were tested, 98 percent showed they could think in divergent ways. By the time they were aged eight to 10, 32 percent could think divergently. When the same test was applied to 13 to 15-year-olds, only 10 percent could think in this way. And when the test was used with 200,000 25-yearolds, only 2 percent could think divergently."

> **Thinking in divergent and non-linear ways is essential for individual and national success in the 21st Century.**
>
> —Sir Ken Robinson

Mihaly Csikszentmihalyi, in his book "Creativity: Flow and the Psychology of Discovery and Invention" (1996), says creativity requires curiosity and interest in new things:

> On this score, children tend to have the advantage over adults. Their curiosity is like a constant beam that highlights and invests with interest anything within range. The object need not be useful, attractive, or previous; as long as it is mysterious it is worthy of attention. With age, most of us lose the sense of wonder, the feeling of awe in confronting the majesty and variety of the world. Yet without awe life becomes routine. Creative individuals are childlike in that their curiosity remains fresh even at ninety years of age. . . .

The research suggests that everyone is born creative. Sir Ken Robinson says that people do not just lose their creativity as a normal part of aging. Rather, he says, we are educated out of our creativity. As we conform to the expectations of schools, parents, employers and other authorities in our lives, we choose safer, less risky ways to express ourselves that will not trigger criticism for being too different, unconventional, outside the box.

> **The artist is not a different kind of person, but every person is a different kind of artist.**
>
> —Eric Gill, Philosopher

Three misconceptions about creativity ▼

1. *Misconception: Creativity is about special people—artists.* In fact, everyone is born creative, not just artists. Some people nurture their creative talents and somehow escape the negative influences that restrain other people's creativity. That is true. But everyone was gifted with creativity at birth, and people who do not use their creative talents still retain them. Many people rediscover their creativity later in life when the pressures of schooling, employment and parenting have lessened. One hears often of seniors who take up painting, gardening, quilting or other activities as creative expressions later in their lives. Creativity may go into a kind of hibernation, but it can be revived.

2. *Misconception: Creativity is about special activities—the arts.* In fact, almost any task can be approached creatively. Sir Ken Robinson's definition of creativity is "the process of having original ideas that have value." Applying that definition, even fairly mundane tasks can be the focus for creative thinking. Toothbrushes are a mundane product, but product designers have created all sorts of variations of the toothbrush. One might approach inventory control in a warehouse with new thinking. Reinventing a procedure could be an act of creativity. It is important to understand that artists and the arts are not the only valid objects for creative thinking.

3. *Misconception: Creativity is about letting yourself go.* This notion suggests that creativity springs out of wild, undisciplined lifestyles and behavior. We think of modern Bohemian artists who chose unconventional lifestyles, such as Picasso, Allen Ginsberg, Jack Kerouac, Hemingway, or F. Scott Fitzgerald. In fact, creative work usually requires discipline. Authors write, edit and rewrite their work many times before publication. A creative inventor like Thomas Edison was a model of discipline. He held nearly 1,100 patents by the end of his life. To get a working filament for a light bulb that would light and not burn up or melt, he tested thousands of materials until he found the one that would light and stay lit. Similarly, adver-

tising teams explore many different ideas before they settle on a strategy for a campaign.

Creative products
▼

Creative products can be ideas, crafts, music, or writing. Do not let the word "product" in this context confuse you. In advertising and public relations, creative products can include advertising designs, press releases, exhibits, speeches, and special events. Strategies, tactics, and plans are all creative products of public relations.

Creative products should satisfy the following three criteria:

1. originality (novelty)
2. relevance (logic and usefulness)
3. elaboration and synthesis (well-crafted, elegance, understandable, skillful)

Originality

Creative products are original. There is newness, a freshness about them. We experience them as different from other similar things. This criterion for creativity is the most intuitive. Nearly everyone recognizes that creativity requires original thinking.

Relevance

Creative products also need relevance. This means they should do whatever their creators intended them to do. A creative advertisement should sell product. A creative exhibit at a trade fair should attract passersby and build on an organization's reputation. To be relevant, a creative product should do its job well, whatever that job is.

If a message is exciting to look at, but it does not persuade the targeted audience, it fails the test of relevance. If a special event attracts considerable attention and attendance but most people do not know who sponsored it, then it is a failure from a public relations point of view.

Elaboration and synthesis

The final criterion for creative products is elaboration and synthesis, which asks whether the creative product was well crafted and skillfully executed. In the case of a print advertisement, for example, elaboration and

synthesis would relate to the ad's design, typography, quality of images, and general appearance. Elaboration and synthesis for a corporate PR publication relates to the quality of the writing, photos, layout, and design.

All three criteria should be present in a successful creative product: originality, relevance, and elaboration and synthesis. If a publication has an original concept that is logical and serves its purpose, but is poorly put together, readers might see it as amateurish. If it is original and well crafted, but not relevant, then it could be great looking but fails to communicate necessary information to a public. If it is relevant and well crafted, but not original, it may get lost in the clutter of other similar messages, and never gain attention.

Creative process
▼

Many people believe that creative ideas spring out of thin air, appearing from nowhere. In fact, most creative ideas are the product of a process. They are the result of a deliberate series of steps. These steps include:

1. fact finding,
2. idea finding,
3. solution finding.

Fact finding

Fact finding involves trying to understand a problem. In public relations and advertising fact finding involves researching the client, product, audiences, and competitors. Public relations plans typically have a section called "situation analysis" that details important facts. Primary and secondary research are the source of this background information.

Idea finding

Idea finding (ideation) refers to **brainstorming**, trying to identify as many ideas as possible in the belief that more ideas will yield better ideas. Idea finding is also called **divergent thinking**, which means allowing thinking to diverge or spread out. The search for ideas goes in all directions.

Alex Osborn founded the advertising firm of Batten, Barton, Dirstine and Osborn (BBD&O). In the early 1940s, Osborn observed that advertising teams got inconsistent results. Sometimes they produced ideas that were remarkably imaginative. At other times, the results were mundane and unoriginal. Osborn wondered if business groups could be more consistently creative. He looked for guidelines that would nurture original thinking.

Over time, Osborn created a process that he called brainstorming to generate more and better ideas. Following his guidelines, people found their natural inhibitions reduced. Inhibitions prevent some people from putting forward ideas that might be "wrong" or "stupid," at least in the eyes of others. Osborn found that "silly" ideas are useful in brainstorming because they spark other ideas by stimulating thinking and encouraging people to springboard from one thought to another. Osborn reflected on his observations about creativity in a 1953 book titled "Applied Imagination." He also founded the Creativity Education Foundation, which still exists today, to encourage the study of creative behavior.

> **The greatest danger you face is becoming a prisoner of familiarity. The more often you see or do anything in the same way, the more difficult it is to think about it in any other way.**
>
> —**Roger von Oech,**
> **author of "A Whack on**
> **the Side of the Head"**

Solution finding

Solution finding is the rational process of evaluating ideas to identify the best, most workable ones. Thinking converges on a solution. Filtering of ideas occurs until a solution emerges and the details are worked out. The goal of convergent thinking is to focus ideas in a single direction. It is logical and critical.

Creative problem solving (CPS) ▾

Dr. Sidney Parnes authored the book "Optimize the Magic of Your Mind" and continued the work of Alex Osborn at the Creative Education Foundation. Together with Osborn, Parnes developed the Creative Problem Solving (CPS) process that outlines six stages of CPS. The purpose was to encourage a deliberate and thoughtful process for examining and solving problems in imaginative ways. Much creative problem solving is haphazard. People toss a handful of ideas around and often accept the first workable idea. Osborn and Parnes hoped that CPS would guide groups through the necessary steps to think consistently outside the box.

Six steps of creative problem solving ▾

1. **Mess finding**
   ▸ What is the objective?
   ▸ What do we want to accomplish?

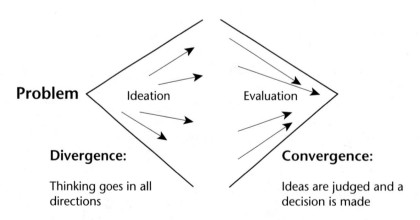

Problem   Ideation   Evaluation

Divergence: **Convergence:**

Thinking goes in all directions   Ideas are judged and a decision is made

▲ *Divergent thinking encourages people to think of many different ideas, allowing their minds to diverge in all directions. Convergent thinking filters and evaluates all the ideas to focus down to one idea and a decision.*

2. **Data finding**
   ▶ What do we know about the problem?
   ▶ What research exists?
   ▶ What research could be done to better understand the problem?

3. **Problem finding**
   ▶ Can we agree that there is a problem?
   ▶ Can we agree on what the problem is?
   ▶ Are there other ways we can express the problem so that we can agree on what the problem is?

4. **Idea finding (brainstorming)**
   ▶ How many ideas can we come up with for solving the problem?

5. **Solution finding**
   ▶ What criteria shall we use to evaluate alternatives?
   ▶ Can we combine ideas to invent new and more acceptable alternatives?

6. **Acceptance finding**
   ▶ What obstacles exist that we must overcome to execute an alternative?
   ▶ What resources are available?
   ▶ What are the timeline, strategy, and plan of action to make the idea a reality?
   ▶ Who is responsible for each action?

Blocks to creativity ▼

Most of the blocks or obstacles to creativity reside within the individual. These blocks hinder people's willingness to think outside the box and to share ideas. Some of the blocks include:

▶ Fear of criticism
▶ Lack of self-confidence
▶ State of mind/body (for example, experiencing negative stress)
▶ Focus on finding the "right answer"
▶ Jumping the gun and adopting one idea too soon, refusing to consider others.
▶ Belief that:
  ■ tradition is preferable to change
  ■ reason, logic, numbers, practicality are good and feelings and intuition are bad
  ■ fantasy and reflection are a waste of time and that playfulness is for children only
  ■ we are not creative

Brainstorming (ideation) in action ▼

Alex Osborn developed the following guidelines for effective brainstorming:

1. Ideation and evaluation are separate. When brainstorming, list as many ideas as possible in the time allowed. Do not discuss, question, criticize, or evaluate ideas. Just list them. Later, in a separate process, the evaluation of ideas occurs.

2. No criticism of ideas is permitted. Discussing ideas damages the brainstorming process. It slows down the pace, makes people feel unsafe, and results in fewer ideas.

3. The goal is to produce as many ideas as possible in the time allowed. This is commonly referred to as **idea fluency**. Research suggests that if a group produces 100 ideas, the second 50 will be the best. Early ideas tend to be safe and familiar variations on things done before. It is important for groups to push past the easy ideas to engage in genuinely original thinking. More ideas yield better ideas.

4. Freewheeling or wild ideas are good. Brainstorming groups that enjoy themselves tend to be the most productive. Sometimes groups feel compelled "to be serious," but seriousness tends to be incompatible with brainstorming. This box limits thinking to ideas that feel practical. Wild ideas can be good because they trigger thinking that leads to breakthrough ideas. A special energy exists in a group that is doing brainstorming effectively. Everyone in the group tosses ideas out, and people take one another's ideas and build on them, creating variations. This stage values **idea flexibility**, the ability to produce ideas that are different from each other. It also values idea novelty, the generation of ideas that are unusual.

5. Recording all ideas on a flipchart, chalkboard, or poster board makes it easy to refer back to them. It is important to record every idea. When some ideas seem to merit recording and others do not, it sends a message to the group that ideas are under judgment. Judgment triggers self-censoring behaviors that limit the willingness of some group members to share their ideas. If enough group members engage in self-censoring the group will be less productive.

Review questions

1. What are the three steps in the process of change?
2. Who is creative? Are you creative?
3. What are the three steps in the creative process?
4. What blocks your creativity? The creativity of others?
5. What are the guidelines for doing brainstorming effectively?
6. What is the difference between divergent and convergent thinking?
7. During a creative problem solving process, why is it important to separate divergent from convergent thinking?
8. What is self-censoring? Why do people self-censor in groups?
9. What is the difference between the fluency of ideas and the flexibility of ideas?
10. What are heuristics? Why are heuristics a barrier to change?

Supplemental resources online

http://www.CreativeEducationFoundation.org	Creativity Education Foundation
http://www.creativityforlife.com	Creativity for Life
http://www.danpink.com	Daniel Pink
http://sirkenrobinson.com/skr/	Sir Ken Robinson
http://www.synecticsworld.com	Synectics technique
http://www.brainstorming.co.uk/tutorials/historyofbrainstorming.html	Brainstorming

Chapter references

Csikszentmihalyi, Mihaly. (1990). *Flow: The psychology of optimal experience.* New York: Harper Perennial.

Csikszentmihalyi, Mihaly. (1996). *Creativity: Flow and the psychology of discovery and invention.* New York: Harper Collins.

DeBono, Edward. (1992). *Serious creativity: Using the power of lateral thinking to create new ideas.* New York: Harper Business.

Johnson, Craig E., & Hackman, Michael Z. (1995). *Creative communication: Principles & applications.* Prospect Heights, IL: Waveland Press.

Osborn, Alex. (1953). *Applied imagination.* New York: Schribner's.

Parnes, Sidney. (1997). *Optimize the magic of your mind.* Buffalo, NY: Bearly Ltd.

Pratkanis, Anthony, & Aronson, Elliot. (2001). *Age of propaganda: The everyday use and abuse of persuasion.* New York: W.H. Freeman and Company.

Smith, Bruce L. (1993). Interpersonal behaviors that damage the productivity of creative problem solving groups. *Journal of Creative Behavior,* pp. 171–187

Von Oech, Roger. (1986). *A kick in the seat of the pants.* New York: Harper & Row.

Von Oech, Roger. (1990). *A whack on the side of the head: How you can be more creative.* New York: Warner Books.

White, Alisa, Smith, Bruce L., & Shen, Fuyuan. (2002). Judging advertising creativity: Using the Creative Product Semantic Scale. *Journal of Creative Behavior,* pp. 241–253.

Name _____

Date _____

Exercise 1

Connect all of the nine dots with four straight lines without lifting your pencil and without re-tracing lines. (Use as many of the boxes below as you need to experiment with answers to this puzzle.)

```
 ○    ○    ○        ○    ○    ○

 ○    ○    ○        ○    ○    ○

 ○    ○    ○        ○    ○    ○
```

Exercise 2

Change this into a 6 by adding one line.

Exercise 1. Solution

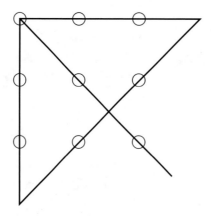

Feel cheated by this solution? Why?

Many people see the nine dots as a box and assume they must keep lines within the box, but the instructions did not say that. Creative thinking means, in part, not creating boxes where they need not exist.

Being creative with public relations requires a willingness to challenge boxes. If a PR team has been using the same strategy and tactics for a long time, for example, the team may become uncomfortable with change. That is a box. In another example, resource limitations or deficiencies in the skills of staff might make a particular tactic appear difficult to execute. Accepting the limitations is a box. Looking for ways to accomplish a task despite the limitations is the outside-the-box approach. Creativity often involves challenging limitations. This can be uncomfortable at first for PR practitioners, clients, and audiences. It involves leaving safe, familiar territory and zones of comfort, but the reward can be breakthrough thinking.

Exercise 2. Solution

Again, feel cheated? Most people assume they are dealing with a Roman numeral problem and try to convert a Roman numeral nine to a six. The decision to see it that way reflects an incorrect assumption. Be careful about assumptions. Assumptions are boxes.

CREATING A PUBLIC RELATIONS PLAN

What is a plan? ▼

The definition of a plan is a series of actions intended to accomplish one or more goals that will enable an organization to move from one set of circumstances to another. Plans are like a detailed roadmap for getting where you are to where you want to be.

Key concepts in this definition are:

▶ Actions
▶ Accomplishing goals
▶ Moving from one set of circumstances (the present) to another (the desired future).

> *A plan is a series of actions intended to accomplish one or more goals that will enable an organization to move from one set of circumstances to another.*

The U.S. Small Business Administration (sba.gov) provides an overview of planning as a vital business task:

> Strategic planning is matching the strengths of your business to available opportunities. To do this effectively, you need to collect, screen and analyze information about the business environment. You also need to have a clear understanding of your business—its strengths and weaknesses—and develop a clear mission, goals and objectives. . . .
>
> In addition, strategic planning has become more important to business managers because technology and competition have made the business environment less stable and less predictable. If you are to survive and prosper, you should take the time to identify the niches in which you are most likely to succeed and to identify the resource demands that must be met.

Types of plans ▼

Informal plans

Marketing plans for products or brands are done annually. PR people may create separate plans for newly introduced products and services. Marketing plans detail how an organization will execute the marketing mix: product, price, placement, and promotion. This mix is termed the "Four P's." Plans must carefully coordinate decisions about product design, packaging, pricing, distribution, advertising, and public relations.

Advertising plan

An advertising plan is part of the promotional component of a marketing campaign. It deals specifically with the strategy for creating, testing, and placing advertisements in various media to reach targeted audiences. Advertising uses purchased media to promote products and services.

Public relations plan

PR plans look very much like advertising plans. Like advertising, public relations has a significant role in marketing campaigns. Public relations, however, has a broader mission than selling products and services, and PR plans must reflect that difference. PR plans take advantage of a wider range of communications channels to achieve results. Targeted publics for a PR

Four P's of the Marketing Mix

Product	design of product, features, warranty, support
Price	cost, discounts (premium or low pricing)
Placement	high or low end retail distribution (Wal-Mart or Nordstrom), online
Promotion	advertising, public relations, sales promotion, IMC

plan often include internal publics such as employees and stockholders as well external publics such as vendors, customers, legislators, government regulators, the community, industry groups, and the media. Public relations plans must reflect the broader scope of communication that makes public relations different from advertising.

While the purpose of plans may differ, they typically have some common elements. Mastering the planning process is a valuable business skill. It is evidence of a disciplined way of thinking and an ability to translate ideas and wishes into specific action steps.

Creating a plan ▼

Effective planning requires honest and specific answers to these important questions:

▶ Where are we now?
▶ What is the present state of things?
▶ What problem(s) do we need to solve?

These questions lead to an understanding of an organization's needs. This part of a plan is the situation analysis. It may also be called the environmental analysis. Think of this as starting *point A.*

The next set of questions clarifies the objectives of a plan. They identify the desired future state of things.

Think of this as point B. The gap between the present situation (point A) and the desired future situation (point B) is the problem.

▶ Where do we want to be in the future?
▶ What outcome do we want?
▶ What do we hope to accomplish?

Present   A ━━━━━━━━▶ B   **Future**

Identifying the problem? ▼

Some people become defensive when the discussion turns to problems. They may insist, "We don't have any problems." In the context of planning, however, a problem is really just the gap between what is happening now and what you wish would happen. For example, sales last year were flat. The company wants sales to increase at a rate of 10 percent a year. The slow growth in sales is the problem.

In another example, a nonprofit food pantry provides free food to needy families. For a variety of reasons, many families do not take advantage of the service. For some it is an issue of not being aware of the Pantry. For others, it is a matter of pride or embarrassment. How can the Pantry overcome the lack of awareness and other problems and deliver services to more

Five reasons to plan

Michael Beckett is a regular contributor to the London Daily Telegraph, writing about business, management, and finance subjects. He says there are "five good reasons to plan and no good reasons not to (http://sme.atalink.co.uk/articles/32):

1. If you do not know where you are going it is hard to know when you have got there.
2. If you have not looked ahead, how can you be sure you are not heading down a dead end or even over a cliff?
3. You need to know the terrain ahead to prepare for the conditions and to know where you are going to need a cash injection or loan.
4. No sensible person is going to get involved in an enterprise without a plan, and you do not want to get tied up with fools.
5. Plans give you a discipline of ensuring you are not letting things drift, correcting mistakes and preventing slackness."

of the families who need help? The gap between the number of families who receive aid and the number who are eligible but do not receive it is the problem in this case. For a public relations practitioner the challenge would be to create awareness of the service in a way that also preserves the dignity of clientele.

Thinking about problems as the difference (gap) between what is happening now and what you want to happen in the future makes people less defensive about talking about "problems."

Present A ■——————➤ B **Future**

gap = the problem

How do we get from point A to point B? How do we solve the "problem?" The detailed answer to these questions becomes the action part of a plan. PR formulates a strategy then executes specific tactics for implementing the strategy. It itemizes a budget that details the costs associated with each action. It creates a timetable or calendar that identifies the order of events and deadlines for accomplishing everything. Together, these steps become the action plan for getting from point A to point B. More discussion about each of these steps will take place later in the chapter.

Situation ■——————➤ **Objectives**

public relations plan

Planning is an essential activity for professionals in every industry and profession. Mastering the planning process is an important skill. Public relations plans are similar to advertising plans and just a bit different in style and presentation from other kinds of plans. The basic elements of plans are much the same and learning one type of planning process is good preparation for creating other types of plans.

Public relations plans ▼

Good public relations is not just about putting out press releases. Public relations solves business problems. Public relations should be proactive and not reactive. That means an organization tries to stay ahead of problems and to avoid them rather than only reacting to events as they happen. Planning helps to avoid crises. The most effective public relations may prevent crises from occurring in the first place. Planning prevents haphazard, ineffective communication. It improves the value of PR to the organization.

Planning is a strategic process. It is a key management task. Most public relations practitioners focus on day-to-day tactics. They send out press releases, organize press conferences, write speeches, and plan special events. Those who develop the PR objectives and strategies are the professionals who give meaning and direction to the effort. Understanding how to develop a public relations plan is one of the main skills that separate entry-level PR technicians from true members of an organization's management team.

> *Understanding how to develop a public relations plan is one of the main skills that separate entry-level PR technicians from true members of an organization's management team.*

Simple planning model ▼

The planning model used in this book is similar to Ketchum's, although sections have different titles. While the format of plans can vary from organization to organization, all should contain these elements:

▶ Research   ▶ Tactics
▶ Objectives   ▶ Evaluation
▶ Strategies

Public relations plans are action-oriented. They involve creating strategies and executing tactics that inform or persuade publics. The process requires the identification of specific desired outcomes and the implementation of different actions intended to accomplish those outcomes.

The timeline for a plan will vary with the client's needs. In some industries, a month or a quarter (three months) is a common planning cycle. This is often the case with high-tech companies, especially startups that operate at a frantic pace. More established organizations in less volatile industries are more comfortable planning for a year.

Each public relations organization has its own style or template for doing a public relations plan. The

Ketchum Planning Process

Ketchum Public Relations (ketchum.com) uses a six-part planning process that it says delivers disciplined and demonstrable results for its clients:

1. **Discover** is the first step in planning. At this stage, Ketchum will (1) clarify the assignment with all client decision makers; (2) investigate beyond the obvious and gain context through research; (3) synthesize knowledge to derive insights; and (4) identify the optimal target and its current and desired mindset.

2. **Set goals** is the second step in planning, based on knowing who the target is and what desired impact communications must have on the target. It is at this point that Ketchum will (1) validate the client's overall business goals; (2) recommend communications goals that include type (awareness, attitudinal), impact (increase by how much), target (among whom), timeframe (by when); and (3) establish success criteria and a measurement plan.

3. **Strategize** is the third and most complex step in planning. With the goal of one focused and bold strategic platform, Ketchum takes a client through several steps that include (1) competitive mapping and/or brand positioning, to identify a client's unique voice; (2) message development and mapping, to craft client messages that are differentiated, motivating and newsworthy; (3) media planning, to select the best reach and frequency channels to have an impact on the target; and (4) influencer planning, to identify the best nonmedia channels to carry key messages. These decisions are captured in a singular worksheet—the communications strategy brief, which serves as an excellent tool for obtaining consensus on strategy.

4. **Create** follows Strategize and unleashes the considerable creative energy at Ketchum to develop original, motivational campaigns that stay on strategy to deliver expected results. Ketchum invites clients to participate in its "informed creativity" process, which includes (1) a brainstorm brief, to synthesize goals, insights, trends and strategies to assure client buy-in on success criteria; (2) a brainstorm network, consisting of Ketchum "insiders" and "outsiders" who can bring relevant and fresh perspective to any brainstorm; (3) trained brainstorm facilitators, who use advanced idea-facilitation tools and techniques to introduce "discontinuity" into the logical, linear way that communicators are trained to think; and (4) a concept evaluation and testing process that helps identify the best idea(s) to address a client's challenge.

5. **Deliver** is the phase of the Ketchum process that puts systems in place to ensure that results are delivered in a way that exceeds expectations. This step entails guidelines for setting expectations; plans for assembling and mobilizing the very best team for the assignment; and best practices for effective and consistent client communications—including project status and budget status reporting.

6. **Evaluate and Evolve** is both the step that sets the highest standards in results reporting and measurement and the step when lessons learned become a chance for discovery again—and Ketchum's commitment to continuous innovation. Ketchum's leadership in this area includes an exclusive online tool that reports media results, including message and tone analysis on a real-time basis; reach/frequency analysis, using MRI data to report percent of the target reached through publicity, and with what frequency; and post-engagement analysis, which prompts the agency and client team to look at work with a critical eye and bring new thinking and thinkers to every assignment. The firm's Strategic and Creative Planners Network collaborate regularly to steward the strategic and creative product on every account."

Reprinted by permission of Ketchum (www.ketchum.com)

structure and presentation of information in plans can vary considerably. There is no standard format in use by all public relations firms or professionals.

Typically, a public relations plan includes the information below. In the model used for this book, there are 10 parts to a plan. This approach helps students become acquainted with the information that goes into a plan and the logical progression of thinking required.

10 part public relations plan ▼

1. Executive Summary
2. Situation Analysis
3. Objectives
4. Audience (Publics)
5. Strategy
6. Tactics
7. Calendar/Timetable
8. Budget
9. Evaluation
10. References

Observe the following logical progression of thinking in the plan.

The 10-part plan (logical flow of thinking) ▼

1. Summary of the plan
2. What is happening now?
3. What do we want to happen?
4. Who do we need to communicate with to accomplish our objectives?
5. What message or theme should we be communicating?
6. How best can we communicate the messages to our target audiences?
7. When should things happen?
8. How much will each activity cost?
9. How will we know if we met the objectives?
10. What sources of information did we rely on for this process?

Plan part 1: Executive summary ▼

Executive summaries are a common component of large documents. An executive summary is very brief,

only a page or two in length. It is the first section a reader encounters in the document and the only part of the document many readers will read.

Busy people often do not have the time to read lengthy documents. An executive's staff may read lengthy documents, but the executive may only want an overview. An executive summary condenses a document into a single page or two, for quick reading. It is, however, more than just a summary. The executive summary must concisely describe the client's needs and sell the proposed solution to those needs. The summary must be both descriptive and persuasive.

In an article titled, "Writing an Executive Summary that Means Business" (2003), for the Harvard Business School, John Clayton writes that a good executive summary balances "efficient delivery of key information with a persuasive, well-substantiated pitch. Above all, the executive summary must demonstrate a clear understanding of the potential client's needs."

Clayton argues that good executive summaries focus on the impact of the plan on performance. Such summaries emphasize outcomes, especially measurable outcomes.

Condensing a document into one persuasive page of text is a challenge. It is easier to say something in several pages than it is to condense thoughts into a clear and concise single page. Executive summaries require careful crafting to make every word count.

Craig Miyamoto is accredited (APR) by the Public Relations Society of America. He runs a successful PR firm in Hawaii and is a member of the prestigious PRSA College of Fellows. Miyamoto regularly speaks to public relations groups and offers advice on PR planning. He suggests the following format for public relations executive summaries (workinpr.com) that "covers several key points most likely to interest the executive who reads your plan. . . .

1. **The Problem:** SState here what you believe the problem to be.
2. **Program Goal:** State here your ultimate goal.
3. **Target Audiences:** (1) Your primary audience, (2) your secondary (intervening) audience(s), and (3) your tertiary (special) audience(s).
4. **Audience Objectives:** (1) What you expect your primary audience to do, (2) what you expect your intervening audience(s) to do, and (3) what you expect your special audience(s) to do.

5. **Major Strategy:** State your major strategy here, listing the key tactics that you will use in your campaign.
6. **Recommended Budget:** State your total anticipated income and sources, your anticipated expenses, and the anticipated net profit or loss.
7. **Evaluation Plans:** State how you expect to evaluate (and expect to know) whether you have achieved each of your campaign and audience objectives."

That is a lot of information to compress into a single page or two. It takes well-crafted writing to create a persuasive summary that is so brief.

Here is a simpler outline for an executive summary:

1. Summarize your understanding of the client's situation and the problem to be solved.
2. State the objectives for the plan and the strategy. What will be the outcome?
3. Summarize the tactics that will be employed to execute the strategy and reach the objectives.
4. Make a persuasive argument that the plan will meet the needs of the client, and that your organization has the capability to execute the plan.

Writing of the executive summary should wait until the rest of a plan is complete. The summary must weave together details from various parts of the plan, and integrate them persuasively. To save time planners sometimes try to write an executive summary while development of the plan is still in progress. The result is likely to be a vague and unpersuasive summary.

Must the summary be only one page? No, but that length is a good goal. A rule of thumb is that summaries can be up to 10 percent of the length of the document they summarize. A 100-page document could have a 10-page summary at the beginning of it. A 10-page document should have no more than a single page. In practice, executive summaries are rarely more than two pages in length regardless of the length of the document they are summarizing.

*P*lan part 2: Situation analysis ▼

The situation analysis defines the public relations problem of the client and the reasons why the client seeks the services of public relations professionals. The purpose of this part of the plan is to make clear the situation as it exists today. You cannot solve a problem unless you understand it clearly and correctly. It is also important that everyone share the same understanding of the situation. Many organizations waste time and resources solving the wrong problem. Sometimes the client and the public relations firm work at cross-purposes trying to solve different problems. Before trying to solve any problem make sure that you are addressing the correct problem and that everyone agrees on what that problem is. This may seem obvious, but it often does not happen.

Type of need

First, identify the public relations need of the client. We may classify needs into three types:

1. Remedial
2. One-time
3. On-going (or standing)

A client may have one type of need or some combination of the three.

Remedial needs

A PR plan requiring remedial action usually is a response to4 some damage to image and reputation that requires a remedy. A typical remedial problem stems from a widely publicized crisis that has resulted in bad press for the organization. Historic crises such as the BP oil spill in the Gulf of Mexico or Tylenol poisoning require remedial action to restore an organization's reputation and credibility. Other examples include the Ford and Firestone handling of deaths resulting from their products; and more recently, the federal government's handling of Hurricane Katrina emergency relief and an alleged sexual assault by Duke University's lacrosse team.

Not every business problem is a crisis requiring remedial action. Remedial strategies make sense when problems are highly publicized and present a risk of lasting damage to the reputation of a product or an institution.

Corporations aren't alone in requiring help to remedy negative publicity. Individuals also experience highly publicized crises that call for remedial public relations. Examples include former Vice President Dick Cheney, after shooting a friend with a shotgun; Tom Cruise, after jumping up and down on Oprah's sofa; and Martha Stewart, after her conviction for trading stocks using insider information.

One-time needs

The client may plan to celebrate a major event such as an anniversary, new product launch, or new facility. The opening of a new library in a community would be an example of a one-time public relations need. Such an event would entail an opening ceremony and other special events. The public relations goal would be to help the client obtain as much publicity and good will from the one-time event as possible.

Ongoing needs

Many organizations have ongoing (also called standing) programs of public relations. There may be no crisis to solve or one-time event to plan. Rather, the organization needs to maintain relationships with various publics and the media to achieve current and long-term objectives. A university, for example, engages continuously in all sorts of public relations activities to communicate with prospective and current students, employees, parents, alumni, donors, residents of the community, and other key publics. A corporation maintains an ongoing program of public relations with its employees, stockholders, vendors, customers, stock market analysts, community leaders, and media, and with various levels of government. Long-term relationships with important publics are crucial to the success of organizations. Such relationships also make it easier

to weather the storms that inevitably occur when a crisis develops. Important publics will likely be more trusting of an organization during a crisis when that organization has maintained an effective ongoing program of public relations.

SWOT Analysis

The next step in the situation analysis is to complete a thorough S-W-O-T analysis. A S-W-O-T analysis is part of most advertising and public relations plans and identifies the client's:

> **S** trengths
> **W** eaknesses
> **O** pportunities
> **T** hreats

Strengths

Strengths are internal to the client. What are the client's overall strengths relative to its competitors? What does it have going for it? What can it brag about? How are its products or services better than those of competitors? Does the client have some advantage that competitors do not have in terms of a new product or a product category—a situation where the client might get the jump on competitors? Does it have other advantages in terms of brand image, manufacturing capability, global reach, and sales trends?

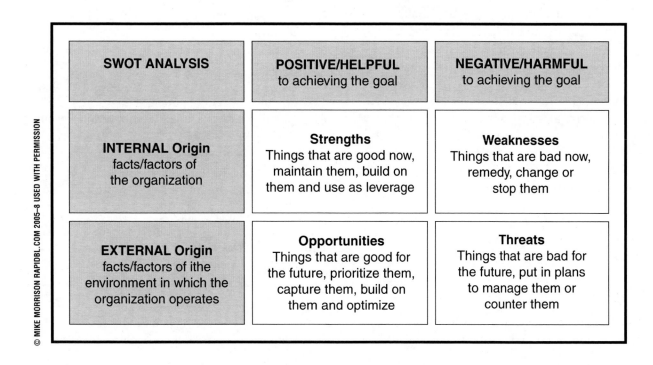

Weaknesses

Weaknesses are internal to the client. What are the client's weaknesses overall and relative to competitors? What are negatives that a competitor can exploit to the client's disadvantage? In what ways are its products, services, image, and sales weaker than those of competitors or of the industry?

Opportunities

Opportunities are external to the client—things outside the client's control. There are always targets of opportunity. What opportunities exist for the client? Are there niche publics not yet served? Are consumers adopting a new product, service, or technology at a rapid rate that will create increased sales for everyone? Organizations should constantly be scanning the environment looking for opportunities that others have missed. Apple Inc. identified and exploited opportunities repeatedly with its computer, iPod, and iPhone technologies. Asian automobile manufacturers also have been ahead of American carmakers in anticipating and exploiting trends in the auto market.

Threats

Threats are also external to the client. The client must respond to threats but cannot control them. What is happening that could dampen prospects for an organization? Perhaps the economy is going into recession and consumers are spending less. A new competitor in the market may be attracting a lot of attention. A new technology may render an older technology obsolete and uncompetitive (DVDs replaced videotape, CDs replaced vinyl recordings, MP3 players like iPod replaced other portable audio technologies). Government might enact legislation that will add to the cost of operations. Community organizations may resist an organization's efforts to expand and build new facilities or retail outlets. Threats can come from many directions and have an effect on an organization's image, production, tax rate, technology, and competitiveness. It is important to identify potential threats so that a public relations plan can respond to those that are most likely to have an impact on the objectives of the organization.

Research

Understanding a situation requires information. Public relations professionals engage in research to pull together information from a variety of sources relevant to understanding the client and its needs. Much of the information is readily available from the client's own files or from other existing sources (secondary research). Other information needs may require original (primary) research.

While research is important to the situation analysis, it permeates many parts of a public relations plan. Tactics, for example, require testing to judge their effectiveness. The evaluation of the plan may require research to measure changes in attitudes and behavior. We should never underestimate the value of research as a building block for a PR plan. Research provides background and facts that stimulate the problem-solving creative process.

Craig Miyamoto worked as a newspaper journalist and public relations professional for 40 years. He recommends gathering as many of the following pieces of information as possible when researching and writing a situation analysis. The situation analysis, he says, "provides details about internal and external contexts (workinpr.com):

Internal information

▶ Statements of the organization's mission, charter, bylaws, history and structure.

▶ Lists, biographical sketches and photos of key individuals—officers, board members, and program managers.

▶ Detailed descriptions of programs, products, services, etc.

▶ Statistics about resources, budget, staffing and programs.

▶ Summaries of interviews with key personnel about the problem situation.

▶ Copies of policy statements and procedures related to the problem.

▶ Complete descriptions of how the organization currently handles the problem.

▶ Lists and descriptions of the organization's controlled communication media.

External information

▶ Clippings from newspapers, magazines, trade publications, and newsletters, tracing print media coverage of organization and problem situation.

▶ Reports of radio, television and cable placements.

▶ Content analyses of media coverage.

▶ Lists of media, journalists, columnists, and freelance writers who report news about the organization and related issues.

▶ Lists and descriptions of individuals and groups that share the organization's concerns, interests, and views (including their controlled print and broadcast media).

▶ Lists and descriptions of individuals and groups that oppose the organization's positions on the issues (including their controlled print and broadcast media).

▶ Survey results of public's awareness, knowledge, opinions, and behaviors related to the organization and problem situation.

▶ Schedules of special events, observances, and other important dates related to the organization and problem.

▶ Lists of government agencies, legislators, and officials with regulatory or legislative power affecting the organization and the problem situation.

▶ Copies of relevant government regulations, legislation, bills pending, referenda, publications, and hearing reports.

▶ Copies of published research on topics related to the problem situation.

▶ Lists of important reference books, records, and directories, as well as their locations in the organization."

Thorough understanding of a situation sets the stage for the creation of realistic objectives, strategies, and tactics.

Plan part 3: Objectives ▼

The situation analysis clarifies the problem(s) that public relations will address. The next part of a public relations plan focuses on desired outcomes. What is the objective of the public relations plan? It is important to know where you want to go to have any chance of getting there. There are two types of objectives:

1. Informational
2. Motivational (also called behavioral)

Informational

The focus of an informational objective is to create awareness, to expand understanding, and generally to inform and educate audiences. For example, an objective might be to create greater awareness of the risks associated with head injuries from falling off a bicycle while not wearing a helmet. The objective is to educate the public about the benefits of wearing helmets and the consequences of not doing so.

Motivational

A motivational objective seeks to persuade people to do something, to engage in some behavior, to take some action. Examples of desired behaviors might include:

▶ sending a donation
▶ buying a product
▶ calling an 800 number
▶ voting for a particular candidate
▶ mailing in a reader response postcard
▶ taking an online survey
▶ buying tickets to a concert
▶ attending an art gallery opening

Motivational objectives are action-oriented. Returning to the example of bicycle helmets, motivational objectives could be to increase helmet sales or increase the percentage of riders who wear helmets.

There are a number of criteria for selecting and expressing an objective. Good objective statements should be:

▶ related to the overall goals of organization
▶ improvement oriented
▶ clearly stated
▶ specific as to what will be accomplished
▶ stated using measurable outcomes
▶ attainable or realistic

Writing objectives

All objective statements should contain two elements:

1. a measurable component,
2. a deadline.

Measurable component

The measurable component is what researchers will measure. It is an outcome that they can quantify in some way. Some examples:

▶ increase awareness by 15 percent
▶ sell 1,000 tickets
▶ raise $10,000 in donations
▶ get 1,000 people to call the 800 number
▶ get 200 column inches of news coverage in area newspapers

Examples of objectives

▶ *Poorly stated* objective:	Increase the number of tickets sold.
▶ *Better stated* objective:	Increase the number of tickets sold by 25 percent.
▶ *Properly stated* objective:	Increase the number of tickets sold in 2007 by 25 percent over sales in 2006.
What is measurable?	Number of tickets sold.
What is the deadline?	The end of 2007 (December 31).

The first objective is too vague. Was the objective achieved if one additional ticket sold? Does the plan have 20 years or 20 minutes to achieve the objective? The second objective states clearly the item being measured (ticket sales) and the quantified goal (25 percent), but there is still no deadline. The third objective makes clear the item being measured and when.

A plan may contain more than one objective. It may include both informational and motivational objectives. Normally, one or two objectives would be sufficient.

It is important to quantify the objective to answer the question later: "Did we achieve the objective?" Yes or no? If the objective was to sell 1,000 tickets, and we sold 1,100 then we met the objective. Had the objective only said, "To increase ticket sales," and sales increased from 500 to 501, would we consider that a successful outcome? Technically, ticket sales increased, but more than likely the outcome would be a disappointment. Specific, quantified objectives make it easier to measure the success (or failure) of public relations plans.

Deadline

There also should be a date specified when researchers measure results and judge success or failure. When will measurement of the outcome of the public relations plan occur? In a week, a month, a year? Be specific. If the objective is to increase awareness by 15 percent and there is no deadline specified, when will the results be tallied?

Some clients measure outcomes once a year. Others want monthly or quarterly reports that quantify results.

Plan part 4: Audience ▼

Public relations plans specify targeted audiences. It is inefficient to target messages to "the general public."

Why? Because most people who would receive a message would be uninterested and unmotivated to pay attention to it.

Mass media messages are expensive. Communicating to the general public is wasteful when the most important targeted groups are only a small subset of the whole population. Why send a letter to 100,000 people when a group of only 1,000 people is important for your purposes? Why broadcast a message on national network television when your audience is a small group in Central Texas?

Targeting smaller groups in a population is called segmenting or segmentation. Different criteria can segment audiences:

Demographic segmentation

Demographics are basic characteristics of a population, including

- ▶ Age
- ▶ Gender
- ▶ Race
- ▶ Ethnicity
- ▶ Language
- ▶ Nationality
- ▶ Family size
- ▶ Marital status
- ▶ Social class
- ▶ Home ownership
- ▶ Geographic location
- ▶ Education
- ▶ Income
- ▶ Religion
- ▶ Political opinions
- ▶ Profession
- ▶ Home ownership
- ▶ Employment status
- ▶ Length of commute

Psychographic segmentation

Psychographics describe consumers or audience members based on psychological characteristics. Together, these characteristics help to construct a psychological profile. Elements of a psychographic profile may include:

- Personality
- Lifestyle
- Memberships
- Values
- Attitudes
- Habits
- Interests

Behavioral segmentation

Behavioral segmentation groups people according to consumer behaviors such as:

- Benefits sought from a product or service
- Usage rate (heavy, moderate, light, nonuser)
- Brand loyalty
- User status (regular, first-time, potential)
- Purchase occasion (events that trigger behavior, such as marriage or graduation)

Communication is more effective when the message source has a clear sense of the audiences who will receive the message. In public relations, there should be identification of primary and secondary publics. They become the targets of messages.

Audience analysis is a process of choosing the key publics to target and profiling them as specifically as possible in terms of their demographics, psychographics and behavior. Such a profile makes it easier for public relations professionals to choose tactics (actions, appropriate words and visuals) that will resonate with targeted audiences.

Audiences today share some common characteristics:

- They are more diverse in terms of age, ethnicity, gender, nationality, language.
- They are visually oriented, forcing message sources to create messages with less text and more visuals.
- They are more likely to focus on single issues such as abortion or the environment. That complicates communication about other issues that are not on the radar of an audience.
- They are more interested in personality and "celebrity." PR commonly uses testimonials from well-known people because they generate interest.
- They distrust authority and are suspicious about conspiracies. It is more of a challenge to be perceived as credible and trustworthy when audiences are quick to mistrust.
- They are global. Pr may need to create messages for audiences in more than one country, using more than one language.

A public relations program targets specific publics. Two types of groups are identified because of their importance to the client:

1. Primary public(s)
2. Secondary public(s) (if any)

Primary publics

Primary publics are those audiences who are most crucial to reach to achieve objectives. Various criteria can identify them, including:

- Age
- Gender
- Race or ethnicity
- Location
- Education
- Income
- Profession
- Political opinions
- Religion
- Consumer preferences
- Lifestyle
- Product consumption habits

Which criteria matter most? What audiences must advertising reach to achieve the client's objectives? Decisions about messages, media, strategy, and tactics depend on the ability to define clearly the target audience. Primary publics are those that PR must reach.

In addition to identifying the primary audiences in stakeholder groups, many PR plans also list the media outlets they will target. The audience section of the plan will contain a list of publications, electronic media, community groups and online sites that will be targeted with messages. If a plan depends on media to communicate with audiences, it is important to know which media vehicles are critical to contact because they serve the primary audiences.

Secondary publics

Other important audiences may exist but be ignored altogether or given secondary status because of limited resources. A plan might target 18 to 25 year olds as a primary audience, for example, but designate the slightly older demographic of 26 to 34 years as a secondary audience. It is critical to reach 18 to 25 year olds in this case. They may be the primary consumers of a product. Resources focus first on reaching that targeted group. If resources permit then public relations may direct some messages at the secondary, older audience as well.

The public relations plan should describe each of the targeted audiences and explain why they are important for the PR effort.

Plan part 5: Strategy ▼

Situation analysis frames or describes the problem. The objectives clarify the outcomes that the client desires. The identification of primary and secondary audiences focuses attention on the specific publics to whom public relations will direct the communication. The next section of a public relations plan is to create a strategy for communicating effectively with the audiences.

The word strategy comes the Greek stratēgiā, *office of a general,* which itself is derived from stratgos, or "general." This was military terminology. The word has come to mean the general or overall plan a major campaign. Strategy is a nonspecific long-term view of what needs doing. Tactics are the short-term activities that execute the strategy.

A strategy statement describes how to achieve an objective. The strategy should state the key themes and messages that public relations will repeat through all media throughout the campaign on publicity materials. The strategy is what will be said.

For example, the Girl Scouts were having some difficulty recruiting new members. Many children and their parents perceived the Girl Scouts as old fashioned. Many had the image of the Girl Scouts as a largely Caucasian group of girls who sold cookies, went camping, and made crafts. The Girl Scouts developed a PR strategy that emphasized the many modern activities that the "new" Girl Scouts engage in, such as rock climbing, whitewater rafting, and creating Web sites. The objective was to revitalize the brand and change the image of the organization to make it attractive to prospective members. The strategy was to communicate that Girl Scouts have evolved with the times and offer modern and meaningful activities for young women today. The tactics for executing the strategy included press releases, along with television and Web content. They also heavily targeted black, Hispanic, and Asian audiences to broaden the demographics and inclusivity of the organization.

Another example is the marketing of Turkey, the country. Turkey is anxious to join the European Union and to increase business investment in the country as well as foreign tourism. Europeans are skeptical about Turkey's readiness to be a partner in the EU. The country has the image of being backward, poor, and tending toward a frightening form of fundamentalist Islamic beliefs. Businesses are not eager to invest in a place where they perceive the politics as unstable and the workforce poorly educated. Tourists are reluctant to take holidays in Turkey because of safety issues and concern about the quality of facilities and hygiene. Many also do not know what there is to see and do in Turkey.

The strategy for advertising and public relations will try to counter misinformation, misperceptions, and prejudice by emphasizing that Turkey has a modern culture and economy that is fully compatible with Europe and with modern business practices. The tourism strategy will emphasize that Turkey has fascinating historical sites, natural beauty, modern accommodations, great shopping, and delicious cuisine. Many different tactics communicate this message to EU politicians, business investors, and prospective tourists.

Strategies describe how public relations will achieve an objective in a general sense. They express the theme or message of a campaign. What, for example, will tactics say about the client? At the end of the plan, what will audiences know about the client? In the case of the Girl Scouts, audiences will know that the Girl Scouts have changed with the times. With regard to Turkey, they will know that Turkey is a modern nation for business investors and tourists and a suitable partner to join the European Union.

Plan part 6: Tactics ▼

Tactics are specific activities and materials that execute a strategy. Most public relations plans involve the use of multiple tactics to achieve objectives. It is important to choose tactics that are effective at reaching the target audiences. Some tactics are relatively inexpensive to execute while others cost a great deal of money. The budget, therefore, is also a factor in choosing tactics for the client. The goal is to use a mix of tactics that will achieve the greatest impact.

Choosing and executing tactics is a creative endeavor. Persuasive messages inundate media audiences. Most messages fail to get noticed or remembered. In Chapter 3, there was a list of requirements for successful PR messages. Applying those requirements to the task of choosing and executing tactics is helpful.

Successful PR tactics should:

1. **Be received (exposure)**
   What media do the primary and secondary audiences use? What can public relations do to gain audience exposure to messages?

2. **Get attention (attention)**
   What device(s) can public relations use to get attention and break through all the message clutter? What can it do to get messages noticed?

3. **Be understood (perception)**
   What concerns are there about accurate understanding of the message? Do audiences include diverse cultures and languages? Is education an issue? Does the client use jargon or acronyms that public relations must handle with care? How can it make messages understandable?

4. **Be believed (credibility)**
   Will the audience question the credibility of the message? Is there a need for expert testimonials, research statistics, or other devices to make messages believable? Are audiences likely to be friendly and accepting or hostile and skeptical?

5. **Be remembered (retention and recall)**
   What devices can researchers use to make messages memorable so the audience will recall them later? Is it possible to achieve repetitive exposure to the message to increase retention and recall?

6. **Be acted upon (action)**
   What can public relations do to get people to take action immediately: provide a coupon,

Common public relations tactics

- ▶ News release (also called press release)
- ▶ Fact Sheet
- ▶ Press kit (also called media kits)
- ▶ Newsletter
- ▶ Company magazine
- ▶ Brochure and pamphlet
- ▶ Handbook
- ▶ Annual report
- ▶ Corporate advertising (also called institutional advertising)
- ▶ Public Service Announcement (PSA)
- ▶ Face-to-face contacts
- ▶ Speeches
- ▶ News conference
- ▶ Media interviews
- ▶ Video news release
- ▶ Media interviews
- ▶ Press parties
- ▶ Letters to the editor
- ▶ Op-ed articles
- ▶ Press tours
- ▶ Meetings
- ▶ Video News Release (VNR)

- ▶ Cable TV
- ▶ Motion Picture
- ▶ Product placement
- ▶ Web site
- ▶ E-mail newsletters
- ▶ Blogs
- ▶ YouTube
- ▶ Social networking
- ▶ Web 2.0
- ▶ E-blast
- ▶ Industry conferences
- ▶ Special events
- ▶ Trade shows
- ▶ Community calendar listings
- ▶ Lobbying
- ▶ Grassroots lobbying
- ▶ Town meetings
- ▶ Guerrilla marketing
- ▶ Viral marketing
- ▶ Media alerts
- ▶ Calendars
- ▶ Feature ideas
- ▶ Direct mail
- ▶ Outdoor advertising

encourage audiences to call an 800 number, provide a self-addressed postcard, direct audiences to a Web site where more information is available? How can audiences be motivated to go from awareness to action now?

Later chapters contain specific suggestions for writing and designing public relations documents.

News releases

The news release is usually a one- or two-page document written in standard journalism style and ready for publication. In theory, a newspaper should be able to copy and paste a news release into its pages and the story would read like any other news story. In practice, news releases rarely get published as written. Large urban newspapers use news releases as a source of story ideas. They often conduct their own interviews to flesh out the story. The news release provides a starting point from which a reporter can construct a story. Small town newspapers may publish a news release as written, especially if it arrives via e-mail so they can easily copy and paste it.

Television requires stories with good visuals. If a story lacks a strong visual element, it will be hard to sell the story to TV journalists. TV also works best with stories that one can explain in a minute or two. Complicated stories with many details are hard to explain in 90 seconds.

What makes for a good news story? Thomas Bivins, in his "Handbook for Public Relations Writing" (1995), says "journalists judge news value based on at least some of the following characteristics:

▶ **Consequence.** Does the information have any importance to the prospective reading, listening or viewing public?
▶ **Interest.** Is the information unusual or entertaining?
▶ **Timeliness.** Is the material current?
▶ **Proximity.** For most public relations people seeking to connect with the media, a local angle is often the only way to do it.
▶ **Prominence.** Events and people of prominence frequently make the news. . . ."

Pratkanis and Aronson (2001) say that "reporters and editors tend to look for stories that

(1) are new and timely, (2) involve conflict or scandal, (3) concern strange and unusual happenings, (4) happen to familiar or famous people, (5) are capable of being made dramatic and personal, (6) are simple to convey in a short space or time, (7) contain visual elements (especially pictures for television), and (8) fit a theme that is currently prominent in the news or society."

News releases must attract the interest of reporters and editors. Most news releases become discarded because they fail to interest journalists. Only a small percentage of news releases become stories. Most do not pass the test for being newsworthy. They appear to journalists as either an attempt to get free advertising or as a story with no local importance.

Public relations can send news releases to highly targeted media (*microdistribution*) in a single city, region, or industry or they could mass distribute them to reach many media outlets and diverse audiences (*macrodistribution*).

In the past news releaseswere distributed by first class mail, fax, personal delivery, or bulk mail. Today, most releases come to media via e-mail, and journalists prefer e-mail to other delivery methods. They can scan e-mails quickly. They can forward them. They can copy portions of them and paste them into a story. Journalists find that e-mail releases give them more flexibility and the ability to handle speedily a large numbers of releases. In addition, e-mail releases minimize the mounds of paper on their desks.

Many organizations do not have a public relations professional on staff and are not comfortable writing releases themselves. There are specialized public relations companies that write and distribute press releases. Examples include:

▶ ereleases.com
▶ businesswire.com
▶ prnewswire.com
▶ pressreleasenetwork.com/
▶ pressflash.com

These services typically charge from $300 to $400 to do a simple one- or two-page news release. The details of a story go to the news release distributor who then writes a release in standard format and distributes it to appropriate media outlets. This is a cost-effective alternative for organizations to generate an occasional news release when they do not have the staff to handle the task internally.

Letters to the editor

Newspapers and magazines regularly publish letters to the editor. Writers can challenge the content of a pub-

News release format

- ▶ White 8-1/2 by 11-inch paper (if printed).
- ▶ Identify contact in upper left of page.
- ▶ Indicate FOR IMMEDIATE RELEASE or the date of release if *embargoed.*
- ▶ An embargoed release is held for publication on a specific future date. Instead of saying "FOR IMMEDIATE RELEASE" the release would read: "HOLD FOR RELEASE: 6 P.M. EDT, Wednesday, July 11, 2007."
- ▶ Double-space.
- ▶ 1.5-inch margins left and right.
- ▶ If the release continues on a second page write *MORE* at the bottom of the first page.
- ▶ Write a one-word description (a *slug line*).
- ▶ Write an active, newsy headline.
- ▶ Use a dateline, noting where the story originates. Do not use postal abbreviations for the state.
- ▶ Use the slug line and page number on pages after the first page. For example, GIFT Page 2.
- ▶ Include a boilerplate paragraph at the end, just above ###, that contains general descriptive information about the organization. For a university, the boilerplate might mention when the university began, the number of students, number of faculty, and the types of degrees offered.
- ▶ At the bottom of the release indicate the end with either ### or -30-.
- ▶ A typical news release format is this:

UNIVERSITY OF XXXXXXX
Office of News & Communications
http://www.XXXuniv.edu

FOR IMMEDIATE RELEASE: Wednesday, July 11, 2007

CONTACT: John Smith
(555) 555-5555
john.smith@XXXuniv.edu

Benefactors

CORPORATION ANNOUNCES $1 MILLION GIFT XXX UNIVERSITY

DALLAS, Texas—An anonymous benefactor has donated $1 million to XXX University to build a new photography laboratory in the Department of Art and Design.

Etc. etc.

Boilerplate paragraph

###

lication or offer opinions contrary to those expressed in editorials. Letters to the editor also endorse candidates for elected office. The authors of letters must identify themselves, and most publications will verify the identity of authors before publishing a letter. Letters to the editor are widely read and a good choice for briefly expressing an opinion or setting the record straight if incorrect information has been published.

Op-ed articles

Op-ed is the name given to guest opinion articles appearing on the page opposite a newspaper's editorial page. Op-ed combines the words "opposite" and "editorial." Regular essays by such syndicated columnists as Charles Krauthammer, Cal Thomas andEllen Goodman occupy much of the space on the op-ed page. Space is also available for well-written local essays by writers who are authorities on a subject. Op-ed pieces are not news. They are expressions of opinion. They are also not editorials. A publication's own staff writes editorials. Op-ed articles can be useful in public relations as vehicles for weighing in on public policy issues. There is no cost to have an op-ed essay published.

Competition for available space is fierce, and op-eds must be well written, timely, and interesting.

Fact sheets

Fact sheets are a quick reference tool in an outline or bulleted format. Media kits generally include them. They provide facts about an organization such as the length of its operation, the number of employees, its annual revenues and products, and the services it provides. Fact sheets provide details that are not appropriate for inclusion in news releases. They supply additional background information for reporters who may be developing a story.

Media kits

Media kits (also called press kits) are a package of materials provided to media at news conferences or other events. Some organizations also make media kits available online at their Web sites. Kits usually consist of a folder that contains such materials as a news release, a fact sheet, background articles, article reprints from publications, brochures, graphic design materials including logos, corporate annual reports,

---

Letterhead format

cMedia advisory
January 29, 2009

Campus Protest over Tuition Rise

Optional short descriptive paragraph about the event here.

WHAT:	Students protest a 15 percent increase in tuition at XXX University.
WHO:	20 student organizations will send representatives; expect more than 1,000 students.
WHEN:	10 A.M. Thursday, Feb 2
WHERE:	Campus Quad, in front of English Building
BACKGROUND:	(optional field, keep it to a single paragraph) blah blah blah . . .
NOTES:	(optional field, keep it to a single paragraph) blah blah blah . . .
CONTACT:	John Smith: (xxx) xxx-xxxx johnsmith@xxxmail.com

###

biographies of key people, and publicity photos. Some also include CDs or DVDs, or other multimedia or promotional materials.

- ▶ hyperion.com/news_events/press_kit/
- ▶ shuttlepresskit.com

Newsletters

Newsletters are an effective tactic for communicating with four target audiences: employees and retirees, stockholders and investors, sales staff and wholesalers, and customers and members. These are audiences with a strong interest in the organization and its products and services. Some organizations save money today by "publishing" employee newsletters exclusively online. These newsletters look like printed publications while the format of other online publications specifically have Internet users in mind, with generous use of headlines and summaries.

Media advisories (or media alerts)

A media advisory gives notice to news media about an upcoming event. It is a one-page brief outline giving journalists advance warning about an event. The format of advisories enables quick reading. They supply journalists with the information necessary to assign a story to a reporter. Advisories should go to the media several days in advance.

It is advisable to indicate whether the event is a photo or story opportunity. A photo opportunity is an event that will probably yield interesting human interest photos but probably no serious story. Television journalists will try to ascertain the availability of video opportunities from the advisory. Describe them if possible.

Company magazines

Large corporations and nonprofit institutions publish institutional magazines. Some magazines target employees to foster better understanding of an organization's goals and activities, and awareness of issues that may impact its operations. Magazines serve as a vehicle for public recognition of employees for good performance and productivity and alert employees to career and education opportunities. In general, they serve to personalize large organizations and to provide a vehicle for the celebration of individual and organizational accomplishments. Among the most widely read company magazines are those produced monthly by commercial airlines.

Company magazines are lengthier and more formal looking than newsletters. Some are lavish in their production values, using four-color print and glossy paper. Journal Communications Inc. (jnlcom.com) produces magazines targeting newcomers, business owners, and executives of major employers. Sponsors of the publications are chambers of commerce, economic development organizations, convention and visitors bureaus, and travel offices throughout North America. One of its magazines is called IMAGES, which reflects life in a particular community. It is targeted for newcomers and relocating companies. IMAGES features original editorial and photography on such topics as health care, education, arts and culture, and business. Journal Communications, Inc. is just one of numerous custom publishers that specialize in this type of magazine.

Oracle, the database software company, publishes a magazine called Oracle. It too is a glossy publication targeted for Oracle stakeholders and others interested in databases and technology. An online version of the publication is available at oracle.com. Sony Magazine is a quarterly magazine published by Haymarket Network and contains stories about film, music, games, television, sound vision, electronic gadgets, and adventure. It is available at Sony Centre stores in the United Kingdom.

Steinway Magazine, produced by Faircount Media Group (faircount.com), boasts a circulation of 70,000 for a publication produced twice a year and writes about the craftsmanship of fine pianos. It targets classical/ jazz artists, pop stars, and a demographic group capable of spending significant sums of money for a top brand piano.

Brochures and pamphlets

Organizations publish brochures and pamphlets for promotional and educational purposes. A pharmaceutical company, for example, may create a pamphlet that describes a medical condition such as arthritis, with information about alternative treatments, including the company's drug products that address the needs of arthritis sufferers. The publications are usually free, and they provide information that does not go out of date quickly. Writing in a clear and concise manner helps consumers with a range of reading skills easily understand the information.

Handbooks

Handbooks are a more elaborate publication. Industries and trade associations publish handbooks that provide background information and statistics about the industry. Many handbooks also contain a directory of members with contact information.

Annual reports

Publicly owned corporations are required to publish an annual report that provides detailed financial information about the corporation. The Securities and Exchange Commission requires that such reports contain certain specific information that informs investors and regulators about each corporation's operations, income, expenses, assets, and liabilities.

A corporation could satisfy SEC requirements by publishing a relatively simple and inexpensive annual report. Most corporations, however, publish annual reports that go well beyond the basic requirements. They use the annual report as a public relations tool to tell the company's story to important audiences. Expensive four-color magazines may impress stockholders, prospective investors, and even prospective employees. One part of the report provides the required financial information, while the rest of the report celebrates a corporation's accomplishments and future plans.

Many people find annual reports boring. As an alternative, some corporations provide a video version with important information in a more interesting format. Video annual reports do not, however, satisfy the SEC requirement for publishing a report. The videos can complement but not replace the required publication.

Corporate (institutional) advertising

Corporate or institutional advertising differs from ordinary advertising. Rather than focusing on selling products or services, corporate advertising promotes an organization's image and reputation to strengthen its identity and its role as a good corporate citizen. A relatively small percentage of ad budgets are devoted to this type of advertising, most of which is spent on television and magazine advertising. The target audiences for such ads include investors, securities analysts, and current and prospective employees. The effect of such ads is difficult to measure.

Some corporate ads engage in advocacy, promoting a position on a public policy issue. Corporations have permission to try to influence public opinion. An organization or industry might, for example, be very concerned about a particular regulation or change in public policy that would affect its operations. Advocacy advertising tries to influence legislation and public opinion, as well as strengthen relations with community leaders and regulators.

Public service announcements (PSA)

Public service announcements are noncommercial advertisements for nonprofit groups that radio and television broadcast for free. Most relate to health and safety, such as messages about drinking and driving, cigarette smoking, and the dangers of using drugs. However, electronic media regularly broadcast PSAs for all sorts of other nonprofit activities and events.

Public relations sends written PSA scripts or prerecorded PSAs to radio and television stations and cable television systems. Announcements must be brief. On radio, on-air talent read many PSAs live as part of their "banter."

Face to face

The most effective interpersonal communication is face to face. A speaker can see the message receiver. The other person's reactions are visible, feedback is immediate, and one can adapt messages easily. In public relations, a common face-to-face exchange is with publication editors. A public relations professional may solicit major coverage of an upcoming event by personally pitching it to an editor. If the editor is interested, the event may generate more coverage before, during, and after the event than might have occurred otherwise. There are some general rules for making face-to-face presentations to editors:

▶ Telephone in advance for an appointment
▶ Identify yourself and your purpose
▶ Be concise
▶ Don't oversell
▶ Express appreciation for the editor's time
▶ Follow-up with a note of appreciation
▶ Leave behind appropriate written material, such as a press kit with a news release, fact sheet, photos, detailed schedule of events, biographical profiles of major personalities, and brochures.

Speechwriting

Many public relations professionals write speeches for executives and clients. Some large organizations employ speechwriters full-time. Well-crafted speeches are especially important if the topic is timely and media coverage expected. A few guidelines for speech writing include:

▶ Research the target audience to understand their views and interests.

▶ Speak using the vocabulary of the target audience.

▶ State and restate major points to help listeners understand. Assume listeners are not 100 percent focused on what is said.

▶ The normal delivery rate is about 150 words per minute. A 10-minute speech, therefore, should be approximately 1,500 words in length (150 wpm × 10 minutes = 1,500 words).

▶ Practice. Practice. Practice.

▶ Check and recheck microphones and other equipment, such as LCD projectors.

▶ If the speech is important or may generate media coverage, bring printed copies of it for the media and others who might want one.

▶ Record the speech as a permanent record. If a speech is misquoted in the media it will be easier to defend the comments if there is a recording of the entire speech available.

Companies such as OverViews (speechwriting.com) specialize in writing public relations speeches for executives. It has written speeches for executives in such Fortune 500 companies as American Express, Eastman Chemical, Ford Motor Company, General Motors, Hilton Hotels, ITT, Sony, and Saturn. Individuals who have little experience writing speeches may benefit from having a firm such as OverViews write a speech for important occasions.

News conferences

News conferences should happen infrequently and only to make major announcements that will generate media interest. It is embarrassing to hold a news conference that generates little media coverage. Suggestions for organizing news conferences include:

▶ Select a convenient location and time, usually 10 A.M. to 3 P.M., to help reporters meet deadlines.

▶ Arrive early to check on room set-up.

▶ Invite the media well in advance if possible.

▶ Prepare a media kit.

▶ Prepare the speaker for likely questions. If the topic is controversial, it is especially important to anticipate difficult or embarrassing questions.

▶ Practice brief answers to questions and think in terms of "sound bites" or comments that television news can easily use.

▶ Make certain the right person represents the organization in front of the media. It should be someone who can handle aggressive questioning without becoming angry or flustered.

▶ Assume that everything said is "on the record" and could appear in the media. That includes informal comments before and after the official news conference that "live" microphones might pick up accidentally. Speakers routinely must defend comments made at events when they thought no one was listening.

Interviews

A valuable opportunity for public relations is the media interview. Newspapers, magazines, radio and television routinely interview personalities and newsmakers. The interview might be brief for use in a newscast or lengthy for a feature-length story. It might be a hard-news interview, or more entertainment oriented, such as for "The Tonight Show," "Letterman," "Howard Stern" (radio) or "Oprah." Media and the press agents for personalities play an interesting game trying to book the personalities into the best venues. Magazines compete to get interviews and photos of major personalities who are in the news. TV talk shows also compete fiercely to get first access to newsmakers and celebrities.

The suggestions for preparing for interviews are similar to those for preparing for news conferences:

▶ Anticipate questions. Rehearse responses to difficult questions.

▶ Prepare clients to minimize camera fright.

▶ Coach clients with practice sessions.

▶ Coach the person on being concise. Practice short responses for television news "sound bites" (30 seconds).

▶ Dress conservatively, avoiding white, black, narrow stripes, loud patterns.

▶ Use gestures to appear animated.

▶ Use eye contact.

▶ Assume a good pose for cameras. Do not slouch.

- Avoid "um," "ah," stumbling, restlessness, and distracting physical behaviors.
- Provide background information to the interviewer in advance.
- When possible, provide background information about the reporter/interviewer to the client. Many people are more relaxed about interviews if they know something about the person who will conduct the interview.
- Make a recording of the interview. If it is edited and there is some controversy about what was said, a recording will provide a record of the full context of the original interview.
- Do not make off-the-record comments in public settings. Someone is likely to overhear, and it will appear in the media. It is always risky to speak "off the record." Assume that every word uttered before, during, and after an interview could appear in the media. Unless a journalist explicitly agrees to go "off the record," assume that every comment is on the record.

Press parties

A meal or reception for journalists, media leaders, and other important guests is a press party. An announcement or statement usually follows some socializing. Press parties are a common tactic for promoting the opening of a new business or facility. A new restaurant, for example, might invite local media, celebrities, and community leaders to show off the restaurant's food and décor. Imaginative food, small gifts for guests, and press kits are usually highlights of a press party.

Press tours (media tours)

Journalists may receive an invitation for a trip to see or experience something. The host pays for transporting, feeding, and sometimes housing journalists. The goal is to familiarize reporters firsthand with something that may be difficult to understand otherwise. For example, when the U.S. Navy brings an aircraft carrier into a non-naval port, where the arrival of such a large ship is news, it sometimes permits public tours and arranges a special press tour for local media.

Press tours may violate the ethical code of journalists, who could view a particular event as an attempt to buy favor. This is a sensitive issue for journalists and needs a careful approach.

Another type of media tour brings clients to the media. The clients could include authors with a new book in print, politicians, actors promoting a new film or television series, and other celebrities. Newsmakers visit major cities for media interviews. For media in smaller markets, PR people may arrange phone interviews instead of in-person visits. One of the ways that PR can "localize" a story is to conduct a media tour that brings interesting people to a community. Their presence in the community is newsworthy and provides the local angle needed to justify coverage.

Meetings

The SEC requires public corporations to conduct an annual meeting for stockholders. These are carefully orchestrated major events. Circumstances may also call for organizing other types of meetings with the general public, employees, or other groups. Town meetings are one type of meeting to solicit feedback from a community about a particular topic. Politicians regularly conduct such public meetings to discuss major pending legislation. A business might sponsor a meeting to explain its plans for expanding a facility, executing layoffs, or to explain upcoming plans that will have an impact on a community

Meetings should be tightly run to start and stop promptly and to move along steadily. Organizers should manage audience involvement so it is fair and no one dominates the discussion.

Here is an example of a news item about a politician's use of a town meeting:

> WASHINGTON—Congressman Harold Ford, Jr. (D-Tenn.) and U.S. Senator Russ Feingold (DWisc.) will host a town hall meeting on campaign finance reform at 5:15 P.M. Friday, September 7, at The University of Memphis, Faulkner Lounge (University Center). The group will hold a press conference at 4:45 P.M. at the Delta Lounge, Room 303 (adjacent to Faulkner Lounge).

Videotape news releases (VNR)

VNRs are a complete video "package" or story that is ready for broadcast. They are similar to printed news releases in the sense that a television station could use them as is, but most will not. If the subject interests TV journalists, they most likely will use the VNR as a story idea and will shoot their own video and produce their own story.

Often PR people make the elements of the VNR package available separately so TV stations can assemble them as they wish. They provide background video, called B-roll. TV journalists are more likely to use the B-roll as part of their story than the complete VNR.

VNRs are controversial because journalists believe they are public relations masquerading as news. Stations seldom use an entire VNR and usually identify on the air the source of the video that they do use. For example, if ExxonMobil provides video for a newscast, it is likely that a station would include this text during the video: "Courtesy ExxonMobil," to make clear the source of the video.

Cable TV

Cable television provides many opportunities for public relations messages to reach audiences. Specialized channels make it easier to target niche groups of views. There are channels for golf, gardening, home improvement, extreme sports, shopping, travel, food, animals, women, science fiction, history, music, fashion and style, weather, science, business and investing, health, tennis, soccer, and auto racing. Channels target the Hispanic and African-American audiences. And, of course, there are many 24-hour news channels. Depending on the client, these specialized channels offer interview opportunities and even a chance to demonstrate products on the air. The proliferation of television channels creates an insatiable demand for programming and program ideas. Public relations people can also purchase advertising on channels that reach narrowly targeted groups, even at the local level where local cable television systems can now insert local commercials into breaks on the national cable channels.

Digital video

Most of the population of the United States now has access to one or more video playback technologies in the home and office. This ubiquitous technology makes possible the low-cost distribution of messages on video. Video is augmenting and sometimes replacing printed materials. Examples include video financial reports from corporations, internal corporate TV newscasts, video training, and video sales messages that serve as "high-tech" brochures. The rapid diffusion of broadband Internet services has created even more opportunities to distribute highly produced video at low cost. Audiences can download streaming video into computers, smart phones, or iPad type devices.

Product placement

Television audiences have more control than ever over the commercial messages that reach them. Remote controls speed the ability to change channels to avoid commercials. TiVo and other digital video recording systems enable viewers to skip commercials in programs. While consumers welcome these technologies, they are a source of frustration to marketers. How do you get your message in front of consumers who are trying so hard to avoid seeing them?

One solution is product placement. Marketers pay television and motion picture producers to put their products in front of the camera as part of a program. The product image appears in the program and is unavoidable.

James Bond, 007, drove an Aston Martin in the film "Die Another Day." Michael J. Fox wore Plantronics telephone headsets in "Spin City." Adam Sandler ate Popeye's Chicken & Biscuits in the film "Little Nicky." Oreo cookies appeared on "Friends." It is no accident that Coke cups appear prominently on "American Idol" each week. In fact, most television programs and films contain product placements.

Internet

Increasingly, consumers expect organizations of all types to maintain Web sites that provide detailed information. They are surprised if a company does not have a Web site. Many sites provide product information and make possible the purchase of products online. Recognizing the importance of the Web, many companies now specialize in developing Web sites that are highly engaging. This area of advertising and public relations is evolving so rapidly that it is difficult to keep up with new developments.

Guerrilla marketing

Jay Conrad Levinson, in his 1982 book "Guerrilla Marketing," popularized the idea of doing public relations and advertising on a very low budget. The emphasis is on free or low cost tactics for small businesses and nonprofits with small marketing budgets. Examples of guerrilla tactics include word of mouth, classified ads, personal letters, leaflets and fliers, T-shirts, promotional items such as pens, refrigerator magnets and calendars, and e-mail. Today we would add web and social media sites and YouTube videos to the list. Levinson's original book has subsequently spawned an industry of spinoff books, including "Guerrilla Marketing Attack," "Guerrilla Publicity," "Guerrilla Marketing Weapons," "Guerrilla Financing," "Guerrilla Marketing Online," and many more.

Viral marketing

Viral marketing is the 21st century extension of word-of-mouth. Designers create Web sites with highly entertaining, odd, and even bizarre content. The content generates buzz or chatter. People e-mail the URL to their friends, who do the same. Knowledge of the site spreads like a virus, hence the name of this tactic. Alternatively, an organization might post a video or commercial on YouTube, allowing the message to spread virally to thousands or even millions of people. The problem with viral marketing is its unreliability. Traditional advertising can largely control the reach (number of people reached) and frequency (number of times the average person sees an ad) of a marketing campaign. A video posted to YouTube, however, might garner an audience of a dozen or an audience of a million viewers. Most videos on YouTube go largely unnoticed. Some go viral and generate incredible publicity. The lack of certainty about response is a frustration for marketers.

Plan part 7: Calendar (timetable) ▼

It is important to plan the scheduling of tactics carefully. Advertising and public relations plans typically become implemented over a period of three to 12 months. Some take even longer. The timetable for a plan must take into account when each activity will happen relative to everything else. The timetable should take into account the planning and execution of each individual tactic.

Here are some questions that help with the planning of a public relations calendar:

▶ When should PR conduct the plan? What will be the beginning and ending dates?

▶ What is the proper order of tactics? Which tactic should PR execute first, second, third, etc.?

▶ What steps need to happen to accomplish each tactic? How much lead time is necessary to prepare each tactic for execution?

The goal is to be certain that everything is done on time and in the proper order. Tactics in a plan are usually not all executed simultaneously. At an early stage, there is preparation work. For example, personnel must write, edit, and design publications, send them to a printer, proof, and print them. A major special event such as an exhibit at an industry trade show can take months to plan. They must allow time for each of the steps required to produce each tactic.

Sometimes selected audiences, such as employees, become targeted for early messages. The rest of the effort may then unfold over a period of time. PR people often refer to the process of executing an advertising or public relations plan as the "roll out." For example, "The campaign will roll out in different markets from August to October."

Tactic/Task	Jan	Feb	Mar	Apr	May	Jun	Jul	Aug	Sept	Oct	Nov	Dec
PUBLISH BROCHURE	■	■	■	■	■	■						
Write copy	■											
Edit copy		■										
Design and layout			■									
Blueline proof from printer				■								
Print brochure					■							
Mail brochure						■						

▲ *Gantt chart*

Gantt chart

Presentation of the calendar in the plan can occur in different ways. One popular method for visually representing the calendar is a Gantt chart. Gantt charts are a type of bar chart that illustrates a project schedule. They are popular in all sorts of project planning. They can include start and finish dates for tactics, as well as intermediary activities necessary to complete each tactic. You can create Gantt charts using commonly available computer software such as Microsoft Project, Excel, or Word. A template for creating a Gantt chart with Microsoft Word is available online at: http://staff.uow.edu.au/cdu/files/project/Gantt_chart.doc. The following simple Gantt chart was created using Microsoft Word.

Plan part 8: Budget ▼

All public relations plans have a limited amount of money to spend. The budget contains not only the total cost of a plan, but also the itemized cost of each major expense associated with the plan. Here are some examples of common public relations expenses:

- ▶ Copying costs
- ▶ Photography
- ▶ Graphics
- ▶ Equipment rentals
- ▶ Promotional materials
- ▶ Videotape cassettes
- ▶ Videotaping charges
- ▶ Letterhead paper
- ▶ Plain bond paper
- ▶ Envelopes
- ▶ Postage
- ▶ Long-distance telephone charges
- ▶ Transportation
- ▶ Business entertaining
- ▶ Rental of meeting space
- ▶ Corporate or institutional advertising
- ▶ Web site design and maintenance
- ▶ Construction of exhibit display

In addition to using budgets as a management tool to control expenses, clients can also use budgets to weigh costs versus benefits. Did the PR plan produce results that justify the expense? Could clients have achieved better results if they had spent the same amount of money on traditional advertising? Does spending more on public relations produce more of an impact? If clients do not track costs, it is impossible to answer questions about the strategic value of public relations. Clients increasing demand accountability from public relations practitioners. They want evidence that money was well spent and produced results.

Budgeting processes will vary depending on whether employees of the organization are executing the public relations plan internally or whether the company has outsourced it to an external public relations firm. If employees are executing the plan, the budget may include both internal and external expenses. Internal expenses include the cost of staff time and overhead items as the cost of space and utilities. External (out-of-pocket) expenses include printing, travel, postage, and payments to various vendors. The organization may choose to ignore internal expenses in a public relations budget and itemize only the out-of-pocket external expenses.

When companies outsource all or part of a plan to PR firms for execution, the budget will detail all of the expenses, including staff costs and out-of-pocket charges. Typically, PR firms will bill staff time on an hourly basis and report expenses on a regular basis, either monthly or quarterly.

Understanding budgets is critical for public relations professionals because competition for resources is intense. Advertising, marketing, and public relations all compete for the limited dollars available for marketing communication. Such professionals also need to associate budgets with objectives realistically. What will it cost, for example, to increase ticket sales for a local nonprofit film festival? If they pull the numbers out of the air as a guess, the numbers are meaningless. They must match resources with the actual cost of executing each of the tactics in the plan. If there are insufficient resources to execute the plan, then they should modify the objectives to make them more realistic. Otherwise, a plan promises more than it can deliver.

Budgets also provide important historical information. Next year's plan can use budget information from this year's plan as a starting point. Professionals may adjust the numbers up or down depending on both the results achieved this year and how ambitious the objectives are for the coming year. Over time, carefully tracked budgets become more useful in the strategic process because the numbers become more precise and more closely associated with outcomes.

Plan part 9: Evaluation ▼

Eventually, it will be necessary to communicate the results of a public relations plan to a client. The question is, "Were the objectives achieved?" In other words, did the plan accomplish what it set out to do?

Sample public relations budget

Category: Out of pocket Expenses	Budget
Printing	$44,650
Paper and stationery	4,500
Postage	13,000
Other office supplies	1,000
Photography and graphics	3,900
Advertising	9,000
Telephone	2,300
Travel and entertainment	12,000
Rental of exhibit space	6,000
Tri-fold exhibit board	7,500
Promotional giveaway items	3,000
Total expenses	**$106,850**

The information can also appear in a graph to illustrate major expense items. In this case there are too many items for the graph to be very meaningful.

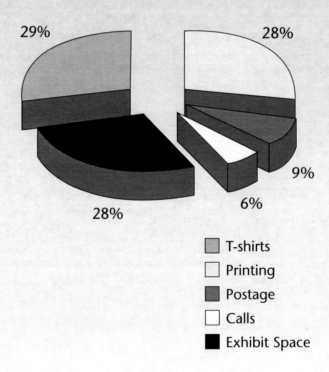

If a budget is small and involves relatively few items, the inclusion of a pie chart or other graphic may be useful to illustrate how money will be spent.

Evaluation is the part of a public relations plan that explains when and how measurements of the results will take place. Clients increasingly demand accountability. They want proof that the money they spend on public relations is getting results. Evaluations report on the outcome of public relations plans. Each objective in a plan should have an evaluation process associated with it.

The information can also appear in a graph to illustrate major expense items. In this case there are too many items for the graph to be very meaningful.

If a budget is small and involves relatively few items, the inclusion of a pie chart or other graphic may be useful to illustrate how money will be spent.

Some companies have made greater use of public relations in recent years because of the rising cost of advertising. They demand proof that they are getting equal or better results than they would have from advertising. They were hoping to achieve similar awareness results with public relations tactics, but at lower cost. If they cannot achieve desired results they may revert to advertising and reduce their support for public relations.

Historically, only about 1 percent of public relations budgets were devoted to evaluation activities. Today, that figure has risen to 5 percent. Some public relations practitioners believe it will rise to 10 percent in the years ahead. The demand for accountability is driving that trend.

Two types of evaluations

1. Formative
2. Summative

Formative evaluation

PR professionals use formative evaluations during a plan's execution as a form of feedback that enables them to make changes in strategy and tactics while they can still affect the end result of a plan.

A test grade in a class is a type of formative evaluation. It gives feedback to the student about the progress she is making. If the test grade is low, the student can try harder or change study habits to improve future performance. Similarly, if early results during a public relations plan suggest that results are lagging, the planners can revise tactics so that they can improve performance before it is too late.

Summative evaluation

Summative evaluations are a measure of the final outcome of something. A final grade in a class is a form of summative evaluation. In the public relations example above, the number of tickets sold as of December 31, 2009, would be a summative outcome for that public relations plan.

How does one evaluate a public relations plan? First, refer back to the objectives of the plan. A proper objective should have two components: a measurable outcome and a deadline. Each objective states what will happen by a specific date.

Example

Objective: To increase awareness of a prostate cancer screening blood test among men in Central Texas by 50 percent in one year.

How would we evaluate this objective?

First, there is a need for baseline data. What percent of men were aware of the test before the PR program began? Evaluating this objective would require doing a survey of men to measure their awareness before implementing the public relations plan.

At the conclusion of the public relations program a second survey of men would measure awareness at that point. Then it is a matter of comparing the pretest and post-test results to see if achievement of the objective occurred. If 20 percent of the men knew about the screening test before the implementation of the public relations plan, what percent would need to know about it afterward to be able to say that the objective was achieved?

▶ Pre-test awareness = 20 percent of men knew about the test
▶ Objective = Increase awareness by 50 percent
▶ Post-test awareness = 30 percent would need to know about the test at the conclusion of the plan for achievement of the objective (20 percent × 1.5 = 30 percent).

Three evaluation techniques

There are three ways to measure the outcome of a public relations plan:

1. Measurement of message production placement
2. Measurement of awareness, understanding, and retention of messages

3. Measurement of changes in attitudes, opinions, and behavior

Message production and placement

While this is changing, this is still the most widely used method to evaluate a public relations plan. It involves counting stuff. Here are some of the things that can be counted and reported to a client as evidence of what the public relations plan accomplished:

▶ Number of press releases created
▶ Number of PSAs created and distributed
▶ Number of letters to the editor written
▶ Number of stories printed
▶ Number of PSAs aired
▶ Number of broadcast talk show interviews
▶ Number of broadcast news stories
▶ Hits on the Internet
▶ Media impressions
▶ Requests for information
▶ Calculation of CPM or cost per person
▶ Attendance at events
▶ 800 number requests

Traditionally, a staff member compiled a portfolio of press clippings, radio-television mentions, and other evidence of media usage of a story. Today, professionals can hire specialized companies such as CyberAlert and BurrellesLuce to monitor and record mentions of an organization in print and electronic media.

The underlying assumption of this kind of evaluation is that greater awareness results from the creation and distribution of more messages. Counting "stuff" is evidence that the public relations professionals are putting out messages.

Advertising equivalencyis another type of evaluation. If an organization adds up the value of free space it obtains through articles and other free mentions in print and electronic media, what would that free space and time be worth?

Advertising equivalency calculates what the same amount of space or time would have cost if purchased as advertising. We can multiply the total number of columns inches of print space by the cost per column inch to arrive at an estimated value for the space. Similarly, we can multiply the number of minutes of free broadcast airtime by the cost of buying a similar amount of time to arrive at a value.

Advertising equivalency is one way of addressing the question: Do we get more exposure through adver-

tising or public relations? It can demonstrate the cost effectiveness of PR.

Evaluating public relations plans by counting stuff has both advantages and disadvantages. The advantages include that it is relatively cheap to do and that it provides a strong incentive to public relations practitioners to get messages out into the media.

The disadvantages of this approach to evaluation include its emphasis on quantity rather than quality of messages. There is a presumption that more messages are better. Another difficulty is that it is impossible to document every use of a message, even when using sophisticated clipping services. Finally, counting stuff does not measure the effectiveness of the message in changing attitudes or creating awareness.

Measuring awareness and attitudes

A second way to evaluate public relations plans is to measure changes in awareness and attitudes. This involves the use of survey research tools, usually emphasizing the recall of messages. The goal is to determine whether the audience remembers a message and what they remember about it. Attitude studies compare attitudes after a PR program to benchmark data collected before the execution of the plan began. Once again, this requires pre and post surveys.

Measuring behavior or action

Public relations is not an end in itself. It is a means to an end. In many cases, an organization wants a public to take some specific action. Examples of desired actions include:

▶ Sales
▶ Letters to the editor
▶ Donations
▶ Attendance at an event
▶ Growth in memberships
▶ Calling an 800 number
▶ Mailing in a postcard soliciting additional information
▶ Winning an election

Evaluations answer the question: Were the objectives of the public relations plan achieved? Ideally, if there were properly written objectives with both a quantitative measure and a deadline it should be possible to answer the question with a yes or no.

Example

The objective was to increase ticket sales by 1,500 tickets by December 31, 2008. If, on January 1, 2009, ticket sales increased by only 900 the plan did not achieve the objective. If the PR people sold 2,000 additional tickets, they met the objective. Success is easier to judge when objectives have a quantified outcome and a deadline.

More examples

▶ Increase awareness by 15 percent. Research would be necessary to first measure awareness before the public relations plan begins. A second piece of research would be necessary after the public relations plan is completed to measure awareness again. There could be a comparison between pre and post plan numbers to see if awareness grew by 15 percent.

▶ Increase media coverage by 25 percent. In this case, one might count the number of square inches of free print media coverage in a year, plus the number of minutes of free broadcast coverage in newscasts. There could be a comparison between the amounts of coverage from one year to the next to see if there was an increase of 25 percent.

▶ A variation on the evaluation method above is advertising equivalency. PR people could translate the amount of print and broadcast coverage to its advertising dollar value. This would answer the question: What would it have cost us to buy this much space and time in advertising? There could be a comparison of the advertising equivalency of one year to the next as a form of evaluation.

▶ In some cases, there may be no direct comparison. The objective may be to have a stated number of consumer contacts. For example, the objective might be to have 1,000 calls to an 800 number, to distribute 5,000 brochures, to receive 500 postcards requesting information, or to raise $1 million in contributions. Sometimes the plan will not state the objective as a comparison with a previous year.

Plan part 10: References ▼

If a public relations group uses images, quotations, or materials of any kind created by someone other than the group, it must make the source of the materials clear. They may do this with footnotes, a sidebar in the text, or a page of citations and references at the end of the plan's book. Somewhere, however, they should make it clear if there is something in the book that the PR team did not create. If the team borrows a few sentences from a client's old pamphlet and uses it in the situation analysis to state the mission of the client, it should put the sentences inside quotation marks and reference the source at the back of the book. It is permissible to make selective use of existing images and quotations, but one be honest about the fact that they are not original creations.

If the situation analysis cites statistics, it must cite the source. A reader may wish to judge the validity of the numbers and the credibility of the source.

Review questions

1. What are the parts of a public relations plan?
2. What is a SWOT analysis? What part of a PR plan contains the SWOT analysis?
3. What is the proper way to write an objective? What should be in the objective statement?
4. What is the difference between information and motivational objectives?
5. How do strategies and tactics differ?
6. What tactics might you use to promote an event by a student group of which you are a member?
7. What is a Gantt chart? Where does it appear in a PR plan?
8. What is the difference between formative and summative evaluations?
9. What is the relationship between objectives and evaluations?
10. What is advertising equivalency?

Supplemental resources online

http://pr.e-agency.com/pdf/elementsofaPRplan.pdf	Elements of a PR plan
http://office.microsoft.com/en-us/excel-help/create-a-gantt-chart-in-excel-HA001034605.aspx	Create Gantt Chart
http://www.bombsite.com	Online magazine
http://www.businesswire.com	Press Release service
http://www.ereleases.com	Press Release service
http://www.pressreleasenetwork.com/	Press Release service
http://www.pressflash.com	Press Release service
http://www.gebbieinc.com/	Media directory
http://www.gmarketing.com/	Guerrilla marketing
http://www.ketchum.com	Ketchum
http://www.nielsenmedia.com	Nielsen Research
http://www.oracle.com/oramag/index.html	Oracle magazine
http://www.prnewswire.com	Press Release service
http://www.rapidbi.com/created/SWOTanalysis.html#SWOTmodel	SWOT analysis
http://www.sba.gov	Small Business Admin.
http://www.speechwriting.com	Speech writing firm
http://custompublishingcouncil.com	Custom publishers

Chapter references

Bivins, Thomas. (1995). *Handbook for public relations writing*. Lincolnwood, IL: NTC Business Books.

Clayton, John. (2003). *Writing an executive summary that means business*. Harvard Management Communication Letter. Boston: Harvard Business School.

Guth, David W., & Marsh, Charles. (2006). *Public relations: A values-driven approach*. Boston: Allyn & Bacon.

Lattimore, Dan, Baskin, Otis, Heiman, Suzette T., Toth, Elizabeth L., & Van Leuven, James K. (2004). *Public relations: The profession and the practice*. New York: McGraw-Hill.

Miyamoto, Craig. *How to write a comprehensive public relations plan*. http://www.geocities.com/WallStreet/8925/prplan1.htm

Seitel, Fraser P. (2007). *The practice of public relations*. Upper Saddle River, NJ: Pearson Education, Inc.

Shelburne, Merry. (2001). *Effective public relations: A practical approach*. Cincinnati, OH: Atomic Dog Publishing.

Weiner, Mark. (2006). *Unleashing the power of PR: A contrarian's guide to marketing and communication*. San Francisco: Jossey-Bass.

Wilcox, Dennis L., Cameron, Glen T., Ault, Phillip H., & Agee, Warren K. (2003). *Public relations: Strategies and tactics*. Boston: Allyn and Bacon.

Wilder, Judith Luther. (1999). *Breaking through the clutter: Business solutions for women, artists, and entrepreneurs*. Los Angeles: National Network for Artist Placement.

Witmer, Diane. (2000). *Spinning the web: A handbook for public relations on the Internet*. New York: Longman.

Notes

Name _____

Date _____

Situation Analysis

Answer the following questions about the client for your public relations plan.

1. What type of need for public relations does the client have?

    ▶ Remedial

    ▶ One-time

    ▶ Standing (on-going)

    ▶ Combination

    Explain:

2. Describe the problem(s) or need(s) facing the client.

3. S-W-O-T analysis:

    a. What are the client's strengths?

    b. What are the client's weaknesses?

    c. What opportunities exist for the client to exploit?

    d. What threats face the client?

4. Who are the client's major competitors?

5. Who are the client's major customers or service recipients?

6. What other background information about the client, the client's products or services, or the client's industry is important to understand this situation?

7. What secondary research exists to help inform this plan?

8. What primary research could be done to better understand the situation?

Objectives

Answer the following questions about the objective(s) for your public relations plan.

1. What type of objective(s) will the plan address?

   ▶ Informational
   ▶ Motivational
   ▶ Combination

   Explain:

   Every objective should be measurable and have a deadline date.

2. Objective statement #1: (write a draft of your first objective)

   _____

   _____

   _____

   What is being measured?

   What is the quantified goal?

   What is the deadline for achieving the goal?

3. Objective statement #2: (write a draft of your second objective if you have more than one.)

   _____

   _____

   _____

   Check whether your objective statement is complete and in the correct format by answering these three questions:

   What is being measured?

   What is the quantified goal?

   What is the deadline for achieving the goal?

Answer the following questions about your objectives statements:

4. How do the objective(s) relate to the overall goals of organization?

5. In what way are the objectives oriented toward improvement?

6. Are they clearly stated and easily understood?

7. Are they specific as to what will be accomplished?

8. Are they stated using measurable outcomes?

9. Are they attainable or realistic? Explain why you believe so.

Audience

1. Profile *each* of your *primary* audiences. Be specific in describing each primary audience.

2. Why are you targeting each of these groups as a primary audience?

3. Describe in detail each of your *secondary* target audiences. Again, be specific.

4. Why are you targeting each of these groups as a secondary audience?

Strategy

1. Brainstorm as many ideas as possible for strategies for the client. The more ideas the better. Make a list of all ideas.

   a.

   b.

   c.

   d.

e.

f.

g.

h.

i.

j.

k.

l.

m.

n.

2. Which of these ideas best target the audiences you identified earlier, and the objectives of this public relations plan? Narrow the list, selecting the most feasible or practical, but be clear that your choices will speak to your primary and secondary audiences and will accomplish the objectives.

3. Create a complete strategy statement for each strategy. Too many strategies will complicate and confuse your efforts. One is usually enough. More may be necessary if there are several targeted primary audiences that are quite different.

    Strategy statement number 1:

Strategy statement number 2, if any:

Strategy statement number 3, if any:

Tactics

List each strategy that you previously identified and brainstorm appropriate tactics for executing that strategy. Think of as many tactics as possible. You can later edit the list. The important thing at this stage is to think of as many ways as possible of effectively communicating the strategies to the target audience(s).

Strategy:

_____

Target Audience(s):

_____

List Possible Tactics:

Calendar/Timetable

▶ What is the beginning date for your PR plan? _____

▶ What is the end date? _____

▶ Organize your major tactics in the order in which they should happen during the plan. Think about the logic of the roll out of the plan and the resources required to do each thing. Don't over burden yourself by trying to do everything at once.

Tactic	Execution Date
1. _____	_____
2. _____	_____
3. _____	_____
4. _____	_____
5. _____	_____

Budget

Itemize the major expenses associated with the execution of the public relations plan.

Expense	Amount $
_____	_____
_____	_____
_____	_____
_____	_____

Evaluation

Restate each objective.

What can you measure quantitatively in each objective?

How can you evaluate the outcome of each objective? What evaluation technique(s) is/are appropriate for each objective? Each objective requires only one measure, but sometimes more than one is appropriate or necessary.

References

List the sources of statistics, images, or other information that the plan used. If you quote text directly it should be clearly in quotes in the narrative.

Material Used   **Source**

_____   _____

_____   _____

_____   _____

WORKING WITH THE MEDIA

Serving as an information source ▼

> "A spokesman for the company said."
> "As first reported on the company's Web site."
> ". . . reported in a news handout. . . ."
> ". . . in an explanation written on her blog. . . ."
> ". . . said in a news conference . . . ."
> "Company XYZ announced today that . . . "

Ane of the most significant tasks performed by public relations specialists is preparing information for public consumption in the media. About half of the content in daily newspapers and their companion websites originate as public relations communications. News releases announce new products, job hires and layoffs, policies, events and meetings. Other public relations announcements include prepared comments in reaction to news developments and statements at press conferences or other forums.

> **Quotations provided will be most useful to media outlets if they relay pertinent information and insightful explanations or observations.**

Public relations specialists write the information in news style, following a structure called the **inverted pyramid**, which presents information from the most important to the least important. Journalists in the United States have favored this journalism style since the Civil War. It is important that public relations professionals use the style that's common to their counterparts in news organizations. Writing in news style lends credibility to the work of the PR professional because it conveys that he or she understands the workings of media. It also makes documents easier for journalists to use if they so choose. An improperly worded document, or one with spelling or grammatical errors, signals to journalists that they are dealing with someone who lacks professional training and experience in the media.

There is a lively tension between public relations practitioners, newsmakers, and the media. Newsmakers and their PR representatives want positive stories that support their agendas. Journalists want stories that reflect real news and appeal to large audiences. They attempt to pursue the truth objectively.

The media generally lack the space or airtime to run lengthy interviews. As a result, public relations specialists need to craft their messages accordingly and get to the point. Clients also need to be prepared to speak succinctly, in sound bites, for the electronic media. Doing so increases the chances that the message a newsmaker wants to communicate is the one that ends up in a story. Newsmakers who ramble are leaving to journalists the task of choosing which 20 seconds to pull from a wordy statement. Having key statements in mind in advance of an interview increases the likelihood that what a newsmaker will say will be included in the news report.

Power quotes ▼

Public relations statements often contain quotes that explain the news story. Generally, reporters prefer to use candid, live quotes they gather themselves instead of sometimes sterile comments prepared by public relations writers.

Interviews conducted by journalists are more likely to generate quotes that reflect an interview subject's personality and the emotions connected with news events. Such interviews also sometimes produce comments that become misstatements. A speaker may not have intended to make a provocative statement, but he or she did. Such misstatements may become the focus of a news story. Interview subjects may later claim that the statements are misquotes or taken out of context. Newsmakers commonly complain that a lengthy interview only yielded a single quote in a news report. What appeared in print was said, they claim, but the person made the comment in the context of another topic or without the explanation provided by an expanded comment.

Quotations provided in a news release will be most useful to media outlets if they relay pertinent information and insightful explanations or observations. Prepared statements usually allow newsmakers to control the tone and content of a statement. They often tell a story that is beneficial to the people or organizations they represent. Some people accept such explanations for a particular position. Others in today's scrutinizing, media-saturated world are likely to call such carefully prepared statements **spin**.

The spin cycle ▼

Spin is a filter through which specialists can transform information that is often negative or vague to create a more positive impression. All sides of a controversy can generate their own spin, creating a many-headed beast. Whose spin is most believable?

The weighty nature of controversial issues and politics, and the responses they evoke, mean that spinning a story requires hours of attention. Writers choose words for these calculated messages with the care, expertise and precision of a surgeon. Thus, the most skilled users of this kind of rhetoric are often called **spin doctors**.

> *Spin is a filter through which specialists can transform information that is often negative or vague to create a more positive impression. All sides of a controversy can generate their own spin, creating a many-headed beast.*

Advocates on every side of an issue employ spin. Edward Bernays, discussed in Chapter 2 as one of the patriarchs of the public relations industry, was dubbed "The Father of Spin" by biographer Larry Tye. Bernays helped the brewing industry explain to the public that beer was "the beverage of moderation." Bernays argued that the public relations professional could "continuously and systematically" perform the task of "regimenting the public mind." He was not talking about lying. He was talking about artfully managing the truth.

Information management ▼

Much media relations work involves providing useful, essential, truthful and newsworthy information for audiences. Reporters often rewrite public relations documents to eliminate wording that they regard as promotional. Most media, from traditional to new media, are businesses that generate revenue through the sale of advertising. The news gathering side of the business, then, is hardly eager to give away free time or space for "news" that is nothing more than thinly disguised promotion. Journalists look for real news in news releases and other PR documents.

The content of a news release may not get published or broadcast exactly as it was submitted. Journalists may use the news release as a starting

point to writing a story but choose to pursue a different news angle as they develop the story with interviews and other information gathering. The focus of a story can change with a single groundbreaking interview that yields a dramatic comment. Chapter 3 discussed the concept of framing a story. Framing means that there is no one story contained in any event. Decisions must occur about which story angle is most important and interesting. Diligent reporters may start with facts or opinion from a news release and balance them with a range of other perspectives. As a story evolves it may go in a very different direction from the one originally envisioned by the public relations practitioner who sent out the news release. PR professionals and their clients need to understand and accept this important reality.

Crisis management ▼

When news events involve highly publicized events and intense human emotions, public information officers must sift through facts and opinion before calmly trying to present the information as accurately and completely as possible. When a student opened fire at Virginia Tech University on April 16, 2007, public relations officials gathered and managed information from various sources to share with the public. The tragic events officially unfolded publicly when spokesperson Larry Hinckler announced on the Virginia Tech Web site, "A gunman is loose on campus. Stay in buildings until further notice. Stay away from all windows."

▲*A throng of media crams a lecture hall at Virginia Tech to receive information about the campus shootings in 2007. The University's initial announcement was brief and to the point.*

Hinckler's announcement had to contend with a whirlwind of information already circulating on social media, much of which included unsubstantiated reports or rumors. The number of hits on the University website was so great that the University created an alternate website just to provide information about the tragedy for the media.

The University wrote media advisories and news releases. It handled inquiries from around the world, and it organized press conferences to facilitate the distribution of information to the media. Interestingly, the fastest way to access information about events at Virginia Tech was through its website. While reporters independently pursued various story angles involving interviews with witnesses and experts, many of the facts about the tragedy and the responses from University officials, police, and other law enforcement officials originated from Virginia Tech public relations professionals.

Some institutions, faced with crises, respond very differently from Virginia Tech. They historically have stonewalled the media in the early stage of their crises. Rather than gather and share accurate information about what they know as events unfold, spokespersons have cooperated minimally with the media and forced journalists to find information elsewhere. This strategy is likely to produce a media frenzy that places an institution on the defensive. It may even assume guilt on the part of the institution and spawn rumors and speculation. The underlying rationale for not cooperating with the media is often concern about managing legal liability. Lawyers usually advocate silence until they know all the facts. Public relations practitioners understand the nature of the news media and the speed, influence and reality of the blogosphere and "tweet-iverse." They understand the need to act in the best interest of the client, but also the appetite of the media and the noise that silence brings. As with a wide range of crises, which are discussed more extensively in Chapter 10, efforts must be coordinated with appropriate leaders. On college campuses, college presidents will often be at the forefront of delivering information concerning matters of great magnitude such as shootings at Virginia Tech, the University of Alabama at Huntsville and Northern Illinois University, the H1N1 swine flu outbreak or the sexual assault charges involving a former assistant football coach at Penn State University.

Chapter 2 discussed the guiding principles of PR pioneers Ivy Lee and Arthur Page. Both men believed institutions are best served by being open and honest with the media. Journalists will pursue a major story with or without the help of those at the center of the story. Telling the truth and cooperating with the media are the best strategies for managing a crisis. It does not make bad news go away, but it does minimize the chances of an adversarial and hostile relationship between an institution and the media. Lee distributed inaccurate information that he had obtained from his client following the Ludlow Massacre. He was accused of deliberately attempting to mislead the public and suffered irreparable damage to his reputation. Thus, he earned the nickname Poison Ivy. In his Declaration of Principles for the practice of public relations, Lee learned from the experience and said, do not lie. Why? Because lies always get uncovered.

Get it right

PR spokespersons and journalists alike must guard against reporting information based on rumors and speculation. The job becomes complex and challenging, however, in today's world of blogs, in which facts, rumors, and opinions circulate freely. While the public may expect news reporters to gather information responsibly, corroborate reports, and check sources, journalists and bloggers both face the temptation and hazards of running with or posting a compelling story prematurely. Media relations specialists, in the face of impatient reporters and editors, must take the time to get the facts right or they will contribute to the confusion that surrounds major breaking stories. As a result, they will lose their credibility. When they officially announce unverified, inaccurate information, PR officials risk accusations of misinforming the public or of setting off a chain of events that can lead to more confusion or tragedy. Communications specialists must be attentive not only to the news but the random comments that often are left behind online in reaction to the news. Reporters increasingly pay attention to these threads of comments, thus media relations specialists must gauge whether comments will have a consequence on news coverage or whether they demand a response. Many news events are dramatic. Sometimes, however, the truth gets lost in the drama.

Creating a crisis plan

In response to terror attacks, campus shootings, natural disasters, oil spills and countless other events and tragedies, various organizations have resorted to creating a media relations **crisis plan**. Like a fire drill or an evacuation plan, a crisis plan helps organizations and employers to plan for unexpected circumstances, so that they can handle the mountain of tasks involved in providing information to the public quickly, efficiently and accurately.

When ice storms or other inclement weather ground airplanes and leave passengers stranded in airports, public relations officials understand the need to have ready information to provide to travelers, reporters and the public. Presidents, corporate executives, celebrities, government officials or other newsmakers need assistance in responding to reporters. The work of public relations specialists in supplying information, fielding and granting interview requests, organizing news conferences, or posting information on websites for public consumption is crucial.

Fleishman-Hillard's Crisis Preparedness Program

Fleishman-Hillard and other global public relations firms recognize that companies today must be ready to deal with issues that can explode into crisis, damaging their hard-earned reputations. Fleishman-Hillard created a Crisis Preparedness program to help clients prepare for potential crises. The program includes:

▶ Using primary and secondary research to fully understand a company's issues, its primary stakeholders, and their interests in the company.
▶ Auditing the company's vulnerability to issues— product liability, workplace disruptions, environmental or labor activism, litigations, and government investigations.
▶ Developing action plans for specific threats.
▶ Producing comprehensive crisis communications manuals, with draft materials, protocols and contact information.
▶ Training employees in crisis communications, including working with the media.
▶ Simulating crises to practice responses.

This "Crisis Preparedness" program shows students how an international public relations firm approaches crisis communications. It suggests that public relations firms think about how they will respond to a variety of fast-moving, intense situations. Public relations works best when practitioners antici-

pate problems and do not wait for them to happen. A prospective client never knows when a crisis will occur (massive floods, power outages, unethical behavior) but that one or more is likely over the life of the company. Part of running a large corporation is preparing for the unexpected. Public relations firms (and students) must learn to think about what to do when negative things happen.

Understanding media ▼

By definition, media relations requires that PR practitioners understand media, how all media work, whom they reach, how they are organized, and why. Clients commonly want to promote their businesses, events or even themselves. Often, they seek media coverage regardless of whether what they want to publicize is really news.

Businesses hire media relations specialists to find the news value in a request and to find media outlets, editors, reporters, bloggers and social media "conversations" that are interested in such information. From a public relations point of view, this publicity is called **free media**. It is media exposure that costs virtually nothing, but it is also content over which PR professionals have little, if any, control. By contrast, advertising involves paying for space or time, which enables advertisers to control the content of their messages.

Getting news coverage of events and messages is highly desirable because news content is supposed to be objective, free of bias. Reporters try to provide coverage that reflects:

▶ Various points of view
▶ Fairness
▶ Balance
▶ Truth

Media consumers value the independence of journalists and regard news content as more credible than advertising. They understand that advertising is paid-for persuasive messages. Advertising has a clear agenda to sell products and services. The purpose of news stories is to inform.

A public relations writer should provide the media with information based on solid research and authoritative support. When the media publish or broadcast such information, consumers perceive the content to have passed the journalistic test of newsworthiness. It is a kind of seal of approval that suggests information is accurate and useful.

Media consumers value the independence of journalists and regard news content as more credible than advertising.

Public relations people usually share with journalists the desire to be accurate and truthful. Reporters are, however, often wary of the distinction between their sense of truth and that of public relations practitioners who may have agendas. Understanding how to deal with journalists who are pursuing stories that involve conflict, controversy or negative events is an important part of media relations. At times, journalists will challenge the content of public relations information. PR people have various options for dealing with such a challenge.

Add to the story

Focusing on positive developments in a story may take some of the sting out of a negative situation. Unfortunately, media people will almost certainly regard shifting the focus to new and more positive information as an effort to spin a story. Similarly, vague, misleading or erroneous information will also trigger accusations of "spin." The handling of the British Petroleum oil spill in the Gulf, discussed fully in Chapter 10, shifted from the poor handling of discussing failures to plug the gushing oil rig to BP's successes in the cleanup of the Mississippi Gulf Coast, the revival of tourism and the revitalization of its local economies.

Public relations specialists can sometimes manage uncomfortable, difficult and negative situations with prepared statements that range from clarifications to outright denials. PR people and clients both must be prepared to discuss a client's past, including conflicts, along with successes. Journalists often ask tough, uncomfortable questions. It is important to be able to answer without becoming flustered or defensive. Under no circumstances should a public relations rep-

Off the record

Going "off the record" means that a news source is going to say something that is not for publication or airing. The information may inform a journalist and help him or her to understand an element of a story that is very sensitive. The source, for one reason or another, does not want to be named in the story.

Is a journalist bound to honor an "off the record" statement if he or she did not agree to its status as off the record? If the source's comment is preceded by the "off the record" declaration, then the rule should be honored. In reality, in today's digital media society, information has a way of surfacing somewhere, even under the cloud of anonymity. Nonetheless, developing sources is like developing relationships. If reliable sources are unhappy, the relationship will become jeopardized. If a journalist does not explicitly acknowledge and confirm the off the record status of a statement, a source should not assume it is off the record.

Usually reporters can take "off the record" information as a tip and find other sources to verify the information "on the record." Once the "off the record" notice is on, the journalist and source must be wary of when comments are no longer "off the record." A reporter respectful of the interview rules should ask, "Are we still 'off the record'" or clarify, "May I quote you on that?" Yet, sources also should be coached by PR media relations experts about asserting when an interview is back on the record. Without this understanding of these rules of an interview, relations between writers and interview subjects will lack trust.

resentative lie. Public relations practitioners who lie erode public confidence in the industry, which has a commitment to ethical standards of professionalism (See Chapter 12). In today's media environment, controversial issues attract scrutiny and criticism. Public relations specialists must be prepared to address tough questions and handle criticism.

"No comment" or "Let me check"

"**No comment**" is a position that means that the source has nothing to say at that moment. While perceptions surround the phrase, "no comment" is neither an admission of guilt nor a denial. Saying "no comment" is risky, though. It makes journalists that much more eager to find the answer to the question. Usually, they will find an answer somewhere. To quell the skepticism surrounding a "no comment" response, the source should expand the response with information that in some way explains issues surrounding issues that prompt the "no comment" in the first place. The impact of social media on any issue presents countless opportunities for others to comment. By not commenting, the target of questioning or criticism will face increased vulnerability to further scrutiny.

Public relations people should not use "no comment" as a substitute for lacking an answer. Not knowing an answer or being unable to discuss a matter is reasonable, if true. For example, disclosing negotiation details or discussing strategies in legal matters obviously harms the ability to attain a result or resolution. Therefore, media can expect officials to state situations in generalities; for example, that "negotiations are ongoing." While public relations officials understand that such a response will encourage reporters to dig around for speculative discussion, they feel the necessity to limit specific disclosures. If a PR professional does not know the answer to a question, it is legitimate, if not preferred, to say to a reporter, "Let me take your question, and I'll get back to you with an answer." Of course, following up with the reporter is part of the source's responsibility and part of maintaining credibility. Pointing a journalist in the right direction or being willing to find the answer for him or her is a key part of media relations.

*P*rint media ▼

The job of the **media relations** specialist is to marry the client's interest with the news judgment of media outlets. Media specialists must understand two primary questions: "What is news?" and "What news angles will meet the news objectives of my client?" Equally important to the legitimate news value of information is identifying opportunities for placements. The first goal is to become familiar with traditional media and new media that may be interested in the information from a news release or an informative but promotional blog. Publications come in a variety of formats with varying publication frequencies. Some publications target general mass audiences. Others focus on highly specialized content for niche publications. Major print media include:

▶ Daily newspapers
▶ Weekly newspapers
▶ Alternative newspapers
▶ Magazines
▶ Trade publications
▶ Newsletters
▶ Books

Daily newspapers reach a general audience. Trade publications reach readers in a particular industry. Magazines such as TIME, Newsweek or U.S. News and World Report target general audiences. Other magazines have a more specialized focus—sports, business, politics, health, automotives, gardening, fashion, travel and other niche interests. Some magazines have demographic targets such as men, women, older adults, young adults, and specific ethnic groups. Newsletters are typically tailored for an even narrower or more specifically defined audience. Each of these publications presents unique opportunities for the media relations specialist.

Dailies

The printed edition of daily newspapers focuses on events that have occurred since the last press run, the day before. Newspapers supplement their printed editions by updating stories continuously on their own websites. This better enables dailies to compete with the 24-hour news cycle of cable news networks, blogs, and other electronic competitors.

Media relations specialists should be familiar with the variety of news products. Newspapers are organized by sections, and each section has its own editor. Common newspaper sections include: Main News, the A section; a local news section, often called "Metro";

▲ *Newspaper front pages present news of the day, allowing the size of headlines and position on a page to signify importance.*

▲ *Editors devote hours to searching for the most appealing cover photography for such publications as Sports Illustrated. Magazines compete for attention at bookstores and newsstands.*

sports, business, and various others covering such features as "lifestyle," food, books, and travel. Some sections offer calendars or "notes" columns. Generally, these columns accept news releases and other promotional content.

Reporters get assigned to certain areas of coverage called **beats**. Each section has at least one editor who manages the content of the section aided by a staff of editors and reporters who cultivate sources to find news. It is important for public relations people to know which reporters cover which beats and to cultivate relationships with those reporters and their editors. The search for appropriate media sources become part of a media list.

Magazines

General interest and niche magazines are generally glossy and published less frequently, usually weekly or monthly. Magazines also typically have long lead times. They need content much further in advance than do daily newspapers. Special-interest niche magazines may have an interest in public relations information if it relates closely to the content of the magazine. For example, a company that manufacturers ski equipment may find skiing magazines receptive to news releases about its new products. Guidelines for submitting news are commonly available on publication websites.

Less frequently published magazines may approach news in terms of trends rather than breaking news. The published versions cannot compete with daily newspapers or electronic media when it comes to reporting the latest news. They must approach issues from a broader, timeless perspective. They, too, work to develop a daily web presence that provides a more timely opportunity to present content. Websites build on their reputations and brands. Sports Illustrated, founded in 1954 and still a staple as a weekly publication among sports enthusiasts, has successfully adapted its publication formula to the Internet, exhibiting the same colorful writing and action photography for which the magazine is famous, but more immediate in terms of timely news.

Trade publications

Trade publications and newsletters present important media relations opportunities. On their own, these publications have important target audiences. Every industry has trade publications that both executives and rank and file workers read. Here are a few of the thousands of trade publication titles. Note how specific the focus of each publication is:

> Bartender Magazine
> Beverage Retailer
> Cleaning and Maintenance Management
> Pastry Art & Design Magazine
> Pizza, Pasta and Italian Food Magazine
> Pizza Today
> Restaurant Business
> Vending Times
> AJM — Jewelry Magazine
> Microwave Product Digest
> Aerospace Engineering Magazine
> Bank Systems and Technology
> Practical Accountant
> Christian Retailing
> Petfood Industry
> Supermarket News
> American Machinist
> Metal Forming Magazine

Suppose that a public relations firm represents a client that manufactures pizza ovens and related hardware. The client has developed an innovative product that it wants to promote. The natural audience for announcements about the product would be pizza restaurants. Sending a news release and photographs to *Pizza, Pasta and Italian Food Magazine* and *Pizza Today* might yield free mentions in the publications that lead to sales. Pizza trade journals — there are actually quite a few of them — would be an important target audience for this client.

Trade journals are also important because they are a reference source for the mainstream media. Beat writers seeking news about a range of subjects, from fashion to aviation, will routinely find news items in trade publications and their websites. Local or national mainstream media then may localize the industry-focused news articles. The client mentioned above, for example, might become the subject of a local news article. The mainstream media audience would be less interested in the specifications for a new pizza oven, but it might be interested in a local company that is expanding and whose products are at the cutting edge of an industry. The story would have a different focus from what might appear in a trade journal, but the coverage would be welcome nevertheless.

Books

One of the certainties of presidential politics is that candidates with presidential ambitions will publish a book. It is almost a requirement today. They can be written quickly and sold as hardbacks, paperbacks or electronically, given the surge in popularity of such devices as the kindle, the iPad and other tablet products. Such books have included:

> "The Audacity of Hope" by Barack Obama
> "Believe in America" by Mitt Romney
> "A Nation Like No Other: Why American
>   Exceptionalism Matters" by Newt Gingrich
> "It Takes a Family: Conservatism and the
>   Common Good" by Rick Santorum
> "The Revolution: A Manifesto" by Ron Paul

Television celebrities and corporate executives also capitalize on their celebrity by publishing books. Martha Stewart, queen of all things Americana, and real estate mogul Donald Trump are among popular figures who use books to build on their personal brands.

Trade groups also publish books to promote an industry. For example, the U.S. Trout Farmers Association published a cookbook featuring—what else—trout. The Wisconsin Cheese Producers Association published a dairy cookbook. The dairy industry folks who sponsor the "got milk?" campaign cooperated in the publication of "Got Milk? The Cookie Book." Cookies go with . . . milk! A natural partnership.

In many cases, publishing a book is not a practical tactic. Newspapers, magazines, trade publications, electronic media and the Internet are probably more accessible media. Still, for some clients, books are a good tactical choice.

Electronic media ▼

The electronic media available to public relations include both old and new media technologies:

▶ New media (Internet, blogs, email, Facebook, Twitter, Tumblr, Reddit, RSS)
▶ Other digital media (interactive CDs, DVDs, Kiosks)
▶ Radio
▶ Television
▶ Video
▶ Video games (product placements)
▶ Motion pictures

New media

New media offer many opportunities to get a message or news into the information marketplace. The 24-hour news cycle in the digital world creates opportunities to have information and opinions instantly distributed and read by millions—or by no one. Specialists can transmit information through the Internet via:

▶ News distribution services
▶ News release distribution services
▶ Social media with seemingly unlimited platforms
▶ Email and listservs
▶ Websites

News distribution services distribute news releases to countless publications and electronic magazines or e-zines. Many of these services offer free distribution to a narrower audience and much broader distribution for a fee. PR Newswire for Journalists (www. prnewswire.com) and PR Web Press Release News Wire (www.prweb.com) are two of many services that electronically distribute news releases to different targets of media, search engines and the general public.

Social media

PR people still highly prize news coverage by the mainstream media. Having a newspaper or a television station report a story can be a cause for celebration. It means free publicity and access to a large potential audience. The problem is that there are too many stories chasing too few opportunities for coverage by **mainstream media**. The media do not cover most stories.

Social media, the newest delivery system for information, emphasize user participation and user generated content. Examples include Web logs, or **blogs**, as well as social networks (Facebook, LinkedIn, Twitter, Google+), video sharing sites (YouTube), online chat rooms, and countless new variations. These sites are ubiquitous and become interconnected through icons called widgets, which allow information to be loaded on multiple social media platforms virtually simultaneously. Thanks to the explosive use of smartphones throughout the world, information travels in infinite directions in milliseconds.

By January 2012, there were 184 million unique online video viewers in the United States who spent an average of about 21.1 hours a month watching video on computers both at work and at home. Online video viewing grew by 40 percent in 2011 over 2010; and it

Print tactics and media

▶ Alternative newspapers
▶ Annual reports
▶ Backgrounders
▶ Books
▶ Brochures and pamphlets
▶ Community newspapers
▶ Company magazines
▶ Contact lists
▶ Fact sheets
▶ Handbooks

▶ Letters to the editors
▶ Media kits
▶ News releases
▶ Newsletters
▶ Op-ed articles
▶ Q&A sheets
▶ Student newspapers
▶ Trade magazines
▶ Urban newspapers

was expected to grow another 40 percent in 2012. It's estimated that 60 percent of all web traffic is derived from online videos. Armed with everything from flip cameras to tablets and smartphones with video capability, it should be no surprise that 48 hours of videos are uploaded to YouTube every minute. A 2011 Intel advertisement boasted in any given 24-hour period, the Internet gained 144,000 new users or 100 every minute; and there are 30 billion instant messages, 35 billion emails and 40 billion SPAM messages.

Just as public relations practitioners develop media strategies for traditional media, they are finding new strategies that take advantage of today's various social media platforms that help stimulate "conversations" among communities of all sizes. The content must be interesting, entertaining and compelling. The interface must foster sharing information through direct placement and through various interfaces in activity called search engine optimization. SEO is an internet marketing strategy that builds on the power of search engines with the goal of improving visibility of a website or web page on search engines such as Google, Yahoo or Bing. The more a site appears as a search result the more visitors the site will experience. Among the popular ways to optimize a website are to edit content to use specific, relevant keywords and to share links with other relevant sites. Using the algorithmic language of the Internet, the digital world uses spiders and web crawlers to find tags and key words to boost visibility. In addition, numerous alert systems, many of them free, can help monitor topics and influencers.

They scour news and blogs and deliver them regularly to an email address.

Having no presence in the social media could render a company invisible to an important segment of the population. Young people read fewer newspapers, if they read them at all, watch less TV news, and spend less time with other traditional mainstream media. Their eyes and ears are elsewhere, notably glued to the screen of a mobile device, a smartphone. Further, they visually leap from platform to platform with a simple touch of a widget or app. With smartphones, consumers also are sent with ease to a web page and website by scanning odd-looking geometric icons called QR Codes.

Blogs

Public relations practitioners who want to create a reservoir of information for their client will add to a web presence by creating a blog, a media platform that allows individuals to express themselves expertly on a variety of topics. The blogosphere is a minefield of opinion about everything from breaking news to debates about politics and sports. Legions of bloggers weigh in on everything, from marketing and management tips to even bad haircuts for pets. Bloggers engage in discourse that can involve countless readers and fellow bloggers. It is becoming a significant part of news coverage and a major source of news for young adults. The Internet-using habits of young people are challenging newspapers and television stations to make their websites more appealing. Traditional media are

Electronic tactics and media

Blogs	Satellite press tours
Cable TV	Social networking Web sites
Corporate or institutional advertising on TV	Teleconferences
E-mail	TV interviews
Electronic newsletters	Video News Release (VNR)
Motion picture	Videotaped brochures and annual reports
Product placement	Viral marketing
Public Service Announcement (PSA)	Web site
Radio and TV calendars	YouTube
Radio interviews	

adapting to the new technologies that young people prefer, from computers and tablets to smartphones.

Though social media are a major media force, they face a world of fierce competition. There are many blogs trying to attract readers. Mass audiences ignore most blogs, which attract only a small group of loyal readers. Blog readers can be fickle, here today and gone (to something new and more exciting) tomorrow, thus the need for an SEO strategy. Blogs also can serve as a springboard, catapulted by widgets, to sending entries to websites and other platforms.

For clients, one of the priorities is to have someone monitor what others are saying about them. The media, from reporters and columnists to television and radio commentators, monitor blogs for facts and as a way of gauging mainstream opinion. Blogs can provide rich insights and excellent reporting; they also can be a source for sloppy, unedited work. The writing on many blogs tends to drift more toward first-person perspective rather than the news style of journalism or news releases. Separating fact from opinion and speculation can become difficult with blog sites. Readers do not have the assurance that the writers have vetted or corroborated their statements and verified information for accuracy and fairness.

A company may find itself the subject of lively debate in the blogosphere. Videos about the company may appear on YouTube; or that same company can create its own channel for videos. If the discussion is positive, companies can celebrate the boost to their reputations and awareness that social media provide. However, what happens if the discussion is negative? Or if people are circulating false and unfair rumors? Or simply "bashing" others? The targets of such rants may be your clients or your own organization or company. It is important that organizations know their critics by tracking the content on these sites. Where there are advocates or critics there are defenders. It may be necessary to execute a remedial PR campaign to correct or to at least balance misinformation on the Internet. Rumors fly, for example, when an airline announces it has filed for bankruptcy. Public relations firms working for airlines in these types of situations are in communications centers monitoring and participating in conversations from blogs and social media.

Blogs and message boards are a veritable playground for people to spread truths, half-truths and falsehoods. The Digital Age has advanced from the old days of simply forwarding email, though that option remains viable and useful. Viral marketing in today's has reached pandemic proportions. The bottom line for public relations is that positive and negative information can spread at an astonishing rate. When the H1N1 Swine Flu virus outbreak occurred in 2009, the Center for Disease Control created a series of short videos discussing the virus, the symptoms, prevention and treatments. The videos generated millions of views in a short period of time. Now millions of people sneeze into their elbows, use hand sanitizing gels and wash their hands with soap and water for as long as it takes to sing "Happy Birthday to You" twice. Far more fun, if not more entertaining, are the much anticipated Super Bowl commercials that reach tens of millions of viewers on the Internet before they air on Super Bowl Sunday.

Motion pictures

What could motion pictures have to do with public relations? Several films have had a significant impact in recent years on public opinion and public policy discussions. Their creators intended these films to be persuasive. Supporters call them educational; opponents of the content have called them propaganda. No one, however, denies the power of a well-produced film to reach a large audience with a compelling message, among them:

▶ "An Inconvenient Truth," by Al Gore. This film about global climate change won Gore an Academy Award and a Nobel Peace Prize.
▶ "SiCKO, Fahrenheit 9/11, Bowling for Columbine," and Roger and Me are just a few of the films that Michael Moore has produced about major social problems in the United States.
▶ "The Unwinking Gaze: The Inside Story of the Dalai Lama's Struggle for Tibet"
▶ "Super Size Me"
▶ "Wal-Mart: The High Cost of Low Price"
▶ "Why Wal-Mart Works & Why That Makes Some People Crazy"
▶ "Outfoxed: Rupert Murdoch's War on Journalism"

A well-produced film can reach a huge audience. They are often highly subjective, point-of-view productions. As a result, they tend to attract audiences predisposed to a particular belief system. The productions stray from the usual standards of journalism in terms of fairness, balance or verification of facts. Their purpose is often to persuade audiences.

Interactive media

CDs and DVDs often do the work one performed by printed materials. Specialists can translate brochures to digital media and integrate them with audio, video and graphics. Users of an interactive medium can quickly search for the content they need. While these physical disks are easily transportable, the content on them is also finding a home in formats that can be downloaded to equally transportable flash drives, tablets and smartphones.

Interactive kiosks are computer terminals that provide people with instant access to information. A well-known kiosk is the ubiquitous ATM machine. Some kiosks enable users to send email and faxes or to access the Internet. Others enable consumers to print digital photographs or coupons. Still others provide maps and visitor information to tourists, including promotional information for tourist sites, restaurants, and hotels. Again, the concepts for such products are commanding even wider audiences more rapidly through apps and scanable QR Codes on smartphones. Other outlets for kiosks are stores, where consumers can research products and make purchases and touchscreens at the gasoline pump. When kiosks are not releasing products, they are displaying ads and other information to a captive audience.

Radio

Most people listen to radio every day, at home, in the office, in their cars, on their computers and mobile devices. Lead time to get material on the radio is shorter than for television or for most publications. Radio offers a variety of opportunities for public relations clients to reach target audiences, including:

▶ Public Service Announcements for nonprofits
▶ In-depth interviews
▶ Listener call-in formats
▶ Calendars of local events
▶ Live broadcast origination from an event or store
▶ Newscasts
▶ DJ "patter" or live comments
▶ Editorials

Radio stations are highly formatted. That means a station broadcasts the same type of programming 24 hours a day. These specialized formats appeal to audiences with some common characteristics, making it possible to target audiences more narrowly than if a station tried to appeal to everyone. Here are some of the common format categories:

▶ News, talk, sports
▶ Country music
▶ Contemporary hit radio (CHR) music
▶ Adult contemporary music
▶ Rock and alternative music
▶ Urban music
▶ Jazz and classical music
▶ Oldies, adult hits, and nostalgia music
▶ Spanish and Latin music
▶ Public and community radio formats
▶ College and other alternative formats
▶ Other ethnic formats

Television

Most people watch television, a lot of television. Nielsen, the viewership ratings company, reports that the average American watches nearly 35 hours of television each week; and there are more television sets in the average American household than people. Also, more than one third of homes (35 percent) have DVRs that record programing; and 85 percent of prime-time viewing is done live. Despite competition from the Internet and other new technologies, television remains a major source of news and entertainment. Network and cable television stations, including the burgeoning array of reality television shows, are finding considerable competition for attention from amateur videos on such sites as YouTube. By the end of 2011 roughly one-third of American consumers streamed "long-form content" (movies, TV shows) from the internet through paid subscription services such as Netflix or Hulu-Plus. Television offers many opportunities for the placement of public relations messages, including:

▶ Newscasts
▶ Interview programs
▶ Product placement
▶ Public Service Announcements
▶ Cable TV bulletin boards of local events
▶ Program episode ideas
▶ Video news releases

Newscasts

Most local television stations broadcast newscasts. Sometimes in larger cities there are 24-hour news channels operated by the local cable TV system. Local newscasters are always looking for story ideas, especially stories with good visuals. PR people can send news releases and media advisories to local newscasters to provide them with story ideas and to alert them about upcoming events.

News releases sent to TV assignment editors should keep viewers in mind. Television news prefers stories with good visual images. Stories with nothing but a spokesperson at a podium are boring. TV news is ideal for stories that will offer interesting video. An old criticism of television news is, "If it bleeds it leads." Violent stories typically have compelling images and air at the top of the newscast to get attention and to hold an audience.

Since most stories are shorter than 90 seconds in length, stories also need brief explanation. Complicated stories get shallow treatment on television because there is not enough time to provide extensive detail. Print media do a better job explaining complicated stories because they have more control over space than television stations have over time. The time of the telecast locks viewers in; readers have control over the time spent with a lengthier, more detailed article.

Television news reports typically lead with tease information. "A car that gets 60 miles per gallon? That's what rolled through town today." More straightforward information will support this tease later. The written release may appear in "script" format, with spoken words written in capital letters on the right half of a

Preparing for television appearances

▶ Prepare clients for television with simulated interviews in front of a camera. Watch the video together to identify problem behaviors such as distracting movements and excessive use of words such as "like," "and," and "uh."

▶ Practice answering questions that the interviewer is likely to ask, especially if you expect the questions to be tough or embarrassing. Anticipating such questions minimizes the chances of a client becoming flustered or angry.

▶ Practice speaking in succinct sound bites of 20 seconds. If an interview will be edited, speaking in sound bites improves the chances that comments will remain in context. Each statement is, to a degree, self-contained.

▶ Wear makeup. Pale skin is unflattering. This applies to men, too. Whiskers show without makeup. Bald heads reflect light.

▶ Do not wear clothing that is white or black or that has narrow stripes or loud patterns. White tends to reflect too much light in a highly lighted TV studio. Black absorbs too much light. Narrow stripes cause an optical illusion called the moiré pattern. A touch of red is okay as an accessory, but most people do not look good on TV wearing a lot of red.

▶ Do not get angry at questions. Stay calm.

▶ Do not use exaggerated gestures. Keep them smaller and appropriate for television close-ups.

▶ Do not wear flashy jewelry. It reflects light and can distract.

▶ Men, wear knee-length socks to cover the shins. Ankles are not attractive.

▶ Women—make sure hair will stay in place so it is not necessary to fuss with it on camera. Be sure to wear clothing that will permit the attachment of a wireless microphone somewhere—dresses with plunging necklines leave little room for the inconspicuous placement of a microphone and its transmitter.

▶ Both men and women look good in conservative outfits, such as suits.

▶ Product placement

page and instructions, such as those introducing graphics, or as video, explained on the left.

National networks also receive public relations materials and may respond if the story idea either has sufficient importance or offers a compelling human interest angle that makes it suitable as a soft news segment.

Interview programs

There is no shortage of talk on television. Talk fills the airwaves morning, noon and night. Local TV stations have their own talk programs. The national broadcast and cable networks have countless programs that provide news and entertainment oriented talk. New to the arena are programs produced for streaming over the Internet. Among the most popular national talk shows are "The Tonight Show," "Late Night With David Letterman," "The Today Show," "The Daily Show," "The Colbert Report," "Anderson Cooper 360," "The O'Reilly Factor," "The View," "Good Morning America," and "The Ellen DeGeneres Show." There are countless others on local stations.

Interview programs compete fiercely for guests. It is a common public relations tactic to book authors, movie stars, musicians and non-celebrities experiencing their 15 minutes of fame onto talk shows. These programs generate considerable free publicity for new books, movies and concert tours. Local programs are more accessible for clients who have a topic that they can discuss interestingly for five to 10 minutes.

It is no accident that Coca Cola cups are conspicuously visible on the judges' table on "American Idol." It is no accident that .007 James Bond drives a particular car, uses a particular model of cell phone, or stays at a particular hotel. It is no accident that Reese's Pieces were used in "E.T. The Extra Terrestrial." When a product appears identifiably in a movie or on a television program the product's manufacturer paid a product placement fee to get it on camera. Most movies and TV shows today are accepting product placements. For the media, the product placement fee is another stream of income. If you need to use a product on camera, why not get paid for using a particular product? Some films contain dozens of product placements. Placements can cost anywhere from thousands to millions of dollars, depending on the amount of exposure the product will receive, which has a basis in part at least on how integral the product is to action in the film. The Ford

Mondeo automobile used in the James Bond film "Casino Royale" cost Ford an estimated $25 million.

Why do companies pay product placement fees? It is an effective way to guarantee that audiences will see the image of their product. Television viewers now regularly avoid advertisements. They leave the room, change channels, or TiVo past them. One cannot avoid product placements. Producers integrate them into the action. If viewers watch the scene, they cannot avoid seeing the product images that are part of the scene.

Video

Public relations specialists now often are translating their information into video. Product brochures become video brochures. They are also producing news releases as video news releases or VNRs, which include file footage that the news station can use, but which they should identify as such. They are producing annual corporate reports for video as well as for print. (The Securities and Exchange Commission still requires print reports.)

The Alaska seafood industry produced a series of videos called "Alaska Seafood Cooking Techniques with Chef John Ash." The series promoted Alaska seafood by providing entertaining tips on using seafood in recipes. In the past, this tactic would have resulted in a printed cookbook.

Video are also useful to distribute corporate news, training instruction, and sales messages. The wide availability of low cost digital camcorders and editing software makes video a reasonably priced alternative to print for many purposes.

Types of news coverage ▼

Exclusives

One of the chief strategies in obtaining news coverage for a client, particularly for a story that has strong newsworthy elements, is to give one news organization an "exclusive." Exclusives give news organizations the opportunity to report something first, before their competitors get the story. They generally contain information that is of wide interest to the public.

The exclusive is also a useful strategy when staging a promotional event. When Dickies, the Western wear manufacturer, was trying to brand itself in the fashion industry, public relations specialists arranged for a Brahma bull to be part of a festive party in Manhattan for people in the fashion and apparel industry, media members, and a few celebrities. The visuals for such an event were attractive for a television station that received an exclusive among electronic media. Publicist Dee Covey, who staged and managed the event, suggested to a *New York Daily News* photographer to use a photo of the bull crossing a busy, morning intersection in New York's financial district. This was similar to the use of the image in the memorable "Abbey Road" album by the legendary rock 'n' roll group, the Beatles. The police cooperated to help pull off this unusual stunt. *The Daily News* photographer got his exclusive photo, albeit with the Dickies logo draped over the bull and similarly adorned apparel on the beast's handlers. The photo splashed across the pages of the New York City tabloid. There is no telling how many other newspapers later received the photograph through news service distribution, but *The New York Daily News* published it first.

Public relations representatives who offer exclusives concerning stories that nobody really wants will raise questions about their news judgment. Journalists are likely to ask, "Doesn't he/she know that isn't news—that isn't an interesting story meriting an exclusive?" An exclusive offer does not make a non-story news. For the offer to mean anything, the representative must establish the newsworthiness of a story.

News organizations generally compete against one another for news. Some stories about the economy, war or conflict command universal attention. Such stories are rarely available as exclusives, and if they do earn the attribution "as first reported by . . . ," the attention is short-lived as the multiple platforms for information swoop in to spread the news as their own. Exclusives are more likely to be used as a branding tactic for a celebrity feature on E! or TMZ and softer news stories.

Offering exclusives is more of a challenge in today's digital world because of the fluidity of communication. With blogs, message boards and 24-hour television news channels and news sites all looking and competing for stories, there are few secrets anymore. Information hits the streets long before the newspaper hits the driveway. Media relations specialists must take the speed of media into consideration when offering exclusives.

One ethical consideration regarding exclusives is that if a journalist has been promised an exclusive, it had better remain so. Sometimes, hoping to drum up interest in a story, a source may offer the same exclusive to more than one news entity. It is certain that journalists will be angry if they discover that their exclusive story was not exclusive after all. PR pioneer Ivy Lee, almost a hundred years ago, had to contend with journalists asking for exclusives. When he gave an exclusive to one reporter, other reporters became offended by the favoritism. Lee used a system of rotation, offering exclusives to a small number of reporters, one at a time. The reporters took turns getting the exclusives. Lee got the enthusiastic coverage of a story he wanted without alienating the journalism community.

Calling a news conference

Events requiring a **news** or **press conference** are open to all media. Public relations specialists should call press conferences only when they have an announcement or an event that truly warrants widespread media coverage. Press conferences are an efficient and effective means for giving multiple news organizations access to newsmakers at the same time. Such gatherings can be live or in-person events, or professionals may mediate them through satellite videoconferencing. Today, they even transmit some as podcasts or live-streamed programing.

In many situations, it would be impossible to grant numerous one-on-one interviews to a world leader, for example, or to a most valuable player of the Super Bowl. In such situations, a press conference makes it possible to make the newsmaker simultaneously available to many journalists at once.

AP PHOTO/WIDE WORLD PHOTOS

▲ *Media day for the Super Bowl is a series of news conferences that give media worldwide an opportunity to gather quotes for their own stories. Given the number of media attending such pre-game festivities, media day tends to be a rather crowded affair.*

The logistics of organizing a press conference can become challenging, from extending invitations and granting credentials to meeting the technical needs of electronic and print reporters. The public relations professional must meet the needs of all media, while also preparing the person who will be facing the press. Speakers at a news conference can expect a lot of questions. Depending on the subject, some of the questions can embarrass, and some of the questioning can be aggressive. PR people should anticipate questions from the media in advance, and, to the extent possible, give considerable thought to the answers.

What is news? What makes news?

Reporters come to stories wondering: "What here is news?" or "What here makes news?" It is the single question that editors in all media ask themselves as they prepare content for publications, newscasts and websites. News is a collection of facts that are interesting, uncommon or extraordinary. News also may be simple information reported as a matter of record.

Philosophically and historically, news organizations see themselves as serving as watchdogs for the public in all kinds of governmental matters, from court filings to police records. This responsibility is the rationale for the protections granted to the press by the First Amendment of the United States Constitution. (See Chapter 11.) While journalists see themselves as protecting the public, public relations has a duty to make sure they protect clients' interests from overzealous reporters.

> *The skilled public relations practitioner will probe and prod, much like a reporter, to find a real story. In doing so, what began as an attempt to drum up publicity actually becomes news.*

The public easily understands that the story trumpeting "Man Bites Dog," a phrase attributed to New York Sun editor John B. Bogard in 1882, is far more unusual than "Dog Bites Man." However, what about a story about a company that is celebrating its 25th or 50th anniversary? That milestone is a great achievement, but

AP PHOTO/WIDE WORLD PHOTOS

▲ *The release of the latest Harry Potter book was a sensational event, but when hundreds, if not thousands, of people jam a bookstore, like this one in Norway, the simple book release becomes a spectacle.*

not particularly unusual. The challenge of the public relations specialist is to find facts and circumstances that make the story more than ordinary. How has the company changed over that period? Perhaps the founder nurtured a small company into one that employs hundreds or thousands of people. Perhaps the company pioneered technological changes that have had a profound effect in its industry and perhaps in the world at large. The media are well aware that audiences perceive them as carrying much "negative" news. As a result, they are eager to learn about success stories.

Everyone has an interesting story to tell. Some stories are more interesting than others. Moreover, some are more newsworthy. The media like human-interest stories. The skilled public relations practitioner will probe and prod, much like a reporter, to find a real story. In doing so, what begins as an attempt to drum up publicity actually becomes news.

News by the numbers

Beyond the unusual, editors are interested in information that affects or interests many people. The release of a novel is not itself necessarily newsworthy. Authors write many novels. What makes one newsworthy may be the celebrity of the author. Alternatively, perhaps the author is local, and the media in that community are eager to cover and perhaps even to cheerlead his efforts. Book lovers often anticipate the release of a novel that is the latest in a series of blockbusters, like the Harry Potter series.

Consider another situation involving numbers. A company that lays off 300 employees faces managing a generally negative news story, one that editors and writers would predictably follow. Job layoffs are a very human story. When people lose jobs it disrupts their lives. Instead of simply bracing for the bad news, the company may choose to organize a job fair to help the former employees find other work in the area. The result? The attention of the layoffs can shift from the harsh reality of job losses to positive efforts of finding jobs for the 300 employees. In this case, two public relations efforts come into play. First, the company creates an event to help former employees, an event in itself that becomes newsworthy. Second, in the process, it transforms a negative story into a more positive one.

Placing the news

While media relations specialists seek major coverage or visibility for their clients, with front-page placement being prime space or online hits, much coverage becomes reduced to brief mentions in notes columns, calendar listings and tweets. Event calendars in publications and online are small but highly visible, and PR people should not ignore them. The public is always eager to know what is happening. Calendars offer an opportunity to publicize visiting guest speakers and events and everything from musical entertainment to conventions.

Announcements of private events are less likely to find their way into print than events that are open to the public. However, a private event that raises funds for a community or nonprofit organization such as a clinic, hospital or museum will likely get some free media attention. In fact, cleverly conceived events can generate major feature space or broadcast time, especially on a slow news day, which will get a bounce online.

The challenge for the public relations professional is to find ways to make something—an idea, a product, a person—interesting and newsworthy. No organization is entitled to news coverage. The media are likely to ignore stories that are strictly promotional and have little or no genuine news value. There are too many real stories to waste time and space on stories that are nothing more than thinly veiled advertising for an organization. Creativity is necessary to find an angle, a way of transforming what is ordinary into something that will merit news coverage.

Becoming part of a larger story

Another strategy to gain media attention for an organization is to become part of a larger story. Reporting on big stories involves multiple sources. Reporters are looking for a variety of experts or credible sources to explain the how and why of a story. A client with appropriate expertise and insight might find her or his way into a news story. This is where the "relations" part of media relations comes into play. By knowing reporters, their beats and the stories they are working and finding popular blogs and online communities, it is possible to connect an authoritative local source that has newsworthy information and insights with reporters working on a story. Local news organizations are also eager to find local angles — or to localize — regional or national stories.

PR practitioners must stay tuned to print, electronic and digital news media to be informed about the world around them. They also have to understand the industries of clients or employers. When they see a story they will ask, "Is there a way to add my client's (or employer's) voice to this story?" A PR specialist with a hospital, health clinic or specialized medical practice may find ample opportunities to be part of an assortment of health-related stories. A reporter working on a story about steroid use, based on a national story, may want a local expert to comment. The expert will not only add insight into the matter and help the reporter with the story, he or she will be getting the name of the expert's employer into the news and into the public consciousness.

Whether the story originates with a PR specialist or a reporter, the task of public relations is to merge the interests of a client with those of news organizations. This is a win-win situation. The client gets media attention and the reporter gets a qualified source to help build a story.

> *The task of public relations is to merge the interests of a client with those of news organizations. This is a win-win situation. The client gets media attention and the reporter gets a qualified source to help build a story.*

Sweating the small stuff

Generally, news organizations with small staffs are more willing to use well-written news releases than those with large staffs. Writers who show a good nose for news and a strong ability to craft a well-organized, thorough and easy-to-read article will win the trust of editors and reporters. The media relations specialist who has the knack, knowledge and reputation for delivering useful, credible sources is helpful to editors and reporters.

Conversely, a consistent lack of news judgment, poorly worded news releases filled with errors, misspellings, and poor grammar—even one error—are likely to lose credibility with deadline-driven editors and reporters. A PR practitioner who consistently sends out emails with badly written releases is likely to find his or her messages redirected, unopened to junk mail folders or just trashed.

If journalists use a story, one caveat for the PR practitioner is this: Do not thank journalists for the *publicity*. Reporters hate to feel they have been used or manipulated. Perhaps an excellent interview revealed an interesting side to a subject. Perhaps the research used in a story showed great depth and detail for a particular subject. Compliments should be substantive. Make the journalists feel good about the quality and substance of the story rather than from the free publicity a client got from it.

Media relations involves an ongoing relationship. It is important to follow up with beat or general assignment reporters from time to time to see what stories they are working on and what sort of help they might find useful. Journalists value public relations more when PR people become a resource rather than obvious press agents striving to worm their way into the news.

Niche markets for stories

Strolling along the magazine racks in a bookstore or searching for ezines online will reveal a large inventory of newspapers, magazines and newsletters. Many child-, family- and fitness-oriented publications are available for free. The printed formats come in various shapes and sizes, from magazines and tabloids to the traditional broadsheets. They are replicated online with the ability to turn electronic pages. Paid magazines range in content from general news publications to publications dealing with every imaginable topic, such as sports, international politics, business, gardening,

collecting and knitting. Think of a topic and there is probably a publication dedicated to that subject. Even celebrities are creating branded publications, such as the magazines of Oprah and Martha Stewart.

In an era of **desktop publishing**, anyone with an idea and funding can publish a special-focus publication. More narrowly defined publications with smaller circulation get disseminated in the form of newsletters. Most of these publications also have some digital content—whether a website or a blog—that appeals to even wider audiences. Contemporary print media can roll off a home or office printer and travel through cyberspace as portable document format (pdf) files. Printed pages increasingly give way to pixels, bytes and megabytes.

Television is similarly expanding and evolving. The proliferation of cable and satellite channels transmitter towers has created many opportunities to distribute information that appeals to niche audiences. The following are some cable TV channels today that illustrate just a few of the niches one can reach via television. In many cases, more than one channel serves a niche—niches within niches.

Animal Planet	Military History Channel
Arab Radio and TV	Biography Channel
Cartoon Network	Legal Television Network
Ecology Channel	Food Network
History Channel	Planet Green
Travel Channel	Wine TV
Fashion TV	Home and Garden TV
BabyFirst TV	BET
Women's Entertainment	Gem Shopping Network
ImaginAsian TV	Fox Soccer Channel
Telemundo	The Golf Channel
FitTV	Horse Racing TV
Military Channel	Tennis Channel

Internet dynamics

One of the great powers of the Internet is the control readers have in choosing what they want to read. Some people visit many different newspapers online. Others identify a few favorite sites and visit them regularly. In effect, readers become the gatekeepers of what they want to read instead of relying on editors to choose their content, based on a traditional definition of news.

The number of pages supported by advertising limit the size of publications and other print media. Available time minus commercials limits the size of newscasts. The space and time on the Internet are seemingly infinite, and online advertisers can buy banner space on websites or find users on various platforms based on user interests and activity.

On the Internet, a message may be available to millions of people, but few readers, if any, will see it. The amount of content available to an audience is astonishing, making the digital space extremely competitive. Internet audiences increasingly expect sophisticated sites with rich content and dynamic interfaces. A static site filled with text and a few photos is unlikely to compete well against more sophisticated efforts to gain and hold attention. Therefore, organizations increasingly hire companies that specialize in web design and operation. A vast number of individuals and small businesses now have the benefit of having a website with great design and functionality through such sites as www.wordpress.com.

Since this is the first generation of the digital revolution, measurements assessing the effectiveness of social media sites are undergoing continuous study and scrutiny. One of the major early challenges to the value of digital media has been the ability to measure actual outcomes, not just impressions. With traditional news coverage, one could always resort to counting circulation figures or viewer ratings to determine the number of impressions. Ratings would provide a mechanism to measure viewers or listeners on television or radio. Websites allowed mass communication practitioners to measure visitors through hits and on counters and direct sales. Social media, to some extent, could be measured by fans, followers and tweets. Media today are visible through the Internet, and they want to understand in a world with plenty of buzz and chatter, the overall impact of a particular message.

This challenge is getting answered through the development of software tools such as Radian6, which monitors and measures the impact of digital and social media by tracking mentions of a product or an issue and those of a competitor. Such results are useful in planning and strategic thinking as to how best to use digital media. The speed and fluidity of social media make it a game-changer in influencing media activity. The use of widgets on various platforms, plus the optimum use of search engine optimization strategies give users the opportunities to derive full benefit of digital media. While content may be king; interfaces are queen.

SocialTwist, a customer acquisition and retention platform that generates viral referrals for businesses,

reported toward the end of 2010 that Twitter users click through 6.6 times more often than do Facebook users, despite Facebook being by far the most popular sharing platform among users. Eventbrite, an online event registration website, however, reports that sharing event information through Facebook is 5.8 times as valuable as doing the same through Twitter. Each time a user shared an event through Facebook it generated $2.52 in ticket sales versus only 43 cents for each Twitter share. In addition to personal outbursts, Twitter is best used as a medium for repurposing content from other media platforms; Facebook excels as a medium for personal communication. . . . at least for now. Both are powerful platforms for communication, and they derive their influence from the creativity of strategists.

The public has more control over what they read and watch. Still, newspaper and broadcasting staffs judge the news based on a fundamental standard of what is news. The basis of journalists' news judgment is the impact an event has on people, the numbers of dollars or lives involved, the actions taken by public officials or public figures, or, more generally, what journalists perceive as most important to a community. Editors have decided for hundreds of years what will go on the front or inside pages of a publication based on these criteria. These journalists have decided what is newsworthy. Traditional news organizations, from the Associated Press and Reuters to The New York Times and The Wall Street Journal continue to provide significant coverage in terms of world and national news. A few online news groups such as *The Huffington Post, The Drudge Report* and *The Daily Beast* offer reporting, blogs, not nearly the muscle yet of the long-standing groups.

Today's young media consumers are using the Internet as a primary source for information, and they are seeking and finding information, independent of editors, based on what they want to know. Information consumers are increasingly serving as their own gate-keepers, no longer relying on the news judgment of editors. This represents a huge change in the information gathering roles of media consumers and journalists. Media consumers are less dependent on journalists at traditional news outlets for their information; and newspapers are less able to set the agenda for public discourse.

There are several ways consumers can get the information they want online. One is to read online publications that target their interests. They connect with such information through apps or simply through desktop searches. Consumers also have information sent to them through such search engines as Google, Yahoo and bing by setting up an **alert** for topics of special interest. "Alerts" can search for the name of a company, a person, or a particular subject. The more specific the keywords for a search, the more likely the search results will be pertinent. This is a useful way to track news about a client or an area of interest. This new way of organizing, presenting and delivering news represents a huge power shift in the media. For the public relations professional, the more he or she understands this dynamic, the better to serve clients as media relations specialists.

Significant changes are also happening in broadcasting and other electronic media. Hundreds of cable and satellite channels have joined the three major networks to compete for attention and viewers. Currently, a new age of television allows users to use their flat screens they way they use computers and mobile devices. The average prime time television program has half the audience it did a couple of decades ago. The proliferation of video choices has led to the fragmentation of audiences. Smaller audiences are often watching programs of specialized interest. Once professionals called television a broadcast media, sent out to mass audiences with broad demographics. Today, many television programs are narrowcasting, targeting much smaller audiences interested in a sport, gardening, home repair, history, science, cartoons, cars, even war.

The boundaries between media are evolving. Newspapers are getting into television. An increasing number of newspapers are equipping news reporters with video equipment, so they can shoot video clips while gathering information for their written reports. The text-only story will appear in the newspaper and tease to video, photos and other data on the publication's website, where space is virtually infinite. The name of this news gathering process that incorporates video online with traditional note taking and information gathering techniques is **convergence**.

National Public Radio and local public radio stations are doing something similar with their websites. They will broadcast an audio story over radio, but make an expanded version of the story with audio, text, graphics, photos, or video available on the website. If a story interests listeners, they can easily learn more. Using websites and social media to expand on stories helps mainstream media overcome the traditional limitations of time and space that force them to compress stories into inches or seconds, leaving out much detail.

Today's media present challenges to both journalists and public relations professionals. Media choices and technologies are evolving. Consumers are using media differently from the way they once did. Understanding media—all media—is crucial to strategic thinking by public relations professionals.

Proactive and reactive ▼

Media relations specialists must be both proactive and reactive. Proactive activity occurs when specialists take information, often newsworthy, and find an audience or a market for it. In considering target audiences, they can determine whether they should direct the news to a mainstream audience or to segmented audiences attracted to niche media, such as a highly specialized trade publication, newsletter or cable channel.

Reactive media relations occurs when professionals create information in reaction to an event or story. Such work requires the media relations specialists to be ready to react anytime, anywhere, and at any moment of any day. In today's blog-infused world, corporations, candidates, and celebrities have public relations specialists who monitor how the information marketplace is treating their name, brand, or image. They must quickly react to, clarify, or expand on information that others are writing or reading.

Review questions

1. What is news?
2. Unflattering rumors are circulating in blogs about your client. There are some truths mixed with falsehoods. How would you deal with allegations on the Internet and questions from the media?
3. Your job is to create awareness for your client. How do you go about finding opportunities to promote the client in a variety of media?
4. What are the positive and negative aspects of giving a news organization an exclusive break on a story?
5. A celebrity couple announces it has given birth to twins. Explain what makes this information news.
6. What makes a media outlet such as YouTube an interesting option for promoting a product, person or idea?

Supplemental resources online

http://www.prweb.com	News release service
http://www.prnewswire.com	News release service
http://www.poynter.org	The Poynter Institute
http://www.burson-marsteller.com	Burson-Marsteller
http://www.edelman.com/	Edelman
http://www.cohnandwolfe.com	Cohn & Wolfe
http://www.ketchum.com	Ketchum
http://www.webershandwick.com/	Weber Shandwick
http://www.blancandotus.com	Blanc & Otus
http://www.b2bpublicrelations.org	Online community for b2b marketers
http://www.lostremote.com	Technology's impact on television
http://www.mediadawn.com	Media dawn / creative multimedia
http://www.westglen.com	West Glen Communications, Inc.
http://www.hitwise.com	hitwise, an Experian Company
http://www.jupiterresearch.com	JupiterResearch
http://www.bulldogreporter.com	Media news and intelligence for PR Pros
http://www.mediapost.com	Media Post publications
http://www.radian6.com	Social Media Monitoring tools

Chapter references

Bergman, Cory. How to write for the Web. Lost Remote's Guide to TV Newsrooms.

Book of Lists 2007. (2007, December 24). *PRWeek*.

Covel, Simona. (2007, December 27). *The Wall Street Journal*, Small Business Link, B4.

Covel, Simona, & Lorber, Laura. (2007, December 31). *The Wall Street Journal*, Small Business Link, B6.

Falkow, Sally. Online PR technology trends. The Leading Edge, Lost Remote TV Blog.

Halpin, Vanessa. (2001), Decoding the secret to effective PR writing. MediaMap, Inc.

Interview with Terry Comer, vice president of finance and operations with American Biosurgical. (2008, February), SKY magazine, 34.

Search engines are driving news traffic. (2007, December 31). *www.hitwise.com*.

To read or not to read? A question of national consequence. (2007). National Endowment for the Arts.

Tye, Larry. (1998). *The father of spin: Edward L. Bernays & the birth of public relations*. New York: Crown Publishers.

Symptoms of H1n1 (Swine Flu), Center for Disease Control, posted April 28, 2009, http://www.youtube.com/watch?v=0wK1127fHQ4

Clean Hands Help Prevent the Flu, Center for Disease Control, posted May 2, 2009, http://www.youtube.com/watch?NR=1&v=XHISh559oho&feature=endscreen

The Dog Strikes Back: 2012 Volkswagen Game Day Commercial, posted Jan. 2, 2012, http://www.youtube.com/watch?v=0-9EYFJ4Clo

"Detailing the Digital Revolution: Social, Streaming and More," Nielsenwire, posted February 24, 2012, http://blog.nielsen.com/nielsenwire/media_entertainment/detailing-the-digital-revolution-social-streaming-and-more/

"100 Ways to Use Social Media Monitoring," http://www.slideshare.net/Radian6/10-categories-to-get-you-started-in-social-media-monitoring-and-enagement-1

Rognon, J. posted Jan. 16, 2012, How Many U.S. Internet Users Watch Online Video Content, http://www.prmarketing.com/blog/how-many-us-internet-users-watch-online-video-content.

Notes

Name _____

Date _____

1. Read articles from all sections of a local daily newspaper and determine how public relations practitioners were involved in the news that day.

2. Discuss how public relations practitioners get involved or could get involved on your campus.

3. New companies and those seeking a new image often see a new name or a new logo as a newsworthy change. Branding the new logo is a key piece to the company's overall marketing strategy. How is this event newsworthy for, say, Wal-Mart and not for a local electronic games store?

4. Consider a trend or program on campus and discuss why it is newsworthy. Write a pitch of the story idea for a local daily newspaper.

5. Identify a front page story from a major newspaper and track how that same story is finding its way on other media platforms..

Notes

chapter

8

CRISIS COMUNICATIONS

*C*risis communications ▼

Sometimes organizations are confronted by circumstances that are drastically different from the norm and manage crisis communications for the groups. Crises can stem from natural disasters, campus shootings, sexual scandals, corporate fraud, labor strikes, political revolution, protests that turn violent and rumors that go viral and take on a life of their own. In recent history, a shocking crisis occurred on Sept. 11, 2001, when commercial airplanes were hijacked by terrorists and flown into two 110-story buildings in New York City

In today's digital world, many activities become well-publicized crises because of acts of indiscretion or recklessness. Statements by high-profile individuals are propelled at break-neck speed along the information highway through new media platforms. They are consumed, digested and redistributed without regard for the truth. Technology can turn private lives into career-damaging public gossip.

Attempts will be made to defuse many crises with the claim that statements were "taken out of context." This reaction is often the first line of defense, but it isn't a very strong one. It does, however, give the accused the opportunity to deflect responsibility for being portrayed as the victim and to transfer blame to the media. Blaming the media is a common strategy for those accused of misdeeds. It rarely works for very long, and is usually about as effective as plugging a hole in a dike with a pebble.

In a crisis there are often two sets of problems:

1. **Managing the crisis itself.** If it is an oil spill, then there is a need to stop the oil from spilling.

If a cruise ship collides with rocks and sinks, then passengers must be offloaded to safety. When terrorists flew aircraft into the towers in New York City, there were all sorts of practical problems related to firefighting, rescue and evacuation, and understanding the scope of the security threat to the country. Public relations professionals don't manage technical and operational problems; they manage information the public needs to know and work with all forms of media.

2. **Managing communication about the crisis.** This is the job of public relations professionals. The organization must communicate to the public, often through journalists and the mass media. Doing an effective job of managing communication can limit damage to an organization's image and reputation. It can also help organizations to distribute life saving information to the community. In some cases, a situation will only require communication management. If a public figure is involved in a sex scandal, for example, then crisis management is focused exclusively on damage control relating to the individual's image or reputation.

Eric Dezenhall in his book "Damage Control" says that crises can really explode into a "perfect storm" when three archetypal story elements are present: (1) disaster, crisis, conflict; (2) vulnerable victims; (3) arrogant or incompetent villains. Many PR crises discussed in this chapter had all three elements, making the crises dramatic and compelling stories for the media and a public relations nightmare for the clients.

The fact is that even the best organizations are likely, at some point, to experience a crisis. Things go wrong. There are, however, ways to handle crises that are truthful, ethical and likely will help an organization weather the storm.

Crisis communications can be managed through planning, particularly if a group or individual is involved in an activity fraught with hazards. It is often possible to anticipate what the most likely crises could be in an industry and develop contingency plans for managing both the crisis itself, and communication about the crisis. Large organizations typically have crisis management plans that identify who will be responsible for handling both the crisis itself and communication about the crisis.

Ken Scudder of Virgil Scudder & Associates in New York believes the successful handling of a crisis is 60 percent preparation and 40 percent execution. Regardless of the disaster, regardless of whether the target of a crisis is the accused or the victim, information must:

▶ Come together quickly, accurately and truthfully;
▶ Be delivered as fully as possible; and
▶ Stay ahead of news reports.

Natural disasters
▼

When natural disasters such as earthquakes, tornadoes and floods occur, crisis communications serves to inform or warn the public. News organizations perform a dual function of reporting the news and delivering information to audiences. Crisis communications workers also receive and often act on information from the public either by phone or through various media platforms. The American Red Cross, other organizations, companies and government agencies use a system that streamlines crisis communications, from communications within the organization to its staff and volunteers, to information releases to the mass media. This system uses a central platform developed by PIER Systems of Bellingham, Wash., to:

▶ Organize document creation and approval processes
▶ Store media lists
▶ Distribute news releases, which are sent not only to traditional media but integrated into social media applications through RSS feeds.
▶ Respond to inquiries from the media, public and other stakeholders.

Plans are useful preparation for managing information during a crisis, but some disasters degenerate into completely chaotic situations that worsen because of poor response coordination. The events surrounding the Katrina Hurricane and various agencies in 2005 have been judged disastrous. Katrina claimed thousands of lives along the Gulf Coast, forced more than 100,000 to flee New Orleans and the Mississippi Gulf Coast, revealed the flawed capabilities of levees in the face of such a forceful hurricane, and overall exceeded the resources and preparation of New Orleans, the State of Louisiana and the federal government.

News organizations, bloggers and the public blamed the handling of Katrina on the lack of cooper-

© CAITLIN MIRRA, 2012. USED UNDER LICENSE FROM SHUTTERSTOCK, INC.

ation and coordination of city, state and federal government bureaucracies. Critics also pointed to a failure of leadership at all levels of government, the "incompetent" work of the Federal Emergency Management Agency (FEMA) and just bad luck. At the same time, the evacuation plan, no matter how flawed, could not resolve circumstances in which some residents simply refused to leave their homes. Studying the communications failures during Hurricane Katrina, Terry Cole of Appalachian State University and Kelli Fellows of the University of North Carolina-Wilmington wrote that "semantic choices used in messages directing the evacuation did not arouse a sufficient amount of concern among residents nor did they imply a level of necessity for action (i.e., the failure to specifically say 'a mandatory evacuation'). The evacuation efforts were further deflated by inconsistent messages regarding evacuation plans. Overall, a sense of surprise among the messengers (local and state government officials) at the event (Hurricane Katrina and the levee failure) was evident in the comedy of errors that was the uncoordinated response."

Cole and Fellows in their article "Risk Communication Failure: A Case Study of New Orleans and

Hurricane Katrina" in the Southern Communication Journal noted three key lessons from the handling of this natural disaster:

1. Effective care communication is to little avail if the subsequent consensus and crisis messages are inadequate. (Messages must be clear so that people under duress can understand them.)
2. Message preparation before the crisis is essential. Specific messages that range in scope from minimal risk to the worst-case scenario should be prepared as part of the disaster management plan. . . . Preplanning, a fundamental function of risk communication, provides an imperative communication arm to the disaster management plan that can be engaged amid other ongoing management functions.
3. To be effective, messages must be credible to their recipient audiences.

A key to handling crisis is to plan for all forms of crises. Communication professionals charged with creating a crisis communication plan learn from the crises of others.

Contingency communications planning happens, for example, where natural disasters are common. In locales with seasonal expectations of hurricanes, tornados or flooding, it is important to create plans that try to expect the unexpected. Evacuating and caring for people displaced by a natural disaster is only one contingency. Disasters affect every aspect of people's lives and the infrastructure that supports them. News releases and alerts are a common way to reach people through traditional media, newspapers, television and radio. Increasingly common today is electronic messaging using smartphones. Relying on smartphones can be problematic, however, because the technology can become inoperable in extreme conditions, and many households lack users of smartphones. There are also language barriers and less than perfect systems for communicating emergency information to people who have visual or hearing disabilities.

Human disasters ▼

Over time in highly publicized, often embarrassing crises, the truth inevitably surfaces. Any attempt to mislead or lie about events is an invitation to a different kind of disaster, one that deals with reputation. The public suspects wrongdoing or a cover-up when the road to the truth follows a circuitous path. Ashley McCown, president of Solomon McCown & Co. in Boston, states: "Most crises can be anticipated and planned for if organizations are willing to take a hard look at simmering issues and deal with them, no matter the 'cost.'" The best route to the truth is a direct one.

By failing to be forthcoming with appropriate levels of factual information, the media will pounce on the possibility that wrongdoing exists. Crisis communicators in these situations find themselves spending substantial amounts of time and energy clarifying or correcting reports and mending internal conflicts when one piece of information does not reconcile with another and that inconsistency fosters suspicion.

Where personal wrongdoing exists, the best response, next to telling the truth, is to take responsibility *and* to offer an apology.

Quickly, accurately, truthfully ▼

News breaks continuously. It's no longer delivered when a newspaper lands on the driveway or when televisions blare in the morning, evening and at night. News is reported almost as fast as it happens. Everything happens in *real time*. A popular smartphone commercial illustrates the speed with which things happen today.

"Did you know that . . . ?" a tailgating sports fan asks.

"That happened so 27 seconds ago," the relaxing tailgaters reply.

Crisis communicators once had hours to assess a situation and calculate how best to manage information. This lapse allowed time for the creation of "spin," an attempt to manage or explain away a problem. In the context of crisis communications "spin" is a term for "damage control."

The speed of message transmission today has changed crisis communications. Silence is no longer an option. Being "unavailable for comment" clears the way for an avalanche of information and disinformation, not to mention aggressive reporting. A reply of "no comment" without a more complete explanation no longer staves off reporters from pursuing information. Saying "no comment" does not stop the telling of the story. Journalists and bloggers and others will still tell the story. What will be missing is the organization's point of view. The organization, by saying "no comment," surrenders the opportunity to influence the content and direction of the story. Journalists and others will tell the story based on other sources of information that may or may not be an accurate, fair or a complete picture of events. An organization might then have to expend energy trying to correct the errors that were reported while they were being silent about the story.

B.D.—before digital ▼

Crisis communications examples are increasing with the complexities of life and the ease of digital communication. Before such digital communication, the most popular case studies involving crisis communications involved the 11 million-plus gallon oil spill from the grounding of the Exxon Valdez off the coast of Alaska at Prince William Sound's Bligh Reef in 1989 or Johnson & Johnson's Tylenol Cyanide Crisis in 1982, when tainted capsules accounted for the deaths of seven people near Chicago.

In the Tylenol case, a reporter knew about the deaths before Johnson & Johnson's public relations department. A Chicago reporter was seeking comment. Johnson & Johnson chairman James Burke formed a seven-member strategy team with the charge, "How do we protect the people?" and "How do we save this product?" First, the company alerted the public not to take any type of Tylenol product and not resume taking it until the extent of the problem could be determined. Tylenol capsules were removed from the shelves in Chicago area and later from throughout the country. A toll-free number was established for customers and news organizations. Open communication on all fronts, from the public to the media, proved beneficial in a crisis situation. News conferences were held via satellite. (Again, social media didn't exist.) Eventually, Tylenol introduced tamper-resistant packaging after the crisis.

The Department of Defense, writing about the Tylenol case, stated: "In most crises, media will focus on the sensational aspects of the crisis, and then follow with the cause as they learn more about what happened." Preparations mean having access to how the public, not the least of which are customers or prospective customers, is reacting to whatever is at stake such as issues or a product. Pay attention to sources that may be generating adverse information. Disinformation or the lack of information can be responsible for a

communications crisis and thus is not an option in managing a crisis. Consider the oil spill that followed a deadly explosion with a British Petroleum rig off the coast of Louisiana.

A different kind of gusher ▼

British Petroleum's oil spill in 2010 generated an avalanche of negative publicity. Stories about the spill focused on its effect on the environment, the economy along the Mississippi Gulf Coast, and the oil company's insensitive executive leadership. BP's public relations team eventually waged an advertising and public relations campaign that offered its "we'll fix this" campaign. Roger L. Martin, author of "Fixing the Game: How Runaway Expectations Broke the Economy and How to get Back to Reality" published by Harvard Business Review Press in 2011, describes the British Petroleum situation as a public relations nightmare, writing, "The lack of a public relations crisis communications plan was evident and, really, the least of BP's problems. The primary problem, of course, was finding a way to cap the well."

BP was initially mum on the problem and ignored media requests. The company, branded for decades as an eco-friendly company, reportedly paid more than $250,000 to create its official YouTube channel. BP began telling its story on May 18, 2010. Tony Hayward, the chief executive officer of British Petroleum during the time, released a statement to the public: "BP is fully committed to taking all possible steps to contain the spread of the oil spill." In the wake of further scrutiny, however, he blamed Transocean, owners of the oil rig, for the safety lapses that caused the explosion and 11 deaths. While the public watched mushrooming

clouds of oil spill into the Gulf for months, Hayward attempted to suggest that the spill from one rig was less than enormous relative to the size of the globe's oceans. "The amount of volume of oil and dispersant we are putting into it is tiny in relation to the total water volume," he announced. After six weeks of criticism and ridicule, Hayward offered an apology. As the calamity continued to take its toll on the ocean, wildlife, coastlines, shrimpers, other businesses and residents, not to mention the grieving families of the 11 dead workers, he revealed his own frustrations from the pressures of the disaster, uttering his infamous comment, "I want my life back." Hayward subsequently lost his job, but got his life back in the form of a reported $18 million severance package and as much time as he wanted to spend aboard his yacht.

The media initially received little information from BP about capping the well or how the explosion occurred. As a result, they were left to focus on the adverse and ugly consequences of the spill and to wonder whether BP was prepared for such disasters at all. Silence spoke volumes in terms of speculation and reporting, most of it negative.

Even comedians had a field day with BP. Los Angeles comedian Josh Simpson created a Twitter site @BPGlobalPR. His first 515 tweets reached 166,825 followers and 8,519 lists, all of which would spread critical barbs as impressively as oil flushed into the Gulf. Doonesbury, the popular, politically hard-hitting cartoon strip, began lampooning BP's daily briefings. Meanwhile, the public watched floating dead sea life and black oil-soaked pelicans and other wildlife gasping for air. BP had much to fix.

BP began providing information through various platforms—its own website, traditional media, on Twitter @BP_America and at www.deepwaterhorizonresponse.com. The company opened a phone line for volunteers (866-488-5816) and to handle claims related to the oil spill (800-440-0858). It bought a sponsored link from Google searches, which went to the BP website. Google created a link to "Crisis Response: Gulf of Mexico Oil Spill." By the fall of 2011, the site's 8,327 tweets attracted more than 30,000 followers. A cursory study of tweets shows BP tweeting news of everything from festivals, fundraisers, United Way activities, travel destinations along the Gulf Coast, restaurants boasting the best Gulf shrimp, sandcastle-building activities, grants supporting conservation and wildlife research. The deepwaterhorizonresponse.com would subsequently redirect viewers to www.restorethegulf.gov.

The corporate website (www.bp.com) features a "Gulf of Mexico Restoration" button with an impressive array of written and video reports with pristine, colorful images of coastal life and evidence of a robust economy. BP's Deepwater Horizon Joint Investigation Team final report was announced Sept. 14, 2011, with the final report posted Sept. 30, 2011, at www.deepwaterinvestigation.com. Five months after the April 20, 2010, disaster, the gushing leak was capped. The transparency that had eluded British Petroleum for two months was resolved. The messaging by BP officials, viewed as callous and condescending by critics, became more responsible, factual and forthcoming. Nonetheless, executives got a chance to see the foolishness of such comments as, "I want my life back" or "We care about the small people." The British Petroleum situation offers insights into handling crisis situations. Among lessons learned from this and other crisis situations are these:

▶ Make key spokespersons available for interviews within one hour of an event.
▶ Make sure interview subjects are prepared for questions from the media.
▶ Prepare news releases and other explanatory materials, to support announcements.
▶ Anticipate media questions and prepare answers or cooperate to find answers.
▶ Expand news coverage through posts on social media and other Internet platforms.

A social media tumble ▼

When Tumblr experienced an outage in 2010, the company had to fend off the problem with apologies—"we're incredibly sorry"—and promises ("be back shortly") as part of a stream of notices announcing "the recovering database cluster is online and healthy." Social media users are either fickle or unforgiving as they have many options for engaging their communities. During the approximately 24-hour outage, Twitter users commented quickly and often, every minute. Some wondered whether Tumblr had "died or something." Others showed such frustration through warnings—"better be fixed" soon. All media have endured interruptions of service and public reaction to them. Cable television outages and late delivery of newspapers have prompted similar reactions for years. Yet younger generations of media consumers were weaned on new media, not traditional media, so they enjoy the

freedom of moving from one free platform to another with little loyalty and no apology.

About the time Apple released its advanced iPhone 4s, the Blackberry phone built by Research in Motion experienced a four-day global outage that, in the face of days of silence by the Canadian company's CEO, drove millions of users to jump to the new Apple phone. Blackberry users registered complaints and jokes on Twitter and threatened to start using Android and iPhones.

On the fourth day of the outage, Mike Lazarides, one of the RIM CEOs, released an apology on YouTube. At the time, experts thought the apology, though sincere, was too little too late.

Maggie Fox, founder and CEO of Social Media Group, a public relations group in Toronto, said, "When it comes to leadership in a crisis, the very first thing you have to do is to show up. They should have set up a hash tag and tried to own the conversation better. Fifteen tweets is not enough, it's just not enough, especially when they have 615,000 followers." Like any product, however, platforms enjoy brand recognition, and patience in the face of a power outage depends on the tolerance level of every user. The dependence of media, traditional and new media, has a history of a cooling off period where disgruntled users return.

A collision with social media ▼

The Chrysler Group invested tens of millions of dollars in 2011 Super Bowl commercials, expanding on its "Imported from Detroit" public relations campaign. Chrysler had momentum. However, an employee with New Media Strategies, a digital public relations and social media agency based in Arlington, Va., had access to Chrysler's Twitter account and tapped a carefree

tweet on March 9, 2011, announcing, "I find it ironic that Detroit is known as the #motorcity and yet no one here knows how to f****** drive." The creator of the message was fired and, ultimately, the Chrysler Group ended its relationship with NMS. Chrysler didn't dodge the public relations nightmare from the tweet. They admitted the mistake using the hashtag (#motorcity), which brought up the automaker's tweeted response. In the "tweetiverse" discussions can take sharp turns and, in this matter, followers wondered whether the firing of the perpetrator was justified. Chrysler joined the exchange, explaining why NMS (not Chrysler) fired the person.

Josh Morgan, vice president of Edelman Digital in Sacramento, and Lori Bertelli, public relations manager of Augustine Ideas in Roseville, Calif., in October 2011, have shared 10 ways to "survive a social media blunder."

1. **Think Before You Speak**—Consider how your blunder affects your entire audience, since not everyone will have the same reaction as your company may.
2. **Post the Rules**—Protect your brand from vicious visitors by posting your policy regarding monitoring practices and lack of tolerance for violations.
3. **Don't Let Your Emotions Take Over**—Keep a clear head if a problem arises and don't respond in a rash way that you'll regret.
4. **Choose the Right Moderator**—It's better to have your social media monitored by someone who knows and cares about your company, instead of someone who's simply hired to handle social media but knows barely anything your brand.
5. **Maintain Back-Up Support**—When a crisis calls, make sure you have multiple people who can access your social media accounts since a rapid response can often save the day.
6. **Create Clear Crisis Policies**—Keep your social media procedures simple and straightforward so everyone is well aware of how to manage a misstep.
7. **Admit When You're Wrong**—Be quick to come clean about your mistake since trying to hide it will only make it worse.
8. **Get an Outside Opinion**—Let a neutral source review your situation to make sure that your response is the right one.
9. **Acknowledge That Anything Can Happen**—Realize that the dynamic and spontaneous

nature of social media makes it impossible to completely control, so just be ready to react if required.

10. **Don't Get Defensive**—Fighting will only fuel the fire, so stay upbeat if you want to downplay the situation.

Source: http://www.franchisemarketingagency.com/blog/10-ways-to-handle-a-social-media-blunder/

By mid-year in 2011, the National Institute of Standards and Technology estimated that a total of 80 percent of companies worldwide felt they are unprepared for a social media crisis.

Social media, including the blogosphere, needs monitoring. Preparations mean having access to how the public, not the least of which are customers or prospective customers, is reacting to whatever is at stake such as issues or a product. Pay attention to sources that may be generating adverse information. Disinformation can be responsible for a crisis.

People at all levels of the organization must be engaged in the workings of social media, and when a crisis develops, communicators must have a process that will promote a quick reaction. It is important to identify who talks to whom and how a proper response, not an empty one, can be quickly developed with useful information and disseminated quickly. A crisis communications plan should be reviewed regularly. Technology changes; positions internally and externally change; people come and go; lists need updating.

Finally, while an organization should have its own crisis communications plan, certain organizations may find it useful to hire an outside crisis communications firm.

Mea culpa statements ▼

To err is human, Shakespeare wrote more than 500 years ago, and to hide behind one's mistakes is equally human. People live lies everyday and speak, post or tweet foolish, reckless thoughts without thinking, but few of those individuals operate under public scrutiny. With whistleblowers and instant communication, including visual communication, those once easily concealed, embarrassing incidents and behaviors are becoming indelibly and instantly etched in the minds of millions or even hundreds of millions. Few incidents simply blow over anymore. Individuals and organizations face this embarrassing dilemma every day: How to deal with the truth of a mistake. They wonder:

▶ "Knowing brands are at risk, do we do nothing nor say anything?"
▶ "Do we make our accusers prove their allegations, no matter how true they are?"
▶ "Do we wait for the media to get distracted by the next sensational story?"
▶ "Do we issue a general, half-hearted statement—'I regret my actions. If I've offended anyone because of my actions . . . .'"
▶ "Does the perpetrator explain why he/she is the victim?"
▶ "Does the accused remain in denial, explaining actions without an apology?"
▶ "Do we release a statement on our website; or on social media?"

Hiding from the truth is not realistic when individuals or institutions are caught in the act of erring, whether it's British Petroleum, a celebrity, a professional athlete or an assortment of public officials.

The maxim "honesty is the best policy" remains the best advice that public relations counselors can offer clients who blundered. That honesty must be couched in mea culpa (Latin for "my fault") statements, which are drafted by attorneys, public relations experts or even the culprits themselves, perhaps with the advice of lawyers or public relations experts. Richard S. Levick, who has handled media for Enron, Napster, the Florida election recount in 2000 and the Catholic Church in handling child molestation allegations, writes, "Apologizing requires strategic thinking. It requires art." In today's media environment and the public's appetite for scandal, publicists or agents for celebrities or corporate entities should have a media relations plan for crisis. Part of that plan is to have someone prepared to apologize publicly or to customers for mistakes. A spokesperson who is informed, direct and contrite will deliver a message that generally will be accepted by an instinctively compassionate audience. "On a long-term basis, you simply cannot sustain a PR program without legitimate facts," Levick writes. "For companies creaking toward obsolescence, or destined to bemire themselves in new rounds of scandal, spin is a bandage, but the bleeding won't stop."

Politicians function in a different spotlight from the general public. Their actions are officially accountable to various constituencies. Usually, voters have their say at the ballot box and are mostly unforgiving. Politicians' aberrant behavior and half-truths or outright lies, such as President Bill Clinton's famed testimony, "I did not have sex with that woman," have tainted his political legacy, but the former two-term president has built on his overall popularity with global public service. He worked with George Herman Walker Bush, whom he defeated to become the 42nd U.S. President, to raise funds and support for natural disasters in Haiti and elsewhere. While politicians such as South Carolina Governor Mark Sanford and New York Governor Eliot Spitzer or Rep. Andrew Weiner lose their positions from sexual scandals despite mea culpa statements, the public tends to be more forgiving or apathetic about the scandalous behavior of celebrities who don't deliberate on issues involving the public trust. Many golf fans and others thought Tiger Woods' promiscuous behavior was a matter between him and his wife, Elin. Despite disappointment, all they really cared about was watching him play golf.

A *public relations bogey* ▼

Tiger Woods' meteoric rise and the world's best golfer of his generation collapsed when he became consumed by an extra-marital sex scandal involving numerous women. He went silent concerning the late night incident at his home, then released general statements through his website. Three months after damaging public comment in the media and throughout the blogosphere, Woods met with the media.

In making his statement of about 900 words, Woods took responsibility for his actions, but his mea culpa statement went beyond what should have been the main focus of his remarks. His apology on Feb. 19, 2010, addressed his personal situation but also his brand, his image, and his business partnerships. "I want to say to each of you simply and directly I am deeply sorry for my selfish and irresponsible behavior I have been engaged in. . . . I am the only person to blame. I stopped living according to my core values. . . ." He continued that he knew what he was doing was wrong and he did it because money and fame gave him a sense of entitlement. He acknowledged that he doesn't get to live by another set of rules. He also acknowledged that he and his wife realized that the only apology that means anything will manifest itself through changed behavior, not words. Still, his apology to her and their children was noticeably implicit, not explicit. Since the mea culpa statement, he underwent sex therapy, took a hiatus from golf, and when he returned his game clearly suffered.

One serious "late night" ▼

For David Letterman, sexual transgressions surfaced when a producer who learned of his affair with women working with the show demanded $2 million to keep quiet. The producer testified before a grand jury and soon went public with his story. In a 10-minute briefing on his "Late Night" show in October 2009, David Letterman admitted, "I have had sex with women who worked on this show."

Letterman told the audience in a matter-of-fact message mixed with humor. "And would it be embarrassing if it were made public? Perhaps it would. Especially for the women." That last comment was poorly received by women's organizations.

During a subsequent show, Letterman added, "Inadvertently, I just wasn't thinking ahead. . . ." He told the audience that his wife, Regina Lasko, has been "horribly hurt" by his behavior and reasoned that he had his work cut out for him to "make some progress and get it fixed" or "fall short and perhaps not get it fixed." Letterman mixed his contrition with claims of being victimized by the producer who wanted millions of dollars in hush money. That person faced his own consequences for his role in the matter.

© NORTHFOTO / SHUTTERSTOCK.COM, 2012. USED UNDER LICENSE FROM SHUTTERSTOCK, INC.

Meanwhile, Letterman's apology actually boosted ratings the next night after his apology by 22 percent, and by going public with his affair with his assistant, Stephanie Birkitt, instead of having reports leaked, the public could condemn the actions in a dismissive way. Dan Schnur, director of USC's Jesse M. Unruh Institute of Politics and a veteran political strategist, told *The Los Angeles Times,* "By bringing up the information himself rather than letting it come out from other sources and being forced to react to it, he did a lot to protect himself."

In general, a mea culpa should be timely and feel authentic. Mea culpa statements that are not genuine seldom do much good, especially if the individual or institution has a history of bad behavior for which they have not taken responsibility and made amends.

Conclusion: Expect the unexpected

It would be nice if public relations could focus exclusively on proactive communication—creating a com-

munication plan with strategies and tactics that achieve the objectives of the organization, such as increasing market share, awareness, or achieving branding goals. Unfortunately, the unexpected happens and public relations must help clients to react to those events. Sometimes the unexpected becomes a crisis. Public relations practitioners must develop proactive plans while also preparing for the worst with a crisis communication plan.

A crisis communications plan protects the reputation of individuals and groups. Positive reputations take years to cultivate and can be tarnished in no time at all in this digital age. Such a plan won't prevent a crisis, but it may avert legal troubles and even help restore public confidence and perceptions.

The following ideas outline a communications plan that will prepare practitioners and their employers or clients before a crisis hits:

▶ Identify a communications crisis team. Who will be part of it? What will each person or team do? Will you designate a space in an office for a war room, where activity can be coordinated?

▶ Present the truth: Explain the situation, why it happened and, if possible, how the situation will get repaired.

▶ Be forthcoming with information: Do not hide. Speed is often crucial in overcoming adversity, and preparation is that much more important in today's instant information age. The 4-, 8-, 12- or 24-hour news cycles of television and newspapers are a thing of the past. All media are live platforms every second of every day.

▶ Consider a separate communications strategy for social media (e.g. twitter, facebook).

▶ Consider tactics that involve using media you can control (websites, social media sites); and media you cannot control (traditional media).

▶ Just as it's crucial to identify a point person for traditional media, it's equally important to identify who will be the "brand voice" online. A 2010 PRWeek Survey reports that more than a third of companies have no one person responsible for social media within the organization. Protect passwords.

▶ Take care in matters that may involve litigation to involve legal counsel in planning media relations. Discuss the importance of presenting helpful information to supplement any "no comment" statements.

Review questions

1. When handling a disaster, companies should not:
   a. Make key spokespersons available interview.
   b. Prepare interview subjects for questions from the media.
   c. Prepare news releases and other supporting materials.
   d. Twist facts to confuse or put off the media.
2. When individuals, groups or organizations are caught acting in error, which of these tactics are viable options?
   a. We do nothing nor say anything.
   b. We make our accusers prove their allegations.

   c. The perpetrator explains why he/she is the victim.
   d. None of the above.
3. Who said what? (Write the letter matching the corresponding name with the comment).
   a. Tiger Woods _____ "I want my life back."
   b. David Letterman _____ "I am the only person to blame."
   c. Tony Hayward _____ "Inadvertently, I wasn't thinking ahead."
4. Name five tactics that should be part of a crisis communications plan.

Supplemental resources online

www.deepwaterinvestigation.com
http://www.brpublicrelations.com/casestudies.html
http://www.ready.gov/business/implementation/crisis
http://www.crisiscommunicationsplans.com/
http://www.macstrategies.com/
http://crisismanagement.com/
http://crisispublicrelations.blogspot.com/
http://blog.ketchum.com/tag/crisis-communications/
http://csrc.nist.gov
http://www.piersystems.com/go/doc/1533/163949/About-PIER-Systems

Chapter references

Cole, T. W. and Fellows K. L., (2008) "Risk Communication Failure: A Case Study of New Orleans and Hurricane Katrina," Southern Communication Journal, Vol. 73, Issue 3, pages 211-228 from http://www.tandfonline.com/doi/full/10.1080/10417940802219702#tabModule

Collins, Scott, "David Letterman admits to affairs, says he was victim of $2 million extortion attempt," Los Angeles Times, Oct. 2, 2009, http://articles.latimes.com/2009/oct/02/business/fi-ct-letterman2

Deepwater Horizon containment and response, from British Petroleum website, June 10, 2010, http://www.bp.com/genericarticle.do?categoryId=2012968&contentId=7062828

Dezenhall, Eric, "Damage Control: Why Everything You Know About Crisis Management Is Wrong," Prospecta Press, 2011

Gold, Matea and Collins, Scott, "David Letterman Affair Is No Joke," Los Angeles Times, Oct. 3, 2009, http://www.latimes.com/entertainment/news/la-et-letterman3-2009oct03,0,878590.story

Lawrence, Dallas, "A Digital Crisis Is Coming Your Way. Are you Ready?" July 6, 2011, http://www.forbes.com/sites/forbesleadershipforum/2011/07/06/a-digital-crisis-is-coming-your-way-are-you-ready/

Levick, Richard S., "The Art of Mea Culpa, How Your Corporate Clients Can Apologize for their Mistake," http://aboutpublicrelations.net/uclevick1.htm

Lukaszewski, James E, "The sound of silence: how inaction makes a crisis worse," January 2012, O'Dwyer's, p. 26

Maj. Harris, U.S. Army; TSgt. Hart, Dawn, U.S. Air Force, MSgt. Hibbard, Brian, U.S. Air Force, Maj. Jurgensen, Jeff, U.S. Marines, "Case Study, The Johnson & Johnson Tylenol Crisis," http://www.ou.edu/deptcomm/dodjcc/groups/02C2/Johnson%20&%20Johnson.htm

McCown, Ashley, "Penn State and Syracuse: a post-game plan for crisis," O'Dwyer's, January 2012, p. 20

Morgan, Josh and Bertelli, Lori, "10 Ways to Handle a Social Media Blunder," Nov. 28, 2010, from http://www.franchisemarketingagency.com/blog/10-ways-to-handle-a-social-media-blunder/

O'Brien, Tim, "Crises you plan for: Preparing for the expected crisis," PRSA Public Relations Tactics, March 16, 2009, http://www.prsa.org/SearchResults/view/7893/105/Crises_you_can_plan_for_Preparing_for_the_expected

Schwab, Stephanie, Social Media Explorer, "Social Media Contingency Planning: The Operational Plan," May 12, 2011, http://www.socialmediaexplorer.com/social-media-marketing/social-media-contingency-planning-the-operational-plan/

Scudder, Ken, "Be prepared: 10 steps to take now for crisis readiness," Public Relations Tactics, January 3, 2012, http://www.prsa.org/Intelligence/Tactics/Articles/view/9530/1041

Simpson, J., Twitter site @BPGlobalPR

chapter 9

PUBLIC RELATIONS WRITING AND TACTICS

No skills are more important in public relations than writing, organizing, packaging information, and thinking strategically. The public relations processes discussed in this book emphasize thinking through action plans. Invariably, writing a variety of documents will become necessary in the execution of any PR plan. Some documents will stand independently, and others will work in tandem and, with varied purposes, with other documents in media kits.

Each document usually entails a different focus, writing style and length. Others will find useful well-crafted bullet points. What documents say and how they are written depend on the reader, viewer or listener. Thus, a fundamental lesson in PR writing—and in all public relations—is to understand and write for an audience.

Documents commonly written by public relations professionals include:

▶ Fact sheets
▶ Backgrounders and position papers
▶ Pitches and proposals
▶ News releases
▶ Feature articles
▶ Magazine articles
▶ Speeches
▶ Editorials
▶ Op-Ed articles
▶ Letters to the editor
▶ Memos and personal letters
▶ Email and other Internet communications, including social media
▶ Blogs
▶ Public service announcements
▶ Brochures
▶ Newsletters
▶ Advertisements
▶ Annual reports
▶ Writing to support visuals materials.

Public relations professionals write each of these pieces as part of a strategy that will help meet the client's goals and objectives. Before writing a brochure, for example, they determine what the piece should accomplish, what format would be useful, and what style and content would best communicate the group's intentions.

When writing a news release, think about what it should accomplish. How does the news release fit into an overall media strategy, and what are the desired outcomes for media exposure from the news release? Ask:

"What is the focus of the news release, and what is the schedule for other related news releases?" In addition to conventional media, what other media (specialty publications, electronic media, digital) should we target, and how should we modify the news releases for each media outlet? The above written products fit into some phase of a public relations plan. A timeline used to plot public relations activity and to chart progress is essential to maintain organization (see Chapter 6).

Pitches to editors ▼

Since working with media is a priority in so many public relations efforts, the public relations practitioner must be able to write in the language of news reporters. Start with a pitch, which is an idea presented to a reporter or editor to sell them on a story:

▶ Make the idea newsworthy
▶ Write in plain, direct language
▶ Get to the point
▶ Do not waste words
▶ Avoid jargon
▶ Discuss what is interesting, even compelling, about an idea
▶ Avoid resorting to hyperbole or "hype"

Editors in news organizations are very sensitive to hype. PR practitioners sometimes try to portray the ordinary as extraordinary. After all, PR people are enthusiastic about the stories they are trying to advance. It is important to remember, however, that the basis of the most successful pitches is solid documented research, data and trends, something out of the ordinary and not vivid language—puffery—and vague facts. For example, quantify the power and speed of new technology, rather than describing features with such superlatives as the "latest," the "fastest," and "revolutionary," unless you can quantify these qualities.

A pitch based on little but hype will get only rejections. Dana Todd of CarterTodd & Associates has said, "When we write pitches to editors, we take out all of the marketing fluff. Try to strip it down to 'Here are the facts.' This is not a marketing brochure. This is news."

Pitch letters also should avoid the jargon pervasive in advertising messages. Avoid descriptions such as "end-to-end solution," "robust," "comprehensive," and "turnkey," said Diana Morrill of Eastwick Communications. "A good way to test whether something is well-

Writing advice from professionals

"Create a 'why should I care?' list before you begin writing. Then, make sure you use all of these points in your pitch. This is the equivalent of needing an oven to bake a cake. No matter how well you mix the ingredients, you can't bake the cake without the oven. If you can't identify at least a couple of good reasons why a journalist should care about your story, they won't get past the first paragraph, let alone want to learn more about it."

—*Christine Payne, Syndesis*

"Proofread. Sad but true. So many don't take the time to proofread. Such a simple thing."

—*Nan Johnson, Edelmann Scott, Inc.*

"I preach religiously 'third-word disturb.' In other words, strike every third word. From a draft copy to final copy, this teaches writers to concisely get their point across with facts, while training them to choose the appropriate word form."

—*Daryl Logullo, Strategic Impact*

"A well-written quote will land directly in a story."

—*Chris Kenneally, Kenneally & Company*

"Journalists need results. Our XYZ Company may claim to make the best widget in the world, but unless that journalist can actually see the widget in action, he's not going to be convinced. A convinced journalist is your best ally."

—*Brad Carmony, Virtual Management, Inc.*

"This is one area where practice truly does make perfect. Writing talent alone is not enough. Not nearly enough. In business communications, which should be kept on the short side, every word counts. And if the words a staff is putting out sound pretty but have no real role in achieving the company's (or client's) objectives, they're worthless."

—*Steve Winston, Comforce Corporation*

Granted by permission of Cision North America

written is to read it out loud and then think, 'Is this something I would actually say to someone?' If it is, great. It is probably being conversational. If not, rewrite."

Words that reflect how consumers might feel about a product should reside in quotes from consumers, industry leaders or other credible sources. Most public relations writing has a different tone and purpose than advertising copy. PR documents written like advertisements do not impress journalists. For PR, stick to facts and pertinent information. Editors will base their judgments about the newsworthiness of a PR document on whether it is factual and unusual rather than hype.

Fact sheets ▼

The **fact sheet** is a useful tool for both the public relations practitioner and the media. It gives reporters and editors a snapshot of an organization, event, product or biographical profile. Fact sheets are best known for their conciseness. Information items are often in bulleted lists to make them jump out to the reader. They use headings and subheadings liberally to make it easy to find important information as the eye moves down the page. While many fact sheets are only one page long, some expand beyond one page. A fact sheet for a new tax provision or other regulatory policy, for example, can become several pages long. Documents that go into even greater depth typically fall under the category of backgrounder.

The fact sheet typically answers the most basic questions of reporters—who, what, when, where, why and how. When it comes to writing a fact sheet for an event or a product, the "who" is less likely to top the list. The most important information for event or product fact sheets is the answer to the question, "what." A fact sheet for the Wii videogame console is available online at http://nsider2.com/wii-fact-sheet/. It illustrates the content and format of this important PR tactic.

Fact sheet sections often go beyond the five W's and H. They might have one section or bullet devoted to ticket information, sponsors, or history. A fact sheet for a disaster relief effort might report the dollar value of local aid distributed during the past 10 years. Nonprofits often want to show that a high percentage of contributions they receive go out as aid rather than being used for salaries and other operating expenses. When the public sees positive and productive outcomes from their donations, they are more likely to open their hearts and checkbooks again later to support the cause. Fact sheets for nonprofits typically bullet the important statistics that illustrate how many people the nonprofits served and how much they spent on aid.

Fact sheets for new products will contain specifications that show the power or capacity that makes a product attractive to consumers and newsworthy to the media. Perhaps a new laptop is thinner or faster or has more capacity than the model it replaces. Perhaps a new car offers improved safety, comfort, or fuel efficiency. Major product improvements can appear in a fact sheet as bullets or subheadings. The product fact sheet also may contain brief, positive reviews from reputable sources.

*B*ackgrounders ▼

A **backgrounder** provides objective historical information and insights concerning a topic. It provides extensive and useful summaries that can save hours of research by reporters, corporate executives, business owners, political leaders, advisers, strategists and others. There are several types of backgrounders. Some provide in-depth background information about an institution or an individual, such as a political candidate. Another type of backgrounder provides background and analysis of a public policy issue or controversy. A lobbyist, for example, might write a backgrounder to help educate and persuade a legislator whose support he or she needs to pass legislation on an issue. Because this research takes a position, such a document is called a **position paper**.

Executives who normally read mainstream or industry publications to stay current on important current events benefit from a compilation of such information that is put together in a **daily briefing**, another form of backgrounder. The staff of the president of the United States prepares such a briefing, for example. Presidents do not have time to read all of the different publications that demand their attention to stay informed about the economy, politics, and world affairs. A **media briefing** is an efficient way to summarize the news.

A business owner who needs to stay abreast of trends in the marketplace, particularly among competitors, will benefit from a backgrounder. Political candidates who wish to know more about opponents benefit from a summary of the record and views of the opponent in the form of a backgrounder. Diplomats or executives contemplating a particular program in another country can obtain the critical information they need to know from a well-researched backgrounder. As an example, imagine the information Microsoft founder and philanthropist Bill Gates needed before he and his Gates Foundation could begin organizing efforts to combat epidemics in Africa.

Executives get the most use from a backgrounder when the writer takes the topic well beyond superficial information. A valuable backgrounder not only provides information from research but also the benefit of the writer's ability to organize comprehensive information and to synthesize it into an understandable and thorough summary. This ability to research and analyze information to make it understood and useful in a practical way is an essential public relations skill.

The backgrounder typically begins with a profile of an organization or its leadership. It might note accomplishments, milestones, and other historical developments. This preliminary information should unearth other facts and raise other interesting questions. How do others perceive something? Who are a group's supporters, competitors, adversaries and critics? A well-researched backgrounder helps decision makers and strategists become more creative and efficient. Chapter 5 had a discussion about creativity and the importance of fact finding in the creative process. The better a team of strategic thinkers understands a problem, the more empowered, and thus more creative, it will become in meeting a goal and serving a client. A shallow understanding of a problem tends to yield strategies, tactics and results that are superficial and mundane.

Consider the time involved in bringing a group of people up to speed on a given topic. Before the group can solve the problem, they must understand it. If each individual must research and organize background information about the problem separately, it will take a long time; and it is likely that different members of the group will define the problem differently based on their individual research results. With the help of a well-researched and organized backgrounder, the group will feel able to act more efficiently and as a team, using a common body of information.

As noted in Chapter 5, creative problem solving occurs by following these six steps:

- ▶ Mess finding
- ▶ Data finding
- ▶ Problem finding
- ▶ Idea finding
- ▶ Solution finding
- ▶ Acceptance finding

A good backgrounder can help with the first three steps, providing a sound foundation for the problem solvers to address the latter three.

The structure of a backgrounder is important in that it keeps the information interesting, like a lengthy magazine article. Headlines typically introduce the information. While the first headings commonly include an "Introduction" and "History," the other section headings will depend on the nature of the information. Headings serve the same purpose as headlines for news stories. They not only introduce the information in a section, but they also serve to hold the reader's attention and to guide him or her through the report.

While backgrounders should be interesting to read, they are not novels. Their purpose is to provide thorough research in a document that readers can digest in a relatively short time.

News releases

The news release is at the core of work produced by public relations practitioners. They write releases in news style, which means they must contain a lead, supporting paragraphs, lively quotes, other details, supporting statistics, and comments to tell a story. The release uses the "inverted pyramid" form of organization in which information generally presents from the most important to the least important facts.

The goal is to include in the lead paragraph or two the most important information, such as who, what, when, where, why, and how. Editors do not have time to read all of a news release before making a judgment about the newsworthiness of the story. It is important that a news release, like a news story in the media, get to the point. Most publication readers also do not read all of every story. They often read only the first paragraphs. The inverted pyramid style places the most important information first, followed by supporting details and elaboration.

Writing in news style does not mean the news releases are objective accounts. They clearly seek to promote or advance a person, a product, a service or an idea. Reporters working for larger newspapers will usually use news releases as a source for story ideas that they may further develop by doing their own interviews and research. Some company announcements, like the announcement of newly hired or promoted staff, may run without further reporting and with little editing. In smaller markets, media often welcome well-written news releases and use them in their entirety.

In gathering information for a news release, blend the information or messages that the client seeks to advance with what an editor will find newsworthy for his or her readers. Stories that are not newsworthy will not make it into the media. If possible, interview a decision maker, maybe an executive or manager, about the announcement to gain insights, details, and quotes.

Public relations people have an advantage over journalists. PR writers have the flexibility to improve on quotes or to manufacture them completely. In writing a news release, the PR writer may create a quote that would be an appropriate comment for an executive or other source within the company. However, the person being quoted should review and approve the comments attributed to him or her.

Reporters may choose to use the interesting and informative quotes provided in a news release, but the most effective news release will prompt a request for an interview. Reporters like to obtain their own quotes, instead of using manufactured material. If the release leads to an interview with its primary source, then it has achieved one of its objectives. If the interview goes well, the release in effect has given the reporter not only information for a story, but a source that future stories can use.

The mainstream media will ignore some news releases. The same release may have greater interest for more local or niche publications, such as small town newspapers, trade journals, and alternative newspapers.

News releases may read like news articles, but they need proper identification. News releases should carry the letterhead of the client or the public relations firm. Atop the page the words "NEWS RELEASE," "PRESS RELEASE" or, simply, "NEWS," should appear. Next, include contact information such as phone numbers for both day and evening and the email address of a person who will field questions. Accessibility is crucial to getting a news release used by the media. Journalists complain that they cannot reach news release contacts and are unable to do a follow-up interview to write a story. They will likely try a few times and then abandon the story. The media business is immediate in today's 24-hour news cycle. Whoever is available and whom a reporter reaches is often the one quoted and whose story gets used.

Along with news releases, writers should anticipate what other information the reporter might need. Attach photographs, such as mug shots, in JPG or TIFF formats. Generally, they should be larger than 50K to provide sufficient resolution for publication.

Many news releases are sent via email these days, but when a news release is sent in an attachment that will get printed it should be formulated in a way to ensure that pages remain identified as being in the correct order. In a two-page news release, for example, write "more" in the center at the end of the first page and —30—or ### to designate the end of the story. At the top left of the second page write a "slug," which contains information indicating the subject of the release and the page number of the release. Examples of slugs include:

SPEECH, 2-2 (meaning second page of two pages)
SPEECH, 2-2-2-2
SPEECH, Page 2
SPEECH/22222

No single format for the slug is used by all publications or writers, just as there are variations in the formatting of the first page as well. If a news release is sent in the body of an email and is likely to be cut and pasted from the email, then the notations differentiating pages are unnecessary.

The body of news releases typically ends with contact information or websites for people seeking addi-

Format news releases correctly

► White 8-1/2 by 11-inch paper
► Identify contact in upper left of page
► Indicate FOR IMMEDIATE RELEASE or when to release if embargoed
► Double space
► 1-1/2 inch margins
► Indicate —more— at the bottom of page one if there is more than one page
► Use a slug line at the top left of each subsequent page.
► Use a compelling title.
► Write like a journalist in the inverted pyramid style.
► The first paragraph is the lead paragraph and must contain key facts of the story.
► Put either -30- or ### at the end of the story.

tional information. Most company and organization news releases end with identifying information often referred to as a **boilerplate paragraph**. Boilerplate paragraphs may contain information about the history, purpose, and performance of a company or organization. The content of a boilerplate might be much the same from one news release to the next for an organization. It is a general statement about an organization.

Scripts for Broadcast

The uniqueness of newswriting for broadcast news releases and public service announcements have been discussed, as they target an audience of viewers and listeners. Stylistically, they differ from news releases prepared for print. The copy generated for prepared news stories is produced as a script, which generally gets read on air. To avoid any confusion or misspoken words scripts follow certain rules:

Text is written in ALL CAPITAL LETTERS

▶ All numerals are spelled out. (Examples: FOUR THOUSAND, ONE DOLLAR AND TWENTY-TWO CENTS.

▶ No words are abbreviated.

▶ Uncommon names that might be mispronounced are written phonetically with accented syllables written in capital letters.

▶ Acronyms that spell words are written as spoken. (Example: NASCAR). Group names with initials that are pronounced by each letter are written with letters separated by hyphens. (Examples: Y-M-C-A, I-B-M, N-C-DOUBLE-A, N-DOUBLE-A-C-P).

▶ Websites are written as pronounced. (Example: W-W-W-DOT-EDELMAN-DOT-COM).

The format for the script is also different from a news release prepared for print. The heading for a script, however, is virtually the same as the heading for a news release, with one exception. Unlike a news release for printed media, the length of the script is measured in time. A script that is one minute long is written in the heading as (:60); a minute and a half would be (:90).

Scripts for television and some radio, in which sound effects are imported, are written with a form that splits the page in half with basically two columns. The right half is the text written in ALL CAPITAL LETTERS that will be read on air. The left half of the page includes production instructions and will be written in regular face, upper and lower cases. Visualize a story produced

on air. While an anchor is reading a teleprompter, a logo or photograph may be placed in the upper left corner of the screen. On the script, the copy is written in ALL CAPS on the right; the production directions will indicate the use of the artwork on the left to match the timing of the spoken words.

During the report, the anchor may cut to a video clip showing someone commenting on something simply a scene that is being described. These events are indicated on the left side of the script at the point when they are added. If the direction involves a quote, merely identify the clip (Example: Clip 1) and the first three words of the quote (Example: "We are shocked . . ."). There is no need to include the entire quote in the script. The partial quote is used so production editors can make sure to put the correct quote in the correct place of a story. Since the time of the report is crucial to a report for broadcast, all aspects of the script are measured in time. Therefore all segments of the script are measured in seconds. For a (:60) broadcast news release, then, all segments are timed separately and should add up to 60 seconds. Generally, a script with only speaking, no video clips, allows for 122 or so words per minute. With the page split in half, allowing for a half-inch space between the columns, each line of text in ALL CAPS (no abbreviations) will allow for five to six words per line. Simple math will give you an idea of time used in reading the news. Clips quoting others can be easily timed. When an anchor or reporter is speaking while video is being shown, the speaking part is referred to as a voiceover and should be designated on the script side as (VO).

The rules for writing scripts are quite different from what PR writers understand from a simple news release. The biggest challenge of the task is understanding the limitations of time, tight storytelling and use of visuals that go along with the overall production. The script is a format that facilitates the sending of video clips. An inventory of video that's often submitted as part of a media kit is called B-roll. Prominent examples of B-roll footage, whose source should be identified, are cars rolling off an assembly line or bottles being filled with some form of content or jets taking off.

Public relations practitioners pitching stories to assignment editors should ask what format do they prefer for clips. Among the choices, they may accept files that can be emailed or on a DVD. They also may be willing to accept the B-roll clips and a news release prepared for print media.

Boilerplate paragraphs

About Whole Foods Market®

Founded in 1980 in Austin, Texas, Whole Foods Market (www.wholefoods market.com) is the world's leading natural and organic foods supermarket and America's first national certified organic grocer. In fiscal year 2007, the company had sales of $6.6 billion and currently has more than 270 stores in the United States, Canada, and the United Kingdom. The Whole Foods Market motto, "Whole Foods, Whole People, Whole Planet"™ captures the company's mission to find success in customer satisfaction and wellness, employee excellence and happiness, enhanced shareholder value, community support and environmental improvement. Whole Foods Market, Fresh & Wild™, and Harry's Farmers Market® are trademarks owned by Whole Foods Market IP, LP. Wild Oats® and Capers Community Market™ are trademarks owned by Wild Marks, Inc. Whole Foods Market employs more than 53,000 Team Members and has been ranked for 11 consecutive years as one of the "100 Best Companies to Work For" in America by FORTUNE magazine.

Courtesy of Whole Foods Market, Inc.

About Edelman

Edelman is the world's largest independent public relations firm, with 3,000 employees in 51 offices worldwide. Edelman was named "Large Agency of the Year" in 2008 by PRWeek and a top-10 firm in the Advertising Age "2007 Agency A-List," the first and only PR firm to receive this recognition. CEO Richard Edelman was honored as "2007 Agency Executive of the Year by both Advertising Age and PRWeek. PRWeek also named Edelman "Large Agency of the Year" in 2006 and awarded the firm its "Editor's Choice" distinction. For more information, visit www.edelman.com.

Courtesy of Edelman

About Cohn & Wolfe

Cohn & Wolfe is a strategic public relations agency dedicated to creating, building and protecting the world's most prolific brands. With offices around the world, the agency is committed to breaking new ground in the delivery of cross-channel media strategies, creative programming, and practice area excellence. Cohn & Wolfe is recognized year after year by clients and the industry for excellence in creativity, client service, digital communications, media strategy, senior management and strategic counsel. Cohn & Wolfe also consistently ranks among the top "Best Agencies to Work For" in an annual, industry-wide employee survey. For more information, visit: www.cohnwolfe.com. Cohn & Wolfe is part of WPP Group plc (Nasdaq: WPPGY), one of the world's largest communications services group.

Granted by permission of Cohn & Wolfe

Localize

When writing a news release, find a local angle and put it in the lead paragraph. Editors receive hundreds of news releases a day. Those most likely to get published have a local angle, giving local readers or TV viewers a reason for their interest. One researcher found that only 10 percent of news releases were localized. Of 174 localized releases, 78 got published or

The "get to the point" profession

The lesson is the same for PR professionals as it is for journalists: keep writing simple. Get right to the point, and keep the news in the first few lines. Consider these comments by public relations specialists:

"Good writing doesn't try to say absolutely everything. What are you trying to accomplish? For example, Moby Dick is written in great detail. Melville uses thousands of words to tell a story. That doesn't work in PR. If you're putting out, say, a bumper sticker, you have to use four or five words to get your message across. So in regards to Moby Dick, you might say, 'Big Fish, Little Man.' The simpler the better."

—*Chris Kenneally, Kenneally & Company*

"Reporters are like the rest of us these days; they don't have time to read long-winded pieces. I tell my staff that they will live or die on their very first sentence, and that they have approximately five to eight seconds to get the reporter's attention."

—*Steve Winston, Comforce Corporation*

"The news should be in the main paragraph. Get down to the nuts and bolts. It's like the old saying, 'Tell them what you're going to tell them, tell them, and then tell them what you told them.' "

—*Alex Zavistovich, Strategic Communications Group*

Granted by permission of Cision North America

about 45 percent. Of 1,174 general (nonlocalized) releases, only 87 got published, or 7 percent. Nothing is more important than finding the local angle to give editors a reason to use your story.

Features: The story behind the story ▼

The search for newsworthy information often produces feature ideas. Features often tell the story behind the story. They explain more extensively and descriptively how and why things happen. They elaborate on the basic facts of who, what, when, where, why and how. The writing in features tends to be more descriptive than the straightforward approach used for news releases. Features show more style, flair and personality, with more entertaining anecdotes and storytelling. They have their own news angles, but they generally fit into the following categories, which sometimes overlap:

▶ Trends; big picture stories
▶ Profiles
▶ Experience
▶ New products
▶ Enterprise

Trend stories, as the name suggests, identify activities or conduct that is increasing in frequency and intensity. For example, more and more people are filing income taxes electronically than mailing hard copies. Other trends include dressing more casually in the work place and commuting to work using some form of mass transit.

If a public relations person has the job of publicizing a new theme park, one of the ways to make an impression would be to invite media to experience a thrilling new "turbo" ride. Instead of a simple article about the opening of a new theme park, the publicist might generate feature stories with exciting photographs and video about journalists riding the big one. A memorable, thrilling experience for a reporter will be reflected in an interesting, entertaining and visually exciting story.

In writing about new products, the public wants to know something unusual about the product. How does it improve on existing products? What will it replace? What is unusual about it? Does it have a funny name? Why? What went into creating the product?

An enterprise feature typically takes a basic piece of information and transforms it into something more interesting as specialists or experts offer insights and explanations. Hybrid automobiles, for example, are getting considerable media attention about their performance and gas mileage. Beyond that basic premise, how can the public relations specialist make this story more interesting? Reporters want something more than specifications and facts, such as some real examples of how hybrids have saved people money or improved their lives. Transform product data into a story about the cost savings experienced by a commuting family. Or perhaps a delivery business has overhauled its fleet of vehicles with hybrids. What went into that decision? What were the estimated costs? What are the anticipated benefits? How has the change made a difference? The answers to these questions will likely yield an interesting story.

Speeches ▼

The best speeches are those that are memorable. Speechwriters write them for, among others, presidents, prime ministers, and premiers, corporate executives and educators. The people who deliver speeches become involved in writing the speeches to varying extents. Many of them employ professional speechwriters to take their concepts, phrases, bullet points, and other information and to transform them all into memorable public addresses.

Speeches are usually the product of much pondering and revising. For speechmakers who are less involved in the writing process, the writer should discuss desired messages and consider the speaker's personality and his or her rhythm in delivering spoken words. Speeches should sound natural, much the way the speechmaker speaks. A person known for a sense of humor, then, should deliver a message with anecdotes. The speechwriter also must understand the audience. An audience of business owners would be more receptive to a speech with complex sentences

and ideas than a casual group attending a company picnic. Knowing your audience, which is key to so many facets of public relations, is equally important for speechwriting.

As for the length of a speech, event organizers will usually provide a time limit. People attending a lunch meeting prefer speeches that last no more than 15 minutes, which will leave time at the end for questions. The average rate of speaking is about 150 words a minute. A 10-minute speech would typically contain 1,500 words. This should be adjusted for the individual speechmaker. Some people amble through a speech at a slow rate and might be able to use only half as many words in 10 minutes. Others practice speed talking and race along saying many more words in the same time period.

Writing a successful speech—beyond providing memorable themes—means making it informative, persuasive and entertaining. Overall, the speechmaker must practice being a good storyteller. The test for a memorable speech is whether the audience will remember a key message, whether people will talk about it over coffee or at the water cooler. Speakers who try to convey too much information will likely bore the audience. Identify three points for the audience to remember and build the speech around those three points, using statistics, humor or impassioned phrasing to inform, entertain or inspire an audience. Chapter 3 had a discussion of Aristotle's idea that persuasive communication requires ethos, logos and pathos—speaker credibility, logic and emotion or passion. A speech that includes all three is more likely to persuade.

Research reported in a speech should be current, with the most recent findings available. Dated references, especially if current research undermines the validity of old research, can become deadly, undermining the credibility of a speaker. Speakers can best make some points with the support of visuals—a flip chart, a PowerPoint slides, a video or a transparency shown on an overhead projector—to reinforce the message or to hold the attention of the audience.

Persuasive writing ▼

All public relations writing is persuasive. The PR tactics previously discussed use clear, plain and direct written language with specific purposes in mind. Writing persuasively is essential in writing speeches, though messages often become infused with emotionally charged words delivered with passion. Persuasive writing by PR professionals, as with editorial writers, is useful for everything from personal correspondence and more widely distributed memos to guest articles written for news publications and company newsletters.

Publications offer guidelines concerning the length of documents such as guest columns or letters to the editor. Letters generally are no longer than 250 words; columns are 500 to 700 words long. It takes organization, research, thinking time, and reviewing and revising to write a cogent, persuasive article, letter to the editor, speech, or position paper that will successfully persuade others.

Changing minds

To understand the art of persuasive writing it is important to differentiate between attitudes, opinions and beliefs. Attitudes are deeply held views, but they are subject to change. The general definition of opinions is as expressions of attitudes. When a person expresses an attitude as an opinion, it tends to become even more deeply held and resistant to change. Beliefs cut to core issues of basic right and wrong and are the most resistant to change.

A key strategy for the persuasive writer is to appeal to the basic belief system of audiences. If a message connects with the beliefs of an audience, the audience is likely to accept the message. If a writer can integrate the message sufficiently with the attitudes and beliefs of an audience so that the audience goes public with its support and expresses an opinion about it, then the audience will become more resistant to changing its point of view. While attitudes, opinions, and beliefs can change, they resist doing so. Public relations is usually better served in finding ways to match prior held views rather than trying to change them radically.

Propaganda or persuasion

Another key element to persuasive writing is credibility. Effective communicators combine authoritative and, hence, convincing information to win credibility with an audience. No matter how passionate one may feel about an idea or an issue, if the message lacks credibility, it will become ineffective and lost on an audience. People consider information tainted by falsehoods or half-truths that harm or disparage individuals, groups,

or nations as propaganda. Propaganda can operate as part of a strategy to persuade people to act in a particular way.

In a world filled with negative campaigns, particularly in politics, and clever rhetoric, it is important for both public relations practitioners and audiences of persuasive communication to understand the tactics of persuasive communication for they must analyze and judge the many messages directed at them. Advocates on both sides of man-made global warming issue, for example, are at great odds. It is an issue ripe for propaganda for each side.

Messages infused the opening ceremonies for the 2008 Olympic Games in China about global peace and the spirit of sportsmanship and fair competition contradicted harsh realities in that country for each of those areas; in addition, the ceremonies featured animated fireworks displays and lip-synched singing, hardly an authentic display. Human rights activists used the same venue to air grievances concerning human rights violations and a range of concerns. On the other side of the spectrum, officials in repressive countries countered by characterizing social disparities in Western countries as mistreatment toward their own citizens. The conflict engendered by these different points of view can become hazardous when conflicting views escalate into violence and other lawlessness. Public relations strategists have abundant options in advancing positions or promoting products and events without instigating violence or hiding behind lies or dishonest rhetorical devices. Artificial fireworks displays alone in China raised many questions about reality in the world's most populous country.

Writing suggestions

Persuasive writing benefits from the following elements:

▶ Appealing to emotions (pathos)
▶ Writing with impact (pathos)
▶ Researching and understanding subjects thoroughly (logos)
▶ Offering facts and opinions from authoritative sources (ethos, logos).

The chief difference between many persuasive public relations documents like a letter to the editor, a guest newspaper column, an Op-Ed article, an article for the company newsletter, or the corporate annual report is length. Generally, each type of writing has an

▼ ▼ ▼

Top 10 speeches ever?

A subject of great debate, the top speeches ever given have shaped world history. No doubt the messengers had varying amounts of influence over their words. Clearly, some verbal gems came during times when oratory was spontaneous. In the public relations world, speechwriters offer measured words everywhere from the boardroom to the halls of Congress that other speeches often inspire, or they quote from other speeches. For your consideration and entertainment, consider the Top 10 speeches, starting with No. 10, made throughout the course of time, according to The List Universe.

❿ *Kennedy Inauguration, 1960.* "And so my fellow Americans, ask not what your country can do for you. Ask what you can do for your country."

❾ *Pericles' Funeral Oration, 5th Century* B.C. "The tribute of deeds has been paid in part; for the dead have them in deeds, and it remains only that their children should be maintained as the public charge until they are grown up: This is the solid prize with which, as with a garland, Athens crowns her sons, living and dead, after a struggle like theirs.

❽ *Emmeline Pankhurst, 1913,* British Suffragette movement leader "Freedom or Death" "You have left it to women in your land, the men of all civilized countries have left it to women, to work out their own salvation. That is the way in which we women of England are doing. Human life for us is sacred, but we say if any life is to be sacrificed it shall be ours; we won't do it ourselves, but we will put the enemy in the position where they have to choose between giving us freedom or giving us death."

❼ *Pope Urban II Speech at Clermont Pope Urban II, 1095* "You have thus far waged unjust wars, at one time and another; you have brandished mad weapons to your mutual destruction, for no other reason than covetousness and pride, as a result of which you have deserved eternal death and sure damnation. We now hold out to you wars which contain the glorious reward of martyrdom, which will retain that tile of praise now and forever."

❻ *William Lyon Phelps, 1933, author* The Pleasure of Books, a speech given over the radio one year before the Nazis began systematic destruction of books that failed to match Nazi ideals.

"A borrowed book is like a guest in the house; it must be treated with punctiliousness, with a certain considerate formality. You must see that it sustains no damage; it must not suffer while under your roof. You cannot leave it carelessly, you cannot mark it, you cannot turn down the pages, you cannot use it familiarly. And then, some day, although this is seldom done, you really ought to return it."

❺ *Sojourner Truth, 1851,* a slave freed by abolition of slavery in New York. The following excerpt was delivered at the Ohio Women's Rights Convention.

"Ain't I a Woman?"

"Nobody ever helps me into carriages or over mud puddles or gives me any best place. And ain't I a woman? Look at me. Look at my arm! I have ploughed and planted, and gathered into barns, and no man could mead me. And ain't I a woman? I could work as much and eat as much as a man—when I could get it—and bear the lash as well. And ain't I a woman? I have borne thirteen children and seen most all sold off to slavery, and when I cried out with my mother's grief, none but Jesus heard me. And ain't I a woman?"

❹ **"I am the first accused."** *Nelson Mandela, 1964,* made these remarks in an opening statement at his trial for alleged sabotage, high treason, and conspiracy to overthrow the government. His imprisonment ultimately would lead to the end of apartheid in South Africa and his ascent to that country's presidency.

"During my lifetime, I have dedicated myself to this struggle of the African people. I have fought against white domination, and I have fought against black domination. I have cherished the ideal of a democratic and free society in which all persons live together in harmony and with equal opportunities. It is an ideal which I hope to live for and to achieve. But if needs be, it is an ideal for which I am prepared to die."

❸ *Martin Luther King, 1963, "I have a dream."* Delivered on the steps of the Lincoln Memorial during the March on Washington

❷ *Abraham Lincoln, 1863* Gettysburg Address, delivered at the dedication of the Soldiers' National Cemetery in Gettysburg, Pa., four and a half months after the Union armies defeated the Confederacy at the decisive Battle of Gettysburg.

"Four score and seven years ago our fathers brought forth on this continent a new nation, conceived in liberty and dedicated to the proposition that all men are created equal. Now we are engaged in a great civil war, testing whether that nation or any nation so conceived and so dedicated, can long endure. We are met on a great battlefield of that war."

❶ *Winston Churchill, 1940,* "We shall fight on the Beaches." Given before he became prime minister.

"We shall go on to the end, we shall fight in France. We shall fight on the seas and oceans. We shall fight with growing confidence and growing strength in the air, we shall defend our Island, whatever the cost may be, we shall fight on the beaches, we shall fight on the landing grounds, we shall fight in the fields and in the streets, we shall fight in the hills. We shall never surrender."

Courtesy of Jamie Frater. From http://listverse.com/history/top-10-great-historic-speeches

COURTESY OF LIBRARY OF CONGRESS

introduction, supporting paragraphs, and a conclusion. The introduction, like the lead sentence or paragraph of a news release written in news style, should grab the attention of the reader. It should be provocative and memorable. What is the point? What does the messenger want to say?

Throughout the article, but particularly in the introduction, keep sentences short, much the way one might speak them. Subsequent paragraphs should offer support for a point of view. Use research, survey results and other statistics to make a point credible.

The next paragraph or section of an article may address the opposing side's best argument. Public relations practitioners commonly refer to this as an **inoculating paragraph**. Like a flu shot, the inoculating paragraph protects one's argument from a predictable criticism from an opposing side, while strengthening the writer's position. The inoculating paragraph raises the anticipated criticism and immediately responds to it. This strategy gives the writer the opportunity not only to make a point, but also to defend against the opposing side's best response. It is the punch and counterpunch rolled into one, often a very persuasive approach to swaying the views of others.

Finally, persuasive writing will close with a sentence or paragraph that is a conclusion. As with other types of essays, the conclusion reconstructs the original points, now supported by convincing arguments and research. Depending on the focus of the article, the writer might find it appropriate to use a well-known quote that captures the essence of the argument. Alternatively, perhaps the writer will make a statement that is a call for action.

One of the best ways to end a persuasive appeal is ask an audience to do something—buy the product, call a toll-free number, visit a website, join a conversation through social media, vote for a particular candidate, or email a message to Congress. If an appeal can persuade an audience to act in some way, it not only demonstrates the effectiveness of the persuasive appeal, it strengthens an audience's conviction about the subject of the action. They feel more positive about the product, candidate or cause. It is common practice at the end of a report on behalf of a natural disaster or a cause to ask for a donation. When people take that simple action, it adds to their conviction. The old saying is true: "Actions speak louder than words." People may say they support something, but when they take action, they are demonstrating and reinforcing their commitment.

Basic rules of writing for public relations ▼

Good writing should be clear, direct, informative, interesting, easy to read and easy to understand. Language has meaning because it follows rules of grammar, syntax, spelling and punctuation. When writers break rules, the quality of writing breaks down, which means the level of communication and understanding becomes diminished.

Writing is a craft taught early in school. Schools teach it throughout the secondary level, even in college and beyond. Good writing is hard work and takes practice. Someone once asked the late Norman Mailer, a "literary journalist," about the value of writing classes. A tough writing teacher or coach toughens you, he surmised. "It's a little bit like a kid who wants to play varsity football but never tries out for the team," Mailer said. "So you go to that writing class and get toughened up a little."

The best-written work is rewritten work. No careful writer writes something once. Why is rewriting or revising work so important? It is important because someone is going to read it. Everyone from middle school English teachers and professors to professional writing coaches preach: "Write to express, not to impress." Poets may like the sound of what they write. Their readers often use their imaginations to discover an underlying message. That is the beauty of poetry. That is not the beauty of writing on behalf of a client for media or public consumption. The late Kurt Vonnegut, a former college newspaper editor and author of dozens of novels, including "Slaughterhouse Five," once pointed out that revisions took place out of respect for the reader.

To facilitate the practice of public relations writing, the practitioner can show discipline by following these simple practices:

▶ Vary the length and complexity of sentences. Doing so will convey and process information in a way that will hold the reader's attention.

▶ Choose words carefully, respectful of their precise meanings. Young writers like to impress by showing off their vocabulary. That is good so long as they really understand the meaning of words. If someone talks about the thrill of a lifetime as the penultimate experience, he or she often thinks "penultimate" means something like the ultimate experience. "Penultimate" actually refers to "the next to the last" as in the penultimate scene of a play. Using words incorrectly clouds the meaning of writing and raises questions about the skills of the writer.

▶ Write economically. Don't waste words. Eliminate redundancies.

▶ Write one thought per sentence, one idea per paragraph.

▶ Write in the affirmative. "Not" is a powerful word that overuse weakens. Use it when it can have the greatest impact. Example:
   - The picnic is not happening.
   - Revised: The picnic is cancelled.

▶ Write in active voice. Is the subject acting or being acted upon? When the subject is acting the voice is active; when the voice is acted upon it is passive. Writing is stronger when writers turn words around in the sentence to place the action closer to the subject of the sentence. The passive voice is effective when you want the person receiving the action to be the subject of the sentence. To be is not really a verb. It indicates existence not action. Its subject does nothing—it just exists. Much writing contains passive voice constructions. However, avoid passive voice when writing a news release, fact sheet, advertisement, or public service announcement. These brief documents must use active, persuasive language. Consider a couple of examples:

▶ *Passive:* The boy was bitten by the dog.

▶ *Active:* The dog bit the boy.

▶ *Passive:* Research will be presented by Goose Einstein at the conference.

▶ *Active:* Goose Einstein will present research at the conference.

▶ Don't split infinitives. The infinitive form of a verb—to fly, to drive, to spend, to study—loses some force as adverbs and other modifiers separate "to" and the verb. Often you can eliminate the word splitting the infinitive or place it elsewhere in the sentence. When placing the modifier elsewhere in the sentence makes the sentence sound awkward rewrite the sentence without using an infinitive. Examples:

▶ *Split:* I plan to diligently keep up with my history assignments.

▶ *Revised:* I plan to keep up diligently with my history assignments.

▶ *Rewritten without an infinitive:* I can do well in history by keeping up with the assignments.

AP style as a standard

Most public relations writing follows rules included in the Associated Press Style Book. The AP style provides a standard to follow for punctuation, abbreviations, capitalization, numerals, titles, and other categories. This style guide encourages consistency that makes it easier for both writers and readers. As with news organizations, some companies have their own style. They may choose to capitalize all titles all of the time. The AP stylebook allows the capitalization of titles before the name but not after. Examples:

▶ Executive Vice President Jane Doe or

▶ Jane Doe, executive vice president

The stylebook has a section of commonly misused words. Some people use composed and comprised synonymously and interchangeably. They are different words with different meanings, dealing with the parts and the whole. Examples:

▶ Nine players comprise a baseball team.

▶ A baseball team is composed of nine players.

Further and farther are commonly treated equally. They are different words with different meanings. Farther deals with physical distance; further refers to the extension of time or degree. Examples:

▶ The student court will look further into the matter.

▶ My car is parked farther away than yours.

While on the subject of using words incorrectly, consider a couple of other common errors. Someone who is apathetic toward something might say, "I could care less." A listener probably knows what this person meant, but it is not what he or she said. By saying, "I could care less," the person is expressing care about something to some degree. If he or she really does not care about something at all, it is more appropriate to say, "I couldn't care less."

Some words need no qualifying. "Unique" is a word used frequently in the public relations world. To prove the uniqueness of a new product or a superlative candidate, one might casually and inaccurately write: "The new car is the most unique vehicle on the market" or "one of the most unique . . ." The word unique refers to something that is one of a kind. There are no degrees of uniqueness. Either it is unique or not.

While discussing "or not," it is important to understand "whether." Implicit in the word "whether" is "or not." In most uses, you can drop the "or not." In the relatively few instances when "whether," used alone, sounds awkward, a little rewriting will eliminate the problem.

▶ *Incorrect:* "I'm not sure whether or not I'll go to the party."
▶ *Correct:* "I'm not sure whether I'll go to the party."

Here are several other common rules for speech and writing:

▶ When comparing two things use "between"; when comparing more than two items, use "among."
▶ Never write "centers around" or "revolves on." Write: "centers on" or "revolves around." By definition, "revolves" and "centers" are verbs that require very specific prepositions.
▶ "Over" and "under" are words that refer to spatial relationships, such as "Somewhere over the rainbow . . . ," and you should reserve it for defining space. Disciplined writers should avoid using these words to quantify something. Instead of writing, "The company spent over (or under) $200 million to automate its factories throughout the world," substitute "more than" or "less than." These words are more precise in meaning than "over" and "under."
▶ It is impossible to promote the "first annual" anything. Announce the inaugural chili cook-off or the first chili cook-off that organizers plan to make an annual event. An event becomes the annual event beginning with the second annual.
▶ Nothing in the word "yet" implies not, though writers commonly use such phrasing as "The team has yet to reach the finals." Instead, write: "The team has not yet reached the finals." Or write around "yet": The team has never reached the finals." Yet is used correctly to project the future, as in "The best is yet to come," but it does not imply "not."

Headlines need a verb

Headlines contain few words but must be compelling and get attention. Every headline should contain a verb. Examples:

▶ *Good headline:* Golden Arches *Offer* Shelter in Storm
▶ *Bad headline:* Farmer Bill Dies in House

The first headline concerns McDonald's having a strong financial quarter and attracting investors in the face of a turbulent stock market. The headline tells the story, and the play on words with arches offering shelter works, too.

The second headline deals with a piece of legislation that failed to receive enough votes in the House of Representatives. At first blush, one might think that Farmer Bill is a neighbor out in the country who expired in his home. Farmer Bill refers to legislation, not someone named William. A better headline would be: *House Rejects Farm Bill.*

Be specific

A poorly written announcement of a new hire might say, "Bob Smith has a long and impressive track record in the public relations profession."

What is the problem? What does long and impressive mean? That is an opinion rather than a statement of fact. Get specific: "Bob Smith has worked in public relations for more than 20 years, handling accounts for more than a dozen Fortune 500 companies.

Watch redundancies over and over and over again

Redundancies are words writers use sloppily that become accepted through regular use:

Bad	Good
advance warning	warning
absolutely essential	essential
funeral service	funeral
completely surround	surround
new record	record
exact replica	replica
former graduate	graduate (former student)
irregardless	regardless (disregarding, irrespective)
join together	join
merge together	merge
overexaggerate	exaggerate
regular routine	routine
undergraduate student	undergraduate

Irregardless, mentioned above, is a special case. The word does not exist. Using it telegraphs to other people a negative message about someone's grasp of vocabulary and word use.

Fumbling over words

One of the best-known American commentators of the English language is William Safire of The New York Times. His columns about word usage and grammar are popular and frequently shared among various communicators, from journalists and public relations practitioners to English teachers. Contemporary grammarians may take exception with some of these rules, but they will promote clarity in writing effectively for an audience. In 1979, Safire solicited from his readers "perverse rules of grammar" that he called Fumblerules. He illustrated rules by breaking them. For example, he wrote, "We never make misteaks" with "misteak" being the mistake. Another example:

▶ "Remember to never split an infinitive," with "never" separating "to split."

Such fun generated 33 additional examples of grammatically incorrect sentences, with each statement more entertaining than the next. Consider these examples:

▶ Don't use no double negatives.

▶ Verbs has to agree with their subjects.

▶ Avoid commas, that are not necessary.

▶ If you reread your work, you will find on rereading that a great deal of repetition can be avoided by rereading and editing.

▶ Place pronouns as close as possible, especially in long sentences, as of 10 or more words, to their antecedents.

▶ It is incumbent on us to avoid archaisms.

▶ If any word is improper at the end of a sentence, a linking verb is.

▶ Everyone should be careful to use a singular pronoun with the singular nouns in their writing.

▶ Don't string too many prepositional phrases together unless you are walking through the valley of the shadow of death.

▶ Avoid clichés like the plague; seek viable alternatives.

Write "Fumblerules" in an Internet search field to find Safire's complete list.

Ease away from "ese"

The evolution of language accelerates in certain segments of the workplace. The legal, government and particularly the technology communities deal with language that affects many people. They read or hear regulations or instructions or conversation and, suddenly, such verbiage gains acceptance. Other sectors of society use language unique to them, from the financial community to the world of auto racing—whose followers are affectionately known as "gear heads."

The language of bureaucrats gets reduced to bureaucratese. Jargon, euphemisms and abstract terminology understood best by bureaucrats fill it. Jargon understood by the legal community is called legalese. Few people understand some jargon and slang. Bureaucratese includes such important sounding phrases or words as "at this point in time," or "utilize." They contributed to the lexicon by using the word "impact" as a verb as in "The new measure impacts the vast majority of people at this point in time as we interface problems." Until bureaucrats got hold of it, the word "impact" was not a verb.

Bureaucratese often results in stilted language. Such problems are creeping into news reports, meetings, classrooms and conversations to the point of becoming part of accepted everyday language. The more bureaucrats—and mass communicators—use such language, the more everyone thinks it is correct.

Use clear, simple words

Some offending words and phrases are unnecessarily wordy. Get rid of the excess verbiage. Some phrases are euphemistic, meaning that expressions hide the real meaning of what people are saying. Avoid euphemisms because they cloud the meaning of messages and raise ethical issues about the intent of communicators to deceive. Acronyms (MADD, UN, BBC, NAACP . . .) and trade jargon are useful shortcuts when communicating with audiences who all understand their meaning. They are a liability to communication when included in messages for the uninitiated, the general audience that does not understand their meaning. Avoid words and phrases that may confuse readers or simply make writing less clear and direct:

Bad	*Better*
aquatic facility	swimming pool
made a suggestion	suggested
in order to	to
free gift	gift
really unique	unique
quality	high or low?
aerial ordnance	bombs and missiles
biosolids	sewage
collateral damage	civilian casualties
IFAK	Individual First Aid Kit
FAQ	frequently asked questions
NCAA	National Collegiate Athletic Association

Keep your eyes on the "ize"

An earlier section addressed the way bureaucrats "bureaucratize" language. Another common error in writing and speaking is to convert nouns into verbs. Strict constructionists of language cringe when the act of setting priorities becomes to "prioritize." A newly automated office becomes "computerized." Intelligent individuals using sophisticated language "intellectualize." Remodelers are "contemporizing" kitchens and bathrooms. A troubled banking industry has regained strength after being "monetized." A company that installs and repairs mufflers wants you to Midasize your car.

Using numbers

Public relations writers should use the journalism style for writing numbers. Spell out numbers zero through nine, and use numerals for numbers 10 and above. Ages are numerals; so are percentage figures.

- ▶ *Incorrect:* Bill went on a 7-day holiday.
- ▶ *Correct:* Bill went on a seven-day holiday.
- ▶ *Incorrect:* Mary took twelve days off.
- ▶ *Correct:* Mary took 12 days off.

Using commas

Journalists do something different for commas in a series. Standard English practice is to use commas after each item in a series before the conjunction. In journalism (AP Style), the last comma is omitted. Punctuation works like traffic signs. It is there to help the reader. For serial commas the final "and" suffices and a comma before it suggests a pause that is unnecessary.

- ▶ *Standard English:* Bob, Bill, and Mary went downtown.
- ▶ *Journalism style:* Bob, Bill and Mary went downtown.

Using titles

Do not use courtesy titles such as Mr. and Mrs. in journalistic writing. Do use them for Dr., Sen., Mayor, Gov. and the Rev.

- ▶ *Incorrect:* The city council selected Mr. Bob Smith as the new mayor.
- ▶ *Correct:* The city council selected Bob Smith as the new mayor.
- ▶ *Correct:* The city council selected Dr. Bob Smith as the new mayor.

Flesch-Kincaid readability statistics

Microsoft Word cannot only spell check a document, it can check grammar and punctuation as well. After it completes the grammar and spelling check, it can display readability statistics for the document using the Flesch-Kincaid readability statistics. A critical statistic is the grade level required to read the document comfortably. A reading level of 12 means a 12th grade education is required to read the document easily. The report also states the percentage of sentences with passive voice constructions. Other statistics include the average number of sentences per paragraph, the average number of words per sentence, and the average number of characters in each word.

Here are some rules of thumb for the readability of news releases:

▶ Average word length: 5 characters or less
▶ Sentence length: 17 words or less
▶ Paragraphs: 2 to 3 sentences each
▶ Passive voice: 5 percent or less
▶ Reading level grade: 9th grade or less

Even journalists do not always live up to these standards. In a study of randomly selected local articles in one issue of a major urban newspaper the readability statistics were problematic because of relatively long sentences that required a 12th grade reading level. Longer sentences often require more punctuation, which adds complexity to the writing. Note that the use of passive voice, paragraph length and word length was excellent. Here are the statistics:

▶ Average word length: 5 characters
▶ Sentence length: 21 words
▶ Paragraphs: 1.7 sentences each
▶ Passive voice: 0 percent
▶ Reading level grade: 12th grade

The study also analyzed news stories on a major broadcast TV network. The results were:

▶ Average word length: 5 characters
▶ Sentence length: 19 words
▶ Paragraphs: 1.5 sentences each
▶ Passive voice: 11 percent
▶ Reading level grade: 11th grade

Finally, the study checked articles from a leading women's magazine. This magazine did best of all. It had a perfect readability score:

▶ Average word length: 5 characters
▶ Sentence length: 13 words
▶ Paragraphs: 2 to 3 sentences each
▶ Passive voice: 0 percent
▶ Reading level grade: 6th grade or less
▶ Use simple, understandable words.
▶ Keep sentences short.
▶ Keep paragraphs short.
▶ Use strong verbs, not passive voice.
▶ Minimize punctuation. Lots of commas and other punctuation are evidence of complicated sentence structures.

Good writing for email and the new media ▼

Ahe world is wired. People move from place to place engaging in **multitasking** of a kind not seen before: talking, texting, searching, sharing, following, "friending," tweeting. Communication today is fast, continuous and heavily mediated. The impact of technology is a topic too large for a single chapter in a textbook, but the importance of communication using today's technology and its interconnectedness is crucial to the public relations industry.

The tendency in today's virtual world, with 24-hour news cycles and endless opportunities on the Internet, and through smartphones and tablets, is to communicate as freely and furiously as dust travels. The reduction of language to codes of initials and acronyms expedites communication. It is easier and faster to type acronyms like "lol," "CUL8R" (laughing out loud, and see you later). Emoticons, the stringing together of punctuation and other symbols, depict emotions like happy, shocked, angry and sad (:-) :-O >:(:-(Cute, perhaps, but not professional or suitable for business communication.

PR clients, even the most tech-savvy, seldom appreciate such technological slang, misspellings and misplaced punctuation. The careless, casual practitioner may be SOL (so out of luck) or out of a job if bad grammar or misspellings become part of an important communication between a PR firm and a client. Sometimes, a public relations campaign may incorporate these language shortcuts deliberately for a product or message targeting youth or others on the cutting edge, but for serious communication, the digital age still requires a solid command of "old school" rules of grammar, spelling and punctuation.

Email subject line

People receive so much email, including unwanted and promotional messages called **spam**, that the importance of an eye-catching heading in the subject field is crucial. Make the heading in the subject field relevant to the reader. Spammers commonly add your "username" or teaser headings beginning with "Re," the normal introduction to an email response, just to make readers curious. When choosing words for the subject field, avoid symbols, a string of numerals and even

> ### When writing email
>
> ▶ Determine what the email is supposed to accomplish.
> ▶ Get to the point.
> ▶ Write clearly.
> ▶ Keep sentences short.
> ▶ Make sure to exercise proper email etiquette by responding to messages, even just to confirm the receipt of the message.

CAPITAL LETTERS, all common practices of spammers. If email headings look like something that most people quickly delete, recipients could miss some important business communications as well. Some form of personalization is a good idea to assure authenticity of the source. One method used is to add one's initials to the end of the heading, such as, "Why the Cowboys will win/ck."

The "from" field

Email is also an excellent way to transmit electronic newsletters, fact sheets and news releases. Many institutions now circulate the traditionally printed newsletter, flier or brochure electronically. Recipients will welcome such communications more readily if they come from a recognized sender. Typically, when the "from field" has an unrecognizable source, something that looks like a jumble of lettering or random numerals or symbols, they will identify it as spam. Companies often purchase email lists, like conventional mailing lists, for a targeted electronic mailing. Make sure the "from field" of these acquired lists shows a name that is credible and recognizable.

Use care before pressing send

Electronic mail is such a fast and facile medium that its users, particularly youthful users, often write whatever private thoughts pop into their heads. Business communication requires a higher level of discretion. All information sent through email has the chance of being forwarded to others, "blogged" or posted independently. One way senders attempt to ward off this practice is by adding a **disclaimer paragraph**. Disclaimer paragraphs put readers on notice that a message is strictly and exclusively for them and that the sender prohibits forwarding the message. The following is an example that one might receive from an attorney:

"Information contained in this transmission is attorney privileged and confidential. It is intended for the use of the individual or entity named above. If the reader of this message is not the intended recipient, you are hereby notified that any dissemination, distribution or copy of this communication is strictly prohibited. If you have received this communication in error, please immediately notify us by telephone."

These stern warnings do a good job of emphasizing the confidentiality of a document and putting the audience on notice against sharing the document. You should share highly sensitive, confidential information with the intended audience in a face-to-face meeting, in a telephone conversation or on paper.

Social media etiquette

The caution discussed about email certainly applies to social media. Social media etiquette can be considered for various audiences—businesses, individuals, college students and, among others, students seeking jobs. Users often feel what they place on social media sites is private. They also know that social media companies alter privacy settings and people accept "friends" easily. Despite warnings, students tend to post information, photos and videos that may seem private and fun, but can harm one's chances to win credibility or jobs. The best advice is to conduct yourself with social media as you would in person. Others suggest, "Ask yourselves whether the information you're posting would be suitable reading or viewing for your grandmother." Again, employers have numerous ways to check one's character.

Final Writing checklist

- ▶ Are your sentences fairly short?
- ▶ Have you avoided stringing together long sentences?
- ▶ Is your writing concise? Wordy?
- ▶ Are there wasted or needless words in your sentences?
- ▶ Have you used familiar words that evoke precise meanings, clear images?
- ▶ Is your language natural, conversational without colloquialisms or trite expressions?
- ▶ Are you varying sentence structure?
- ▶ Is your writing free from bias?
- ▶ Have you read your work out loud?
- ▶ Does the writing flow easily from sentence to sentence?
- ▶ Are you proud of your work?

Part of the joy of social media is the art of sharing. Consider how the information you're sharing will reflect on you. Posts also can be posted on one's various social media sites through widgets, the linked icons that post information instantly to Twitter, Reddit, Blogger, Tumblr, Gmail, LinkedIn and literally hundreds of other social media sites that people can create for themselves. Social media is as widely abused as it is used. Rethink posting private information on Facebook or other networking sites. The guilty parties of such playful, casual communications are no longer students or pranksters. Elected officials and celebrities have dealt with the embarrassment of sharing too much through social media.

Review questions

1. What are backgrounders and position papers? How are they similar? How are they different?
2. What makes a news release ineffective?
3. What is the benefit of the "inoculating paragraph" in a piece of persuasive writing?
4. A graduate is writing an email to a prospective employer. What are the do's and don'ts in writing that note?
5. What are the benefits and hazards of social media?

Supplemental resources online

http://www.clarityir.com/index.html
http://www.plainlanguage.gov
http://www.b2bpublicrelations.org
http://www.websitetips.com
http://www.dailywritingtips.com

Chapter references

Bernays, Edward. (1928). *Propaganda.* New York: H. Liveright.

Newman, Edwin. (1974). *Strictly Speaking: Will America be the death of English?* New York: Bobbs-Merrill Company.

Newman, Edwin. (1976). *A Civil Tongue.* New York: Bobbs-Merrill.

Newman, Edwin. (1988). *I must say: On English, the news and other matters.* New York: Warner Books.

Norman Mailer Interview. (2004, June 12). The Academy of Achievement.

Safire, William. (1990). *Fumblerules.* New York: Doubleday.

Sparks, Suzanne D. Sparks. *The manager's guide to business writing.* New York: McGraw-Hill.

Stepp, Carl Sessions. (2007). *Writing as craft and magic.* Oxford, United Kingdom: Oxford University Press.

Strunk, William Jr., & E. B. White. (1972). *The elements of style.* New York: Macmillan Publishing Co., Inc.

The American heritage® dictionary of the English language, Fourth Edition. (2006). New York: Houghton Mifflin Company.

1. Take a story idea and create a fact sheet, then write a news release, incorporating the comments of at least two sources and a boilerplate paragraph.

2. Find five fact sheets reflecting different kinds of announcements. Note similarities and differences. Do the same with backgrounders.

3. Take an issue and examine the arguments that advance the idea. Quantify the strengths and weaknesses of each side.

4. Discuss characteristics of and habits with e-mailing that senders and receivers find bothersome, if not irritating.

5. Take a worthy cause and develop a plan using social media? Discuss how it can be used to generate outcomes.

Notes

chapter 10

PUBLICATION LAYOUT AND DESIGN

Marshall McLuhan, philosopher and author of the phrase "the medium is the message," never lived to see the Internet. He died in 1980. Yet, the effects of speed and time shaped his vision of communication and media. He once said, "People don't actually read newspapers. They step into them every morning like a hot bath." At that time, newspapers and television had not yet given way to the Internet, social media, round-the-clock television or YouTube channels. Mobile devices are things of fantasy and science fiction. American news readers, however, were about to experience a new kind of newspaper, a national publication called *USA Today*.

When *USA Today* rolled off the press in 1982, the industry braced for an experiment, a reaction to conventional newspapers, those with black and white photos and an overall gray appearance. *USA Today* presented news in condensed stories, much briefer than was common in most other dailies. Visually, *USA Today* offered splashy color, graphs and charts. They told stories through data. The industry viewed it as a comic book of sorts. Its detractors called it, "McPaper," the first newspaper equivalent of fast food. However, on-the-go newsreaders, like business people traveling through airports and others in an increasingly mobile society, found the *USA Today* format attractive and easier to read. Its editors gave readers news that was brief, visual and relevant to their needs and interests. Other newspapers looked dreary by comparison and, over time, changed their formats to look more and more like *USA Today*. The mobile society it tapped more than three decades ago is getting news on-the-go more today than ever through smartphone apps.

Creating collateral ▼

This snapshot of newspaper evolution to the digital age is important for public relations practitioners to understand, not simply for the sake of history, but as an example of how easily one can translate information to other media. The elements that comprise newspapers or magazines translate easily into digital media. Just as headlines and artwork tell a story in a conventional newspaper or magazine, they also combine to communicate effectively in other formats. PR professionals can print newsletters, brochures, fliers and other collateral material and hand them out at trade shows, conferences or meetings. They can send the same printed pieces by email or post them on the Internet. They create much material today for distribution in both printed and digital form. They can include the graphic element of a QR Code that, once scanned on a smartphone, can take a reader to a website laden with multimedia material.

Stages of layout ▼

As with writing, layouts also go through a series of drafts. The design effort for this type of project is similar to the way a painter works—from rough sketches to drawings to under paintings and finally to the finished work. Layout artists begin with a thumbnail, then proceed to a rough layout, a comprehensive, and finally, a mechanical. Each offers more detail than the preceding version. Today's paginated documents are delivered or transmitted to a printer as a Portable Document Format (PDF) file. The process is all very seamless. In today's world of pagination software, skilled designers can make changes or corrections quickly and resend the new PDF file to the printer or anywhere.

Visual language ▼

Good headlines, body copy (text) and graphics remain sturdy elements for communicating messages today. Writers create sentences and paragraphs that will hold the reader's attention and interest. Editors and designers take the words and combine them with visual elements in a format that makes the content even more attractive to readers. The media magic happens in print, online, in blogs and on mobile devices.

For news publications, the size of a headline and its position on a page indicate the importance of the story. This has always been part of the visual language of print. Over the years, readers came to understand this language, even if only subconsciously. Public relations adopted this visual language, using it in the design of brochures, newsletters, blogs and other web content. Clearly, readers want content with strong visual components. Capturing a reader's attention graphically and clear writing remains crucial in today's media environment, which is cluttered with competing publications, websites and advertising. Sterile, gray, textual publications are virtually invisible in this environment.

Another element to publication design are references to digital content. Editorial content often

▲ *The Fort Worth Star-Telegram's redesign shows similarities of a home page with stacked vertical elements and a high story count, with various headlines and photographs.*

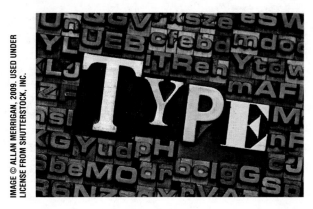

includes references to available video on websites and will site the URL or web address for audiences. They also may reference a photo gallery to augment the availability of additional photographs. When visiting such links, readers will have an opportunity to comment or join the conversation about a particular topic, making the experience highly interactive with a community. Advertising will incorporate QR Codes that are scanned to transport readers to the dynamic content of a website.

Some things do not change, however. As public relations products take shape, the process still begins with the same questions asked for years: What is the goal? Who are we trying to reach? What do we know about our target audience that allows us to connect with them? It is critical to begin by understanding both the objective and the audience.

Text size

Printed material, regardless of the medium, usually contains a combination of headlines, subheads and text. Larger, bold headlines signify something that is more important than content beneath a smaller headline. Font size signals importance.

A measurement called **points** defines the size of a headline. An inch equals 72 points. Body copy, the words contained in paragraphs, typically is 10 to 12 points in size. Older readers benefit from a larger font size—12 points, sometimes larger. Older people may find body copy printed at 10 points unreadable. Printers call the tabular material commonly found in sports pages or with stocks listings agate. Agate is as small as 6 points.

Point size measurements move from the top of the ascending stem of a character to the bottom of the descending stem of a character. Software used to create publications, such as Adobe InDesign or Microsoft Publisher, will give the user choices for size of text and headlines. The measurement typically used to define the width of columns, a page or the size of a photo is the **pica**. One pica equals 12 points or one-sixth of an inch; six picas equal 72 points or one inch. Once the editor or designer understands how to measure elements manually, he or she can use design software to create the publication.

Readability and legibility

Readability relates to how easily one can read a large amount of text in a document or online. As the word implies, a readable document is easy to read. The text is large enough. The font style is easy to read. Decisions about leading and kerning of text do not interfere with readability. In general, the layout respects the physical act of reading.

Legibility and readability advice:

DON'T USE ALL CAPS FOR LARGE AMOUNTS OF TEXT.

Don't use a very small type size.

Avoid italics for large amounts of text.

Avoid boldface for large amounts of text.

<u>Avoid underlining large amounts of text.</u>

Avoid script fonts for large amounts of text.

AVOID DECORATIVE FONTS FOR LARGE AMOUNTS OF TEXT.

Avoid reverse type for large amounts of text.

Avoid black on gray for large amounts of text.

SOURCE: Wheildon, Colin. 2005. Type & Layout: Are You Communicating or Just Making Pretty Shapes. Mentone, Australia: The Worsley Press.

Some decisions render documents unreadable or difficult to read. High chroma fonts, like lime green and hot pink, are exceedingly difficult to read. Small type is hard for older people to read. Reverse type—white type on a black, gray, or colored background—is more difficult to read than conventional black ink on a white page. Some layouts focus more on the visual impact of the elements on a page than on the readability of body copy. These layouts treat the text like an image rather than as information content. This is a mistake if the text is an important part of the document because if the text is not readable it cannot communicate effectively and part of the client's message becomes lost.

For body copy, serif fonts are the most common and easiest to read as is black type on white paper. Most people can read with ease type that is at least 12 points. Upper and lower case type is easier to read than all CAPS. Italics, bold face and underlined text are harder to read than standard text. Decorative and script fonts are extremely difficult to read if used for large amounts of text.

Legibility relates to the ease with which one can read and quickly understand a small amount of text. The classic situations requiring legibility are headlines and billboards. Headlines are supposed to capture the reader's attention. They should be easy to read quickly. Billboards have to be read in four or five seconds at significant distances by motorists traveling 70 miles an hour, often in crowded traffic. Odd-looking fonts, too many words, and other distracting typography and design decisions can limit legibility. Readers cannot digest a handful of words quickly when the layout is distracting or when they cannot decipher the type itself in seconds. Design decisions guide the eye and brain to consume information.

Leading

Another measurement that affects the presentation of type is **leading** or the space between the lines. Allowing more leading can create easy-to-read displays; less leading will make more lines fit into a smaller space. Commonly, one point of leading is allowed between each line of text. The written instructions for a typical news column, then, would be 12-point type over 13-point leading or, simply, "12 over 13."

Research shows that too little and too much leading negatively affects readability. Too little kerning presses lines too close together and they overlap. Too much leading spreads lines far apart, which seems to slow the rhythm of reading.

Kerning

Kerning is the space between letters, also referred to as character spacing. Sometimes we can reduce the space between characters to compress a bit more text into a given amount of space. Expanding kerning can create an attractive visual effect with text.

As with leading, too much and too little kerning makes text difficult to read. Too little kerning forces letters too close together and they can overlap. Too much leading, especially in body copy, can spread the letters out so much that it becomes difficult to discern words, which slows reading.

Font styles and use

Another element in the design of printed materials is the selection of a font or typeface. Microsoft Word provides a directory of fonts. Some of the fonts have **serifs**, the pointed tails or strokes that finish a letter. These

---

Leading

This is normal leading, also called line spacing. It is easy to read.

Leading in this example needs expansion. Lines are too close together to read easily.

Kerning

This is normal kerning or character spacing.

This is compressed kerning.

This is expanded kerning.

Serif and sans serif

This is a serif font, Times New Roman

This is a sans serif font, Arial

Reverse type

Reverse type, white on black

strokes are marked by ascenders and descenders. Times and Garamond are two common serif fonts. Fonts without the strokes are sans serif fonts, or fonts without serifs, such as Arial or Helvetica. Still other fonts are decorative and reflect a very stylized personality. They have names like Smoke and Stencil and conjure up obvious images inherent in the font. Still others are script fonts, which mimic handwritten text or calligraphy. Font designs are as varied as the imaginations of the font designers who create them.

Most publications use a serif font for body copy and a san serif font for **cutlines** (also called captions). Type commonly appears in an upright or Roman format. PR people use italics to add emphasis to words or to conform to certain rules of style. Some publications prefer to use italics for foreign phrases or the titles of newspapers, for example. In headlines, italics contrast Roman typefaces.

Reverse type

A few additional design strategies can help make a printed product visually appealing. **Reversing** text or a headline within blank background space in a photograph can draw a reader into the page. Color or text in a tinted box also offers another visual variation for the reader. Designers create a tinted box by setting a percentage of a desired solid color. It should be light enough or dark enough to allow for the reading of displayed text. Typically, the tint for a box that makes type easy to read is a 10 percent screen. Anything much darker will compete with the black text. When text is difficult to read the reader will move to another article or lose interest in the publication altogether. Any tint that is darker than 40 percent likely will require the use of reversed text, making the words look light against a darker background.

White space

Another important use of space is **white space**. The use of an image and a couple of words—for example, "got milk?" or simply the Nike swoosh—may speak volumes. White space or blank space is another way of drawing the eye to a particular element. Of course, the size of attractive artwork is an instant eye grabber. A large photograph arranged with a smaller photograph can move the eye toward another element on a page. Too many elements on a page can create distract-

ing visual competition. The eye does not know where to go first and next.

Bleed

Images with a surrounding white space border are slightly more distracting to the eye than a **bleed**, an image or background that goes to the edge of a page. In other words, a bleed is a page without margins on the sides, top and bottom. It is common in magazine-format publications. Professionals set the image beyond the designated page size, so when the printer prints, folds and trims the publication the image or background extends to the edge of the paper.

Bleeds require using and trimming a larger sheet of paper. This additional effort and wasted paper often make bleeds more expensive to print and, as a result, magazines typically charge more for ads that require bleeds.

Text as a design element

Publications contain various design elements: headlines, subheads, body copy, charts, graphs, photo captions (also called cutlines), and **readouts** (also called **pull quotes**.) All publications, whether a newspaper or a newsletter, a mainstream magazine or a corporate annual report, require careful blending of these elements to create a document that is attractive and easy to read. Public relations documents also need to reflect institutional branding. A document should have the look and feel of other documents from the institution consistent with the principles of integrated marketing communication.

> *Pull quotes are used to add emphasis to a significant point or colorful quote in an article or to fill space and 'break of the gray.'*

Generally, photographs accompanying a story will have a short, one-sentence caption. A publication may run a photograph without a story, sometimes referred to as a "cutlines only" element, with a short headline and a longer caption. Editors and designers incorporate charts and graphs to present statistical information in a readable format that consumes a small amount of space. Readouts or "pull quotes" are direct quota-

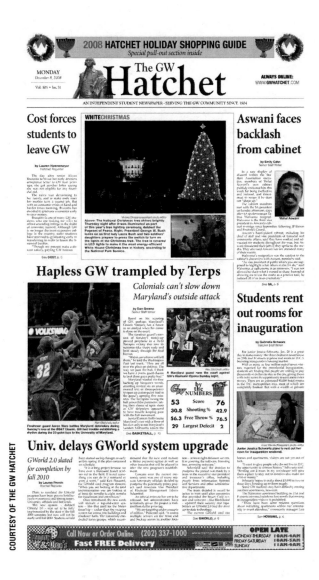

teenaged music lovers. Identifying the audience is an important part of layout and design. Generally, layout and design follow four approaches:

► Vertical design
► Horizontal design
► Modular design
► Open design

Vertical design will appear dominated by one- or two-column elements in a multi-column format. The design generally guides the eye from the top of the page to the bottom of the page.

Horizontal design will appear dominated by multi-column elements that extend beyond half of the page's width, often the full width of a page. The reader's eye tends to move from left to right in following the news down a page.

Modular design combines horizontal and vertical elements in a format that squares elements off with other elements on a page, such as a photograph, a boxed item or maybe an advertisement. Modular design, adopted by most newspapers throughout the United States, allows the eye to move down the page in a logical way. Typically, the eye follows a backwards 6, beginning in the upper right part of a page and ending toward the middle and bottom of a page. Design also can take the reader from the top to the bottom of a page in the shape of a Z.

An **open design** is one that may have only one large, impressive photograph, a large headline and text. Smaller format publications—a magazine or newsletter—or a print advertisement will arrange elements using an open design, often called magazine layouts, with the page serving as a blank canvas.

Balance

Regardless of the approach, the design of a brochure or any other printed product should be balanced. Balance refers to the visual or optical weight of elements on a page. The left and right side of a page should feel in balance. There are two types of balance: formal (also called symmetric) and informal (asymmetric.)

Formal balance exists when the left and right sides of a page are almost mirror images of one another. If you draw a line down the center of a page from top to bottom, the left and right sides of the page would appear almost like copies of one another. Informal balance occurs when a page contains an uneven distribution of

tions taken from the text. They add emphasis to a significant point or a colorful quote in an article or to fill space and "break up the gray," an old newspaper expression that means giving the eye a break from inches and inches of text only. Dense text is daunting to look at and fatiguing. Visual elements provide places for the eye to rest. White space makes the layout seem less crowded and intimidating to a reader.

Layout and design ▼

Professionals consider all of these visual and textual elements as they design publications for public relations. They organize each publication to appeal to the reader. A publication for lawyers may have a different design and organization than a publication for

▲ *Formal balance: left and right sides are like mirror images.*

▲ *Informal balance: the various elements together create balance through their distribution on the page.*

elements. The left and right sides of the page are quite different, yet the elements balance one another.

Contrast

Contrast is the relationship of elements on the page in terms of size, shape, tone, texture, direction, and color. We usually think of contrast just in terms of black and white, but contrast also exists with regard to the size of elements, differences in shapes, use of color, and use of texture.

The absence of contrast means that a page has kind of an uninteresting uniformity, a grayness in which nothing stands out and captures the attention of the eye. It is boring and does not invite readership.

Flow or movement

Layouts should guide the eye across and down the page. Earlier this chapter discussed the "backwards 6" and "Z format" flow of layout in newspapers and advertisements. In ads, the eye often comes to rest on the product logo in the lower right side of the page.

Researchers now use sophisticated eye tracking technology to test how readers look at printed documents and computer images. It is possible to follow the eye of a viewer across a page or a computer monitor and record how the eyes tracks—what it sees first, second, third, and so on. Newspapers are using this technology to test new layout concepts. Advertising and public relations use it to test print layouts and websites.

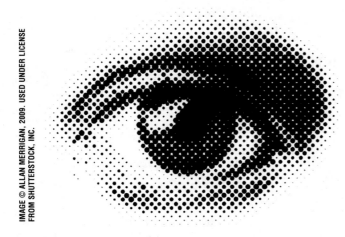

◄ *The black dots in a halftone image are rarely this obvious today, although you can still sometimes see the dots.*

*I*mages ▼

A picture may be worth a thousand words, but in print pictures actually consist of dots of various intensities. Specialists must convert a black-and-white photograph for publication into a **halftone**. Real black and white photographs contain an infinite pallet of grays. Printing presses, on the other hand, can only print black and white. Grays in a printed photograph are actually an arrangement of black dots. This was once apparent in newspapers. The dots were visible. Modern printing makes the dot formations in halftones much less conspicuous.

There are two types of color printing: spot color and process color (also called four-color printing). Spot color enables a layout to include black and one or more specific colors. The printer can combine individual colors and black to create some shades of color. It is apparent, however, that spot color publications do not contain the full spectrum of colors. This type of printing is cheaper, however, making documents more affordable for many purposes. It is also usually cheaper to place an ad with spot color rather than process color. Publications usually charge more for process color.

The palette of colors used for spot color is called **Pantone**. The process of selecting colors is more complex and sophisticated, with seemingly infinite variables, than choosing them at a paint store. Each Pantone color has a unique number. In theory, every printer should be able to produce the same color. Aside from simple usage in layouts, precise use of color plays an important role in the branding of an institution. Many organizations, from universities to corporations, have adopted standard colors for their logos and other promotional materials. McDonald's uses Pantone gold PMS 123. The U.S. Government Printing Office specifies Pantone 186 and 288 for the red and blue colors used in the American flag.

Process color uses a combination of four colors—cyan, magenta, yellow and black—sometimes called CMYK. The four CMYK inks can create a full spectrum of color. Printers use this process for more expensive publications. Not only is the printing process itself more expensive, but the best process color requires better paper, which adds to the expense. Designers may manipulate the CMYK colors further to achieve many different visual effects.

*C*onclusion ▼

All of these design elements collide in an effort to draw attention to the content of a publication, a blog, a social media site or a website. The challenge for designers of printed pieces, from simple brochures and annual reports to large circulation newsletters and newspapers, is to create documents that have visual appeal and that effectively communicate content to achieve public relations objectives. Today, publications must compete for attention with video, animation, and dynamic graphics—media that move. How can print create visual excitement to compete with the video and animation of the Internet? It does so by understanding all forms of media and adapting visual effects to the uniqueness of those platforms. Certain design elements, notably banners, connect the aesthetic of print to all electronic media. The Old English banner for *The New York Times*, for example, has been branded as an app, using only the "T" from the Old English font. The respective font and letters "WP" serve as the app for *The Washington Post*. These examples represent the melding of old visual elements with new platforms.

Publishers and broadcasting companies use design elements to connect readers and viewers to supporting media platforms. It's part of today's media business model. The newspaper industry is suffering as advertising and readership shift to the Internet. As a result, publishers face cost-cutting measures such as reducing the width of the page, finding less expensive inks, and cutting employees. On the other side of the ledger, publishers are seeking new revenue streams from the Internet versions of publications and by creating new sections that will appeal to both readers and advertisers. Not lost in the discussion is how to make a two-dimensional product—a printed publication—more like the dynamic experience in the digital world, something that appeals to a new generation of readers. Many metropolitan newspapers are redesigning their publications with teases, label headings, larger photographs, mixed media, and more design elements that allow the eye to move quickly across or down a page. Designers are attempting to replicate the linking feature on websites by adding links that refer to galleries of photos and related stories on the Internet.

Consider what a wide, brightly colored ribbon does to an ordinary white box. That is what designers try to do with all sorts of printed materials. In a printed document, the words and pictures are static, but designers can have an effect on the way the eye moves across the page. It is possible through effective layout to influence how the eye moves from a heading to a photograph to a story—an attempt to replicate the visual experience of visitors to the Internet.

The approach is the same for a daily or a weekly publication as it is for an annual report or a single sheet that PR professionals will hand out at a trade show. Good design fosters readership, whether it's a publication, a blog or a website, but it must always complement the true strength of publications—content. Cosmetic changes that ignore content will appeal only to the creative side of the brain. They may do little to advance a message or stimulate thinking. Ultimately, well-composed photographs and informative, entertaining and well-written articles, headlines and captions will determine the success of a publication.

Printed materials are an important part of the work of public relations. They require careful thought and planning. Publishing is an art form, from conception to organizing content, to writing and designing in a way that is not only visually appealing but that also achieves desired objectives for a client.

Competition for public attention and the resulting clutter that we live with today make it ever more important that professionals effectively translate ideas into publications and digital media that are both well-written and visually engaging. For electronic media, the challenge is to transport viewers to content that is appealing and informative. For print media like newspapers the challenge is to compete with dynamic new technologies while retaining an experience that Marshall McLuhan compared to a warm, welcoming bath.

Review questions

1. Considering the various design elements discussed in this chapter, identify two newspapers, two television stations, and two Web sites and discuss why these media outlets attract your eye.
2. How do pull quotes and reversed type draw the reader's eye into media? Cite examples.
3. In terms of design, what attracts you to some media and not to others? What might you do in terms of design to stimulate interest in your least favorite medium?
4. Three inches are how many points? Picas?
5. What are the differences in making text legibility and text readability?

Supplemental resources online

www.marshallmcluhan.com	Official McLuhan website
http://www.creatingonline.com	Free webmaster resource
http://www.newseum.org/todaysfrontpages/default.asp	View daily front pages
http://www.mydesignprimer.com	Graphics basics
http://photography.nationalgeographic.com/photography	Superior examples
http://www.collegefrontpage.com/	Link to 264 college newspapers
http://www.newsdesigner.com/	Blog about newspaper design

Chapter references

42nd Publication Design Annual. The Society of Publication Designers. Rockport Publishers. (2007).

Branczyk, Alexander, Nachtwey, Jutta, Nehl, Heike, Schlach, Sibylle, & Siebert, Jurgen. (1999). *Emotional digital: A sourcebook of contemporary typo-graphics.* New York: Thames & Hudson.

Bringhurst, Robert. (2004). *The elements of typography style,* 3rd Edition. Vancouver, BC, Canada: Hartley and Marks Publishers.

The Society for News Design, 29th Edition. (2008). Rockport Publishers.

Wheildon, Colin. (2005). *Type & layout: Are you communicating or just making pretty shapes.* Mentone, Australia: The Worsley Press.

Notes

Name _____

Date _____

1. Measure the width of a newspaper front page, measure its width in inches, and subtract the space for margins and the space between the columns or gutters (1 pica). How wide is each column for a five-column format? State the answer in inches and in picas.

2. Study the way your eye moves down the page of a news publication. What elements draw your attention initially and then pull it down the page?

3. Scan your school newspaper and local community newspaper. How is the layout vertical? Horizontal? Modular? Open design? Explain.

4. Look at the way designers combine text with photographs and how they use headlines as a visual element.

5. Check with your university's communications office or website to find the PANTONE number used in logos.

Notes

chapter 11

PUBLIC RELATIONS LAW AND REGULATION

Many people feel intimidated when confronted with legal issues or topics. That feeling of trepidation is well placed. Legal problems can spell the end of an individual's employment or a company's existence. In a criminal context, they may result in loss of personal freedom or even death. In civil cases, thousands or even millions of dollars may be at stake.

Public relations practitioners must understand pertinent laws and regulations to reduce their exposure to lawsuits or to pursue protection for themselves and their clients. This is true whether an individual handles PR in-house for an organization or has employment with a PR firm or whether the organization is for profit or not for profit.

PR law involves not only standard business law but also a variety of First Amendment issues. Many of the laws and regulations are purposely vague; others are quite clear in their intent and meaning. What would a chapter on law be without a caveat? The information in this chapter should be taken as general legal knowledge, not as specific advice for a legal situation. Legal problems require a licensed lawyer who can provide the appropriate legal perspective and options.

Potential legal problems ▼

What sorts of problems might get a PR practitioner into trouble? Generally, one area would be errors of commission, those that come about through carelessness, recklessness or a lack of performance. For example, the spread of false information, in print or electronically, can become devastating financially or organizationally to a client. In addition, errors of omission can attract legal problems. A firm that fails to do what it promised to do, resulting in damaging problems, will suffer consequences. The vast majority of legal concerns in the public relations industry fall under the following categories:

- ▶ Defamation
- ▶ False and misleading claims
- ▶ Invasion of privacy
- ▶ Copyright violation
- ▶ Trademark infringement
- ▶ Violation of SEC regulations

First Amendment ▼

A good place to start an examination of journalism and public relations law is the First Amendment to the U.S. Constitution. It contains some of the most cherished rights in the United States. The first 10 amendments, collectively called the Bill of Rights, outline limits on government power. They serve to stop the government from infringing on the rights of American citizens.

The First Amendment, ratified in 1791, has never been altered or amended:

"Congress shall make no law respecting an establishment of religion, or prohibiting the free exercise thereof; or abridging the freedom of speech, or of the press; or the right of the people peaceably to assemble, and to petition the Government for a redress of grievances."

Most people are familiar with some of the five freedoms protected in the First Amendment, but they do not recall them all:

1. freedom of religion
2. freedom of speech
3. freedom of the press
4. right to peaceably assemble
5. right to petition the government

Historically, colonial Americans felt oppressed by the British government. The British tightly controlled the press through licensing printing presses. They also vigorously prosecuted speech that was critical of those in power. In the intervening years, oppressive governments all over the world have limited the right of their people to assemble, to criticize the government, to access a free press or, in some cases, to exercise freely their religious beliefs. In their grand democracy experiment, the founders of the United States sought to turn the monarchy on its head. Instead of all power in one person, the monarch, the founders gave ultimate power to the people.

This is why the Constitution calls for three branches of government: so that each one —executive, legislative, and judicial—serves as a check on the others. We know them as the three estates of power. However, the original 13 states were wary of placing too much power in a federal government. They worried they were creating another monarchy. Before some states would ratify the Constitution, they wanted assurances that the government would not oppress the people and the states.

In writing the Bill of Rights, the framers gave the people the power to hold government accountable and to change the leadership peacefully through regular elections. With freedom of speech, people could

openly criticize the government. With freedom of the press, the people could stay informed of government actions. The press, then, as the "fourth estate," would serve as a check on the three branches of government.

> *The press, then, as the "fourth estate," would serve as a check on the three branches of government.*

For journalists and public relations practitioners, the most important clause involves freedom of speech and press. In theory, this clause prevents the government from censoring free speech or a free press. The Amendment literally says *no law* may limit these freedoms. In practice, there are a number of laws that do limit speech and press rights. Over the years, the Supreme Court of the United States, the highest and, thus, the most powerful court in the country, has interpreted the freedoms guaranteed under the First Amendment repeatedly. The Supreme Court is the final arbiter when it comes to interpreting constitutional rights.

The First Amendment protects most of what a public relations professional says or releases to the media and the public. However, even though the wording of the First Amendment suggests that government may not infringe on those rights, it is important to note that a majority of the justices on the Supreme Court has never interpreted the First Amendment to be absolute. Indeed, there are a number of areas where Congress may make a law that abridges freedom of speech or of the press.

For example, the government may stop newspapers from publishing certain stories in the name of national security. In New York Times v. United States (403 U.S. 713, 1971), the Supreme Court ruled that President Richard Nixon could not stop The New York Times and The Washington Post from publishing the "Pentagon Papers," a collection of a classified government study about America's foreign policy with Vietnam. The papers proved embarrassing to the government because they outlined how the United States became engaged in the Vietnam War. They also included a frank assessment of U.S. foreign policy and revealed a number of occasions in which the U.S. government misled its citizens to maintain support for the war.

Nixon argued that publishing the papers would harm national security, but the Supreme Court ruled

THE WHITE HOUSE HISTORICAL ASSOCIATION (WHITE HOUSE COLLECTION)

that the government could not prove that the papers harmed national security, so they allowed the newspapers to continue publishing the top-secret study. Nevertheless, a majority of the Court said that the government may stop a newspaper from publishing information if there is harm to national security.

The following are other regulations and laws that limit freedoms of speech and press:

Fairness Doctrine

These three laws have imposed limits on First Amendment freedoms in broadcasting: the **Fairness Doctrine**, the **Personal Attack Rule** and the **Equal Time Rule**.

The Federal Communications Commission (FCC) adopted the Fairness Doctrine in 1949. It required broadcasters to provide balanced coverage of controversial issues and a reasonable opportunity for the presentation of contrasting views. The Doctrine was a reaction to one of the realities of early broadcasting: That there were a limited number of radio and television frequencies available. In theory, anyone with enough money can become a publisher and print a newspaper. In over-the-air broadcasting, however, there were a fixed number of channels available. Most communities had access to only a few radio and television stations. If the stations pursued a highly political agenda and only carried one side of controversial issues, that

would deny people in the community access to the information they might need to make informed decisions. The FCC imposed the Fairness Doctrine to guarantee that the few stations in each community were balanced in their treatment of controversial issues, giving each side a fair opportunity to present its point of view.

The Doctrine came under attack for many years. Evolving technology made possible the entry of more and more stations over the air and on cable and satellite systems. The limited access argument that justified the Fairness Doctrine became less defensible when there were many more voices available on electronic media. Viewers and listeners had choices. If someone did not like certain programming, he or she could simply change the channel. In 1987, the FCC formally abolished the Fairness Doctrine, calling it an infringement on the First Amendment rights of broadcasters.

The elimination of the Fairness Doctrine does not mean broadcasters do not have to be fair anymore. It does mean broadcasters have more leeway in what they put on the air. For PR practitioners, the demise of the Fairness Doctrine can sometimes make it more difficult for them to gain access to the airwaves to provide balance on controversial issues. If a news report or documentary were highly critical of a company, for example, the Fairness Doctrine would have made it relatively incumbent on a broadcaster to offer some airtime to the company for its point of view. Today, broadcasters no longer need to make those opportunities available. Many of them do, but there is no longer a Fairness Doctrine that requires it. Of course, practitioners have numerous opportunities to promote a position through various social media platforms, from blogs and social media to YouTube.

Personal Attack Rule

Closely related to the Fairness Doctrine was the Personal Attack Rule, which the FCC adopted in 1967. The rule said that when an attack occurred over the airwaves on the honesty, character or integrity of an individual, or a group during a broadcast about an issue of public importance, the broadcaster had to notify the attacked party and offer a reasonable opportunity to respond.

The rule applied to any personal attack at first. Later, it was narrowed to attacks that related only to issues of public concern. Over time, the FCC interpreted the rule more and more narrowly, until, in 2000, it rescinded it completely.

While both the Fairness Doctrine and the Personal Attack Rule are gone, their rescission does not mean broadcasters can attack people with impunity. Individuals and groups who are the subject of personal attacks on radio and TV can still seek remedy under defamation laws, discussed later in this chapter. Public relations practitioners who engage in media relations for associations, businesses, other groups or even political candidates keep their eyes and ears open to criticism against any of these parties as clients, much the way they do in tracking comments on social media, blogs or online bulletin boards. When opponents challenge remarks, stations can hardly ignore the public and usually will respond in some way.

Equal Time Rule

One rule the FCC has not repealed is the Equal Time Rule. This rule states that broadcasters must offer all candidates for a particular elected office equal time. If a station sells five minutes of airtime for commercials to candidate A, it must make a similar amount of time of comparable quality available to other candidates for the same office. If stations do a news story about one candidate, they are obliged to give similar coverage to that candidate's competitors.

In theory, the rule applies only if a broadcaster makes its airwaves available. A station could decide not to broadcast political commercials or to do news reports about candidates for a particular elected office. In that case, it would incur no obligation under the Equal Time Rule, with one exception. Federal law dating back to 1934 guarantees candidates for federal office the right to reasonable access to the airwaves. Stations cannot deny federal candidates access to their airwaves, and they must give competing candidates similar access under the Equal Time Rule.

The interpretation of the guarantee of equal time is very literal. This can become a problem for on-air personalities such as TV and movie stars, newscasters, and radio disc jockeys. A newscaster who runs for office, for example, must give up his or her on-air position during the election or the employing station will incur the obligation to give competitors in the election an equal amount of time. That is what happened to conservative political pundit Patrick Buchanan who had to give up hosting the CNN Crossfire show when he ran for president. When Arnold Schwarzenegger ran for governor in California, stations in California could not run his old movies for fear of incurring the

© RON SACHS/CNP/CORBIS

equal time liability. During the 2008 Republican primary campaign, when Fred Thompson was a candidate to be the Republican nominee for president, network and cable television stations were preparing to suspend broadcast of "Law & Order" episodes in which Thompson appeared as a recurring character.

Confidentiality ▼

The Code of Ethics of the Public Relations Society of America contains a provision requiring PR practitioners to protect confidential and private information. It would be an ethical violation for a PR professional to give a client's confidential information to one of its competitors. In many cases, PR professionals sign confidentiality agreements. When public relations firms learn all about clients, they have to ask questions that reveal strategic thinking and facts that will help them conduct desired public relations activity. The free flow of information boosts the creative work performed by public relations practitioners. Consider a grocer or a telephone company that needs public relations support for a certain goal. The PR firm needs to understand the client's role in the marketplace in order for the firm to perform at the highest levels and help its client reach its goals. Understood in the counseling relationship with clients is an agreement concerning confidentiality. Violating the confidentiality of an employer or client is both unethical and can subject a practitioner to legal action.

> **Most states define trade secrets as information not generally known by others and that has economic value that disclosure or use could compromise.**

If the confidential information qualifies as a trade secret or some other proprietary information, the liability may become even greater. Most states define trade secrets as information not generally known by others that has economic value that disclosure or use could compromise. Most states use similar language that provides additional protection for business secrets beyond what common law protects. Revealing new product specifications to a competitor before the launch of the product, for example, would incur substantial legal liability.

Consider the creative work that goes into the release of the latest electronic tablet or device or a more efficient fuel system in a hybrid vehicle. Any disclosure of information prior to the release of new products could jeopardize the effectiveness of the release or tip off the competition as to how companies create or market such products.

What about the disclosure of confidential information in a legal proceeding? *Privilege* protects some professions. Attorneys cannot compel lawyers, doctors and clergy, for example, to reveal confidential information in court. Physician-patient privilege protects doctors from having to reveal information obtained from conversations with patients. Qualified privilege may protect journalists from revealing sources or their notes, depending on the jurisdiction. These professionals have a protected relationship. However, the doctrine of privilege does not protect PR practitioners. The law can require them to disclose confidential information. If they refuse to do so, they can be cited for contempt of court, fined and even jailed.

Libel

One commits libel by damaging a person's reputation in the public eye. Traditionally, libel has referred to written defamation, while slander involved spoken defamation. Today, libel is the broader term and encompasses both written and spoken defamation. Defamation involves harming the reputation of a person or company with a false statement.

In a successful libel lawsuit, the following libel elements must be present and proven:

1. There was a written or oral communication that is false and harms the reputation of a person, company or product.
2. The communication identifies the intended victim.
3. The communication was disseminated to at least one other person other than the accused and the victim.
4. There was a level of fault, either actual malice or negligence, on the part of the accused.
5. There is proof of damages.

False statement

Defamation involves a false statement that harms a person's reputation. Accusing someone of murder or of having a contagious, loathsome disease are examples of defamation. Remember, to meet the first test of libel, the statement must be false, meaning that the person is not, in fact, a convicted murderer or infected with the disease.

There are two types of defamatory statements: **libel per se** and **libel per quod**. Libel per se means that the words themselves harm a person's reputation, such as falsely calling someone a murderer.

Libel per quod means that the harm to reputation is not so clear. The quintessential example of libel per quod happened in Fellows v. National Enquirer (42 C.3d 234, 1986), a California Supreme Court case involving a television producer and actress Angie Dickinson. The National Enquirer published a photograph of Arthur Fellows and Dickinson leaving a swanky Beverly Hills restaurant with the caption that read, "Angie Dickinson Dating a Producer." A brief two-sentence article referred to Fellows as Dickinson's "new man" that she was "steady-dating."

However, Fellows was not dating Dickinson, and he had been happily married to his wife, Phyllis, for

AP/WORLD WIDE PHOTOS

18 years. Someone who did not know that Fellows was married would not think that the publication harmed his reputation. However, someone who did know that he was married would likely think less of him for the implication that he was cheating on his wife. Therefore, libel per quod requires additional information before understanding the defamation, as in the Fellows case.

Identification

Identifying the intended victim is fairly straightforward: The person targeted by the defamatory statement must be identifiable so that people who hear or read the statement know to whom the statement refers. Identification usually happens by name or nickname. But, if the identification is very general in referring to the woman with the blue hat, for example, then it may not meet this test. Most people might not know to whom the defamatory statement refers. Or, if the statement is about a group that is so large—say all the police officers in a major metropolitan city—then the statement cannot reasonable be understood to apply to any particular police officer.

Publication

Communicating the defamatory statement is also pretty straightforward. The false statement must be published or broadcast so that people—other than the speaker and the victim—read, see or hear the defamatory statement. In cases involving the mass media, this is usually easy to show—a newspaper article, a television broadcast or a post on a Web site are all examples of "publication."

Though new technologies sometimes raise new legal questions, it is important to note that social media networks, such as Twitter and Facebook, are not immune to libel laws. Statements posted on networks like these easily meet the publication criteria and may be libelous if the other elements are proven.

Fault

The intended victim also needs to show that the defendant published or broadcast the statement with a level of fault. The key question is whether the defendant knowingly published a false statement that caused harm to the intended victim. There are two levels of fault: actual malice and negligence. The status of the intended victim determines what level of fault the victim must prove on the part of the defendant. For public figures, such as elected officials and celebrities and those who place themselves in the public eye, the level of fault that requires proving is actual malice.

In New York Times v. Sullivan (376 U.S. 254, 1964), the U.S. Supreme Court defined actual malice as knowingly publishing a false statement, or publishing it with reckless disregard for the truth. This is a difficult standard to prove, and it makes it harder for public officials and public figures to prevail in libel lawsuits against media defendants. In its opinion, the Court reasoned that American citizens rely on the First Amendment to criticize public officials. The Court ruled that allowing officials to prevail in libel suits too easily would limit free speech.

> *In New York Times v. Sullivan (376 U.S. 254, 1964), the U.S. Supreme Court defined actual malice as knowingly publishing a false statement, or publishing it with reckless disregard for the truth.*

Comedian Carol Burnett sued the National Enquirer for libel in 1981 (Burnett v. National Enquirer, 193 Cal. Rptr. 206), after the tabloid alleged public drunkenness purportedly with former Secretary of State Henry Kissinger. Burnett's parents suffered from alcoholism and thus the comedian/actress was sensitive to the allegation. The unprecedented $1.6 million verdict for Burnett in the landmark case subsequently got reduced and settled out of court.

What if the intended victim is not an elected official or public figure? For them, the Supreme Court ruled that the victim must prove that the media defendant acted with negligence. One is negligent if he or she does not act with reasonable or ordinary care. That means not acting in accord with sound journalism judgment such as not checking facts or striving for balance. Though not an easy standard, negligence is easier to prove than actual malice. Part of the Court's rationale for the easier standard is that the intended victims in these cases, people who are not elected officials and those who have not thrust themselves into the public spotlight, need more protection. This also serves as an incentive for media outlets to take extra care when reporting on private people.

Damages

The last element to prove is damages. The intended victim must show that the defamatory statement harmed the person's reputation. Many celebrities who have sued publications for libel have had their cases dismissed for failing to prove that the published falsehood damaged their reputations. It used to be that damages were presumed. If the victim could show the above elements, then monetary damages would be awarded. Now, in most cases, the victim must show that harm has occurred. How can a plaintiff show harm? Witnesses may testify that a plaintiff's reputation has deteriorated as a direct result of the defamatory publication.

There are several types of damages that could be involved in a libel case. *Actual damages,* the most common type of damages in a libel case, are those that the victim seeks to recover from loss of reputation or from mental anguish, to list two examples. Actual damages, also called general damages, are usually subjective and determined by a judge or jury, subject to certain statutory limitations. **Special damages** are those that have an exact monetary figure, such as medical bills. **Punitive damages** are "punishment" damages that a jury might add to the total damage award when a defendant's behavior is especially egregious. The purpose of punitive damages is to send a message to the defendant and anyone else that such behavior is not acceptable.

Libel defenses

There are three main defenses to a libel claim:

1. truth
2. privilege
3. fair comment and criticism

Truth is the strongest and most effective defense against a libel claim. If the statement about the person is true, then the libel case dissolves. Remember, a libel claim must involve a false statement about the intended victim. Without falsity, there is no actionable claim. In addition, the U.S. Supreme Court has ruled that plaintiff must prove that the statements in question were false. This provides an additional protection for news outlets since they do not have the burden of proving the statements true.

The second defense, privilege, is a bit more complicated. First, privilege refers to immunity from legal action. In some cases, privilege is said to be absolute. For example, executive privilege, often ruled absolute, covers communications between the president and advisers. This means that attorneys cannot subpoena either the president or the advisers to testify in court. Such communication is protected so that the president can consider a wide range of options without having the advisers worry later about revealing their discussions. Other examples of absolute privilege generally recognized by the law include attorney-client privilege (to protect all discussions between a lawyer and a client) and clergy privilege (to protect all communications between a person and his or her religious adviser).

The idea that reporters protect their sources is popular in mass media, but it is not a universal protection for journalists in the United States. Nearly 40 states, including Texas and the District of Columbia, have a shield law that protects news gatherers from testifying in civil or criminal cases, revealing their sources or handing over their notes and materials. However, there is no federal shield law. What this means is a judge may fine or send to jail a journalist who refuses to testify, to reveal a source, or to hand over notebooks. In recent years, Congress has considered a federal shield law for reporters, but no legislation has passed.

Public relations practitioners should be aware that even if an existing state shield law protects journalists, it does not protect them. No state protects PR practitioners in their shield laws. Clients periodically find themselves involved in legal actions that will have public relations consequences. To ensure such protections, sensitive conversations between executives and public relations advisers have occurred in the presence of corporate counsels to preserve the attorney-client privilege.

The third major defense to a libel claim is **fair comment** and criticism. The U.S. Supreme Court has long recognized the importance of a free press in a free and open democratic society, so it is reluctant to issue decisions that hamper or harm the press. In order for the public to make informed decisions about important issues, they rely on an independent press to hold government accountable and ask tough questions. Therefore, media relations advisers to public officials and public figures should expect fair comment and criticism about elected officials and celebrities.

In addition, the Court has also ruled that the First Amendment protects statements of opinion and that these cannot be the basis for libel claims. Libel involves statements that may be proven true or false, but one cannot prove an opinion true or false. For example, if a public relations adviser writes a guest column or letter to the editor, taking a position or defending one on behalf of a client, the fair comment and criticism defense would protect the writer. Of course, if a writer states that "in my opinion, the mayor is a murderer," when, in fact, the mayor has not been convicted of murder, then the fair comment and criticism defense would not protect that statement. The words "in my opinion" do not automatically protect the statement. It is important to differentiate between statements of opinion (such as, "She is a bad governor" or "He is a bad leader") and statements that make factual allegations that one can prove true or false. These examples are couched in language that looks like opinions, but are actually factual allegations that may be libelous: "In my opinion, he lied under oath" or "In my opinion, he killed his neighbor."

Public relations advisers pride themselves on being able to construct messages that are forceful, tough, challenging and civil in issuing criticism of something or someone. Fair comment and criticism is a protection that gives public relations firms great ammunition in serving their clients publicly.

Herbert v. Lando

Public relations practitioners should stay apprised of court rulings affecting libel and other communications issues. Actions involving media organizations are relevant to the public relations world, as PR firms assume responsibilities for producing electronic and print materials for a broad range of media with widespread audiences.

A significant libel case decided in 1979 made many journalists nervous because the U.S. Supreme Court ruled that there are limits to First Amendment protection.

In Herbert v. Lando (441 U.S. 153, 1979), Anthony Herbert was a retired Army officer who served in the Vietnam War. In the CBS news magazine show, "60 Minutes," Herbert accused his superior officers of committing atrocities and other war crimes related to a massacre of civilians.

However, when the show aired, Herbert was upset that Barry Lando, the producer and editor of the segment, left out portions of the interview that Herbert thought exonerated him. He therefore sued "60 Minutes" and Lando for defamation of character.

The case went to trial. Herbert's lawyers called journalist Mike Wallace and Lando to testify. Because Herbert was a public figure, he had to prove that Wallace and Lando acted with actual malice. In other words, he had to show that "60 Minutes" broadcast the edited interview knowing it was false, or that they did so with a reckless disregard for the truth.

Wallace and Lando refused to answer questions because they said it violated freedom of the press. Herbert's lawyers pressed the issue and appealed to the Supreme Court to compel the journalists to testify.

In a landmark ruling, the Supreme Court ruled that the First Amendment did not protect Wallace and Lando from testifying. As a plaintiff seeking state-of-mind evidence in an attempt to prove that the journalists acted with actual malice, Herbert had a right to question those journalists.

Wayne Overbeck, author of "Major Principles of Media Law," writes that the decision did not result in a significant change for media outlets. Journalists would still have to answer to discovery requests during a lawsuit just as they always had. However, Overbeck notes that the case provided a significant psychological impact on media defendants in libel cases. Following the Herbert decision, complying with discovery demands has become an increasing burden on journalists and media outlets.

Still, the significance of the ruling is not lost on journalists. The Supreme Court, in effect, ruled that journalists may not block questions about the editorial process in libel cases. Writing the Court's majority opinion, Justice Byron R. White ruled that allowing journalists to refuse to testify about editorial decisions would only add to plaintiffs' already substantial burden to prove actual malice. White reasoned that opening the door for a plaintiff to question journalists in this way would only affect journalism conducted with a reckless disregard for the truth, not honest journalism. In this way, White did not see the decision as a threat to freedom of the press.

What does this mean for PR practitioners? If a public relations firm issues a news release, or produces a video or a publication that libels someone, the agency could be at risk for a libel lawsuit. Any media outlet that publishes or broadcasts the release may also be held liable for the defamatory content. That is a good reason to be careful about what goes into news releases and other media products.

Privacy ▼

Privacy is a broad topic that encompasses a wide-range of legal issues, including the right to make intimate decisions about one's life. For example, a public relations practitioner working in a medical setting would

have to exercise care and seek permissions in writing about patients or procedures. Publicists work zealously to gain media attention for public figures, many of whom are in the spotlight in today's media-saturated society. The line between public and private life is one that the legal system will continue to review on a case-by-case basis. Yet, the courts have addressed privacy issues in many categories, among them:

▶ Appropriation
▶ Intrusion
▶ Disclosure of private facts
▶ False light

Appropriation

One aspect of privacy of particular concern to public relations practitioners is **appropriation**. Appropriation, or misappropriation, involves using someone's name, image, likeness or voice for commercial purposes without the person's permission. The idea of appropriation is said to be a right of publicity. A person has a right to benefit from lending his or her name or likeness to a product for commercial purposes.

This often arises with public figures and celebrities. For example, a person in the business of selling baseballs, gloves, and bats could certainly sell more products with a celebrity-athlete's name attached to them. New York Yankees third baseman Alex Rodriguez is a good example. Rodriguez has a right of publicity, a right to decide what products to endorse. So, how would one obtain that endorsement? It would likely involve a large

© WILLIAM PERLMAN/STAR LEDGER/CORBIS

In 1988, Bette Midler won a $400,000 award from Ford Motor Company for appropriation of her voice. Ford had secured permission to use Midler's hit song, "Do You Want to Dance?" but they also wanted her to sing in their car commercial. When she refused the offer, the automobile company then went to Midler's long-time backup singer and asked her to sing in the commercial, and to try to sound as much like Midler as possible. The U.S. Court of Appeals for the Ninth Circuit held in the decision that "when a distinctive voice of a professional singer is widely known and is deliberately imitated in order to sell a product, the sellers have appropriated what is not theirs…" The Court expanded the concept of appropriation to include the protection of one's distinctive voice. Also, the Court found that the public would likely think it was Midler singing in the commercial and the great potential for that confusion is why Ford lost. We should note that Ford did have permission to remake the song because they got permission from the copyright owner of the song (more on copyright later in this chapter).

The lesson for public relations is that we cannot use the images, likenesses and voices of people without their permission. It is always safest to have a signed agreement. Imitation in this case is not flattery; it could be appropriation of identity and result in substantial legal liability.

Intrusion

Other types of privacy claims may result in a civil lawsuit. They include intruding on a person's solitude or private affairs. Examples include trespassing, eavesdropping or using a hidden camera or recorder. If a person has a reasonable expectation of privacy—in a bathroom at home, for example—then any uninvited breach of that space would likely be an intrusion. Technological advances in surveillance equipment have given rise to a rash of privacy claims. Hidden cameras that capture images of unsuspecting women changing clothes in department stores or visiting restrooms have led to civil and criminal complaints.

Disclosure of private facts

Another privacy claim is the public **disclosure of private facts**. With libel, one is dealing with falsity, a false statement that harms someone's reputation. What happens when the statement is true? Is the plaintiff out of luck? No, in such a situation, a plaintiff could file a

monetary payment. Without his permission, however, the baseball equipment business would be in danger of being sued by Rodriguez for appropriation.

A dramatic example of a misappropriation case involves Russell Christoff and Nestle, the company that makes Taster's Choice coffee. In 1986, Christoff was a model who posed for some photos for Nestle. He received $250 for the photo shoot, and his contract specified future payments if Nestle used the images on its products. Christoff never heard from Nestle and assumed nothing had come from the photo shoot.

Then in 2002, a woman told Christoff that he looked just like the man sniffing a warm cup of coffee on the label of Taster's Choice package. Unfamiliar with the product, he sought it out on the shelves and recognized himself from the photo shoot nearly 16 years before.

A jury awarded him $15.6 million because Nestle had used an image of Christoff without his permission. After the trial, Nestle officials said they thought they had Christoff's consent to use the image. However, in 2007, a California appellate court limited the award to $330,000 in actual damages.

private facts claim under the idea that the information is not newsworthy and should not have received publicity. Examples include reporting that a private person has a certain medical condition that the person did not want revealed. It is difficult to predict what would constitute an embarrassing private fact, so the best protection is to ask two questions:

1. Is the information newsworthy?
2. Is it related to the public interest and the public's right to know?

One area of public relations where this might be relevant is informal, gossipy newsletters. It was once common practice for organizations to have chatty newsletters that encouraged familiarity among coworkers. Publishing and distributing embarrassing information might create a liability. Organizations that continue to do such newsletters generally now require a signed release from an employee before publishing private information.

False light

Another privacy claim is **false light** publicity, defined as placing someone in a false light in the public eye. An example is publishing a stock photograph of a street in a city that is notorious for prostitution. The photograph might randomly capture an individual whose inclusion inadvertently creates the impression that he was on the street to frequent the prostitutes discussed in the article. It creates a false impression. The publicity does not need to be negative—even if the publicity is positive, if it creates a false impression, then a false light lawsuit could follow.

In some states, false light is substantially similar to libel (a false statement about someone that harms his or her reputation), so the law does not recognize this type of claim as a privacy claim, but instead as a libel claim. In Texas, for example, courts have ruled that plaintiffs should file a false light claim as a libel claim.

Defenses to privacy

In general, there are two main defenses to privacy, newsworthiness and consent. Newsworthiness is a legal term that courts define broadly. Nearly anything that has to do with the public interest or is of public concern would be considered newsworthy. Suppose a newspaper published an article about a man who had Severe Acute Respiratory Syndrome (SARS), a highly

contagious disease. Later, the man might argue that the disclosure invaded his privacy. However, the newspaper would likely win with the argument that informing the public about the disease was of great public interest and concern and, therefore, newsworthy. Note, however, that a newsworthiness defense would not overcome civil and criminal trespassing charges. In most cases, the newsworthiness defense would arise in a private facts case.

Consent could apply to any of the privacy torts. If the media defendant can show it had the plaintiff's consent to publish or broadcast the information, then that might preclude a privacy lawsuit. Such actions most often come up in appropriation cases. The defendant argues that they had plaintiff's permission to use the image or likeness. Remember in the case involving Russell Christoff and Nestle, the coffee company thought they had Christoff's consent to use his image on their jars, but their mistake was costly.

Intellectual property ▼

Copyright

Copyright and trademark fall under an area of law called **intellectual property**. **Copyright** is meant to protect creative works so that the creator may benefit from his or her hard work. In fact, copyright law has a long American tradition. The original U.S. Constitution included a provision granting Congress the power to protect creative works through copyright.

While copyright law has changed significantly since the founding of the United States, the Copyright Act of 1976 is the basis of modern copyright law. Even so, the innovations in digital technology have exceeded

the limits of copyright law, and some legal scholars predict that a sea change in copyright law is imminent.

The purpose of copyright is twofold—to protect creative works and to encourage innovation so that society benefits. We can copyright many things, including books, movies, poems, photographs, songs, videos, computer software, newspapers and Web sites.

Copyright law protects works that are "fixed in any tangible medium of expression." Work printed so that others can read it, or displayed on a screen so that people can view it, are examples of tangible works. There are, however, limits to copyright. It does not protect ideas or history. For example, if a major earthquake claimed many lives and destroyed a city, a media outlet that reports on the disaster may copyright its account of the disaster. Copyright cannot protect the details of the disaster, such as the number of people killed and the amount of property destroyed.

Copyright notices usually occur at the beginning of a book and include this symbol: ©. This means it is a protected work, and one must obtain permission to use any part of the work. Getting permission often involves payment or a portion of the profits of the new work.

Another example of copyrighted work relates to sporting events. At some point during the broadcast of a baseball game, announcers will inform the audience that Major League Baseball requires permission to rebroadcast or duplicate the images and accounts of the game. This is true of the other major professional sports as well.

Public relations practitioners work hard to come up with promotional themes for campaigns, new products, or a company's services. They must use great care in making sure that promotional themes are not someone else's property. PR firms also will want to advise clients concerning what creative work from public relations and advertising efforts copyright should protect.

Another copyright issue is the duplication of the works of others as part of a marketing effort. An automobile dealer might be excited to see an article in a national magazine that extols the virtues of a car model handled by the dealership. The dealer decides to reproduce the article and put copies on the showroom floor for prospective customers. This would be a copyright violation if the dealership did not obtain permission to duplicate the article, which almost certainly would have involved some expense.

Fair Use Doctrine

There are some exceptions to copyright law that allow for use of copyrighted material without the permission of the copyright owner. The main exception involves what is called the Fair Use Doctrine. The Fair Use Defense, the most common defense in copyright cases, is difficult to define. In the 1976 Copyright Act, the Fair Use Defense was defined as involving four criteria:

1. The purpose and character of the use: whether the use is for profit or nonprofit.
2. The nature of the copyrighted work: whether the use is fictional or factual. Courts have tended to protect fictional works more than factual ones.
3. The amount of the copyrighted work that is used: whether a substantial part of the entire work is used. The greater the percentage of the work that is used, the lesser the possibility that it would qualify as a fair use. In addition to amount, courts review what was used. If the portion used is the most important part of the work, then its use without permission may not be a fair use.
4. The potential impact on the profit-making ability of the original work: whether the new work decreases the value of the original work. If the new work is offered for "free," and sales of the original work drop, then it is likely that fair use would not apply.

Scholars, publishers, and teachers often rely on a fair use argument when they use copyrighted material, without permission, in the classroom, in research articles or in written accounts.

In recent years, a movement to reconcile changes in technology with copyright law that predates digital technology has gained momentum. Because digital technology makes it virtually impossible to distinguish between an original work and a copy, some argue that copyright law is ill suited to handle issues involving file-sharing and digital copies.

A nonprofit organization, Creative Commons, is encouraging creators to consider an alternative to copyright law. Under traditional copyright law, a copyright owner has the exclusive right to a work, and every time someone wants to use it or alter it he or she must seek permission. Under the Creative Commons model, creators would retain some rights but allow anyone to use the works under certain conditions. For example, a rock and roll band would allow anyone to use part or most of its song without permission, so long the band is credited and the new work is not created for profit. Such works would be marked with a symbol similar to the copyright symbol, but instead of one "C" in a circle, it would have "CC" in a circle, and "Some rights reserved."

Creative Commons also provides for creators who do not want to reserve any rights over the work. The symbol for that is the same as above with "No rights reserved." This means that anyone may use the work for any purpose, whether for profit or not.

The founders of Creative Commons argue that this alternative is needed to encourage creativity and avoid legal liability under current copyright law.

Photographs

With so much material available online, it is tempting to grab images and other content from websites, but much of that information is copyrighted and using it without permission is illegal. PR people should take extra care that the information they disseminate is original or that they have permission to use it.

Sometimes a user slightly alters copyright material, such as digital photographs, and argues that the altered work is new and different from the original copyrighted photograph. The courts have frowned on such arguments. If, however, the person uses the altered material for satire or parody, then courts have ruled that such use may be a fair use. Courts recognize a First Amendment right of free speech and expression when people use copyrighted works for social commentary. The court is less likely to find a fair use when people alter the works for commercial purposes.

SOPA and PROTECT IP Act

In late 2011, Congress considered two legislative proposals that would have altered how we interact with the Internet every day. The two bills—Stop Online Privacy Act and the Preventing Real Online Threats to Economic Creativity and Theft of Intellectual Property Act—would have given unprecedented power to corporations to shut down websites suspected of providing copyrighted material without authorization. In January 2012, many online advocates were alarmed by these measures and held a day of protest on the Internet. Some major web companies, such as Google, WordPress, Mozilla and Wikipedia, joined in the protest on Jan. 18, 2012, by informing web users of their position and, in some cases, blocking access to their online content for 12 to 24 hours.

After the mass online protest, Congress tabled these bills, effectively killing them. But intellectual property and online experts warn that even though SOPA and PIPA appear dead, other similar bills may soon be proposed.

Trademark

A trademark is a word, name, symbol or design used to identify business products. Advertisers use trademarks to clearly identify products and avoid confusion with similar products.

Trademarks are customarily accompanied by this symbol: ™. Examples include the Honda "H" on its automobiles and the "N" on New Balance shoes. The trademark covers the distinctive style of these letters, not the letters themselves. In other words, the stylized letters are recognized and associated with the brand. Words, logos, slogans, and most everything else associated with branding falls under trademark. The symbol

IMAGE © PEDRO TALENS MASSIP, 2009. USED UNDER LICENSE FROM SHUTTERSTOCK, INC.

®, can also identify trademarks. It means that the trademark is registered with the U.S. Patent and Trademark Office. The symbol SM identifies service marks, which protect a service that a company provides.

Interestingly, the courts have ruled that a competitor may use trademarks, such as in an advertisement, without permission. For example, in soft drink advertisements that purport to be taste tests with regular people, the participants choose the product of the company putting on the advertisement. Does Pepsi, for example, have to get permission to use the name and trademark of Coca-Cola? Did the authors of this book have to get permission to use Pepsi and Coca-Cola in this sentence? The answer to both questions is the same: No. The First Amendment permits some use of a trademark, courts have ruled, so long as there is no altering of the trademark.

Corporations spend considerable time, effort, and money protecting their trademarks. Xerox, for example, is ever vigilant about protecting its name and making sure that others use the name properly—as a noun. Therefore, when they see inappropriate references to their company—such as referring to making copies as "Xeroxing"—they send letters admonishing the offender. Xerox also places advertisements in trade publications to show they are defending their brand name and trademark.

"The Associated Press Stylebook" discourages reporters from using a trademarked word unless it is essential to the story. For instance, if the story involves a Dumpster, a large, metal trash bin, the reporter should use the trademark term only if such use is necessary for the story. If not, he or she should use the generic term—large, metal trash bin. The Stylebook substitutes real estate agent for Realtor, which is not a generic word for people who sell land and is a trademark for a licensed member of the National Association of Realtors. PR writers should refer to the Stylebook for guidance in using trademarks.

Some companies have lost trademarks, in part, because they failed to vigorously defend them. For example, aspirin, trampoline, and zipper were all protected trademarks until they fell into common use and could no longer receive protection as trademarks.

A good resource for checking on current and lapsed trademarks is the International Trademark Association (inta.org). Composed of trademark owners around the world, the nonprofit organization maintains a list of trademarks on their Web site and words that have fallen into the public domain.

Protecting material

PR professionals create proposals that involve logos, themes, jingles, ads, reports, campaign plans, and other PR work products. Practitioners are concerned about losing ownership of their creative ideas as, for example, when a PR firm makes a proposal to land a new client. The proposal includes elaborate materials complete with logos, layouts, slogans, and research. If the potential client declines the firm and takes its ideas to another PR firm, is the original firm out of luck?

Maybe—but one way to protect ideas is to put a copyright notice on proposals. Using the traditional copyright symbol, ©, with the year and name of the copyright owner serves notice of a claim to ownership of the materials. One can use them only by permission. As a practical matter, materials become copyrighted as soon as they are put to paper (or on the computer screen), but the copyright symbol informs everyone of ownership and may help discourage unauthorized use.

> *Using the traditional copyright symbol, ©, with the year and name of the copyright owner serves notice of a claim to ownership of the materials.*

It is important to note that copyright protects only the particular expression of ideas, not the ideas themselves. Therefore, even though a proposal has a copyright, the copyright probably will not prevent a prospective client from taking the ideas. Images and designs, specific text and other permanent expressions of the ideas can receive protection. The thinking cannot.

Another way to prevent the giveaway of ideas is by changing proposals from a focus on the creative aspects of the plan to the firm's capability and experience. By focusing on why a firm is the best public relations practitioner for the client's needs, the firm will not waste valuable resources and time on creative proposals for clients they may not win. However, if a client does sign with a firm, then the work the firm pours into creating a creative plan belongs to the client anyway.

Securities and Exchange Commission

The Securities and Exchange Commission, a federal agency, has the charge of regulating the financial industries. They review and regulate publicly traded companies to ensure that the companies' practices are not misleading. This is a complex area of law that has seen significant changes in recent years. Public relations practitioners need to become familiar with regulations that relate to corporate communications, including:

▶ Timely disclosure
▶ Insider trading
▶ Quiet registration period

Timely disclosure

Companies that sell securities are required to make timely disclosures to the public. The disclosures must be done in a way that give investors time to make important investment decisions. Further, the disclosures must be released to everyone—investors, analysts, the public, and others. Public relations professionals who specialize in investor relations should be very careful about when and how they release documents. PR firms often get involved in creating annual reports and planning annual meetings. Legal departments or outside counsel and accounting firms become involved in documentation dealing with financial and other corporate moves during the year. Public relations professionals help to create readable and visually appealing annual reports for corporations, which often take on the appearance of glossy magazines. Annual reports can boast about the past successes of a company but should not make statements that allude to the future success of the company. Such information could be construed as a prediction of future performance. SEC regulators disallow such statements because they can significantly affect the value of a stock based on information about future events that is still speculative.

Insider trading

Timely disclosures are necessary because of insider trading. Insider trading occurs when someone who has access to information that is not publicly available acts on that information to sell stock, often for great profit.

The SEC focused on homemaker guru Martha Stewart after she sold nearly 4,000 shares of a stock that dropped significantly in value the following day. By selling while the stock still had its value, federal prosecutors said she profited by some $45,000. Prosecutors accused her of benefiting from an illegal insider tip that the stock's value was about to plummet and it would be a good time to sell. In a highly publicized trial, a federal jury found Stewart guilty of conspiracy, obstruction, and lying to investigators. She served five months in a federal prison.

Quiet registration period

A third area of regulation that PR professionals must understand is the **quiet registration period**. This time period begins after a company makes a new securities offering, but it occurs before the registration with the SEC has become effective. During that time, the company cannot issue any written communication to sell securities, except for a preliminary prospectus. For PR practitioners, the danger is releasing information that would generate publicity for an upcoming securities offering. Again, companies must avoid communications that would suggest a company's future performance.

Historically, the release of information about future products, profits and other business changes have manipulated stock prices. The SEC's goal is to minimize such manipulation by emphasizing factual, historical information and by releasing information to everyone at the same time, rather than by allowing a few people to gain insights ahead of everyone else and profiting from them.

In terms of public policy, meaning what is best for the public welfare, actions based on speculation can become disruptive to financial markets. Journalists and public relations officials must also be careful about reporting on banking and investment issues. Reporting based on rumors and speculation concerning the financial industries has historically led to runs on the banks. Words that spark fear among consumers have and can prompt people to withdraw funds from banks, leaving the banks with a huge imbalance in handling bank business. It can also cause people to buy and sell stock, causing dramatic inflation or deflation of stock prices. Any information that sparks fear can prompt countless consumers to act in a manner that adversely affects the life of a company and, consequently, the welfare of its employees. The markets have experienced such havoc in the past, which prompted the regulatory efforts of the SEC and other federal agencies.

Financial communications can be a complicated area. PR practitioners should become familiar with the regulations to avoid legal problems. A useful guide is a government publication titled, "A Plain English Handbook: How to create clear SEC disclosure documents" (available free at www.sec.gov/news/extra/handbook.htm).

Sarbanes-Oxley

One final topic relating to financial communications is the Sarbanes-Oxley Act of 2002, which became law in the wake of several securities scandals. After the collapse of corporate giants such as Enron and WorldCom, Congress acted to help restore confidence in the securities markets. Sarbanes-Oxley requires corporate executives to certify personally the accuracy of financial reports. Public relations practitioners should be aware that corporate executives are exceptionally interested in the corporate documents coming out of the investor relations departments, since the executives now have personal liability if the documents are in error.

Sarbanes-Oxley was designed to help prevent another Enron, but there is some debate whether the new regulations are effective. Business Week reported in 2005 that compliance with all of the requirements of Sarbanes-Oxley costs large corporations an average of $35 million a year.

Conflicting advice from PR and legal counselors ▼

PR spokespersons often find themselves in a tough spot, especially during a company crisis. Management may receive legal advice that tells them to take a tightlipped approach. Sometimes, this legal advice is appropriate, especially if it involves a criminal investigation or a potentially large fine. Crisis management was discussed earlier in this book, with emphasis on the impact of crises on reputations and brands. The focus here is on the conflicting advice that might be forthcoming from legal and public relations counselors.

In the face of a crisis, a demanding press and public want to know what happened, and fast. Some companies handle controversies well; others fail miserably. The companies that handle conflict well tend to lean on the side of admitting mistakes and telling the truth.

Public relations problems arise or become exacerbated when companies shy away from the truth or misinform or flat out lie to the public. Many public relations practitioners would agree that honesty is the best policy. When troubles head toward the courtroom, lawyers and public relations officials agree that information is best reserved for hearings or trials over having matters played out in the press, in the court of public opinion.

PR advisers, legal counsel, and company management should explore the ramifications of sharing information with the public or through the media. Media relations seeks to cultivate relationships with all forms of media and to help reporters understand a company's business. Legal counsel advises companies about legal issues, some of which involve public disclosure. PR advisers are in the better position to read a situation as to how it will play in the media. Sometimes PR and legal advisers disagree, and legal counsel will prevail, leaving PR officials to manage the situation with the press. PR specialists and legal counsel both work to represent the best interest of the company or client.

Recent history is filled with examples of managing a legal and public relations crisis simultaneously. O'Dwyer's, an online and print news outlet that covers the PR industry, identified the top public relations blunders in 2011. These blunders have proven costly because they received lots of negative publicity and turned public opinion against these institutions and individuals.

For example, when allegations of sexual harassment by Republican presidential candidate Herman Cain surfaced, he and his staff were unprepared and evasive. Worse, rather than answering questions directly, Cain pointed fingers elsewhere, accusing other campaigns of trying to smear him. Soon thereafter, Cain suspended his campaign and fell out of the race.

Another example involved accusations of sexual abuse by former Penn State assistant football coach Jerry Sandusky. The university's poorly planned response seemed to be an attempt to justify why administrators had done nothing about the allegations, despite knowing about them for more than 10 years. As Sandusky's case proceeds through the criminal justice system, Penn State's image has been badly damaged.

What is the lesson in all of this? Sometimes, the best way to deal with a PR nightmare is head on and with the truth. A public statement may not be the best legal strategy. In fact, it may conflict with the legal strategy, but winning the public opinion battle may be the more effective strategy. Eric Dezenhall, author of "Damage Control," says that both lawyers and public relations counselors are right within the context of their disciplines when they give advice. Ultimately, he says, it is up to the chief crisis officer in the organization, who is usually the chief executive officer, "to determine where along the silence-openness continuum public statements must fall."

Those who find themselves in the middle of a crisis might consider practicing **mea culpa**, a Latin term meaning "my fault" or "the fault is mine." Sometimes the best strategy in a crisis is to accept responsibility quickly and honestly when you do indeed have some responsibility for the problem. It can act as a highly effective form of damage control. Polls show that Americans are remarkably willing to forgive people who make mistakes and who appear genuine in their expressions of regret.

Eric Dezenhall says mea culpa works best "when the behavior in question is viewed as aberrant versus revelatory." If people view the incident as aberrant, meaning isolated, they are more likely to forgive.

If, on the other hand, there is a pattern of misbehavior, denials and evasion, then the law is more likely to see the mea culpa as revelatory; it reveals more about the character of an individual or institution. The media and public are less forgiving of attempts to hide behind mea culpa.

Dezenhall says that some crises are archetypal narratives. There is "a vulnerable victim pitted against an arrogant or incompetent villain." The victim suffers, and the villain purposely caused the suffering or did little to stop it. Such a narrative makes for a great story. Corporations are easy to tag as villains. Victims are easy to find, too, whether they suffered directly or more indirectly, like baseball fans disillusioned by the steroid use of athletes they admire. Mea culpa works best, according to Dezenhall, under these circumstances:

1. When the client has clearly done something wrong. "Fix the problem, explain your actions, apologize, and make amends."
2. Early in the controversy. It is hard to make amends after months of denials and verbal warfare. The key, Dezenhall says, is to mea culpa soon enough to have an impact. Late in the day confessions ring hollow.
3. When the issue is not worth fighting for. Pick your battles. Some battles are not worth spending a lot time, money, and good will on.
4. When the client does not have the fight in them. Dezenhall says, "You can't turn Bambi into Rambo." Mea culpa if you do not have the will and resources to fight an extended battle in the court of public opinion, with the media, and of course within the judicial system.

When mea culpa is not an option, clients need to listen carefully to the advice of lawyers because the most important audiences they may now need to persuade are judges and juries. Having failed to exit gracefully from a crisis, it is now time to prepare a strong legal defense.

Review questions

1. What are the five essential freedoms guaranteed by the First Amendment?
2. Which institution ultimately decides Constitutional issues?
3. Describe the circumstances and give examples in which a professional may legally refuse to reveal information in a court proceeding. Are PR practitioners protected by such a privilege?
4. What are the elements of libel? What are the main defenses to libel?
5. What are the four legal claims that fall broadly under privacy?
6. What are the two main defenses to privacy?
7. What is the purpose of copyright?
8. Name a significant exception to copyright law and give examples when the exception may apply.
9. What is Creative Commons and how is it different from traditional copyright law?
10. What is trademark?
11. Why did Martha Stewart gain the attention of the SEC? What happened in her case?

Supplemental resources online

http://www.apstylebook.com	Associated Press Stylebook
http://www.creativecommons.org	Creative Commons
http://www.findlaw.com	FindLaw
http://www.inta.org	International Trademark Association
http://www.soxalw.com	Sarbanes-Oxley Act of 2002
http://www.sec.gov	Securities and Exchange Commission
http://www.supremecourtus.gov	The Supreme Court of the United States
http://www.oyez.org	United States Supreme Court Media

Chapter references

Bagin, Don, & Fulginiti, Anthony. (2005). *Practical Public Relations: Theories and techniques that make a difference.* Dubuque, Ia: Kendall/Hunt Publishing.

Black, Henry Campbell. (1990). *Black's Law Dictionary.* St. Paul, Minn.: West.

Dezenhall, Eric, & Weber, John. (2007). *Damage control: Why everything you know about crisis management is wrong.* New York: Penguin Books.

Christian, Darrell, Sally Jacobsen and David Minthorn. (2011). *The Associated Press Stylebook and Briefing on Media Law.* New York: Basic Books.

Fineman, Michael. "Penn State, Herman Cain, Oakland top 2011 PR blunders." (January 2012). *O'Dwyer's.* (www.odwyerpr.com)

"Model finds coffee label looks familiar: It's him!" (2005, Feb. 2). *Chicago Sun-Times,* 4.

Overbeck, Wayne. (2007). *Major Principles of Media Law.* Belmont, Calif.: Thomson Wadsworth.

Trager, Robert, Russomanno, Joseph, & Dente Ross, Susan. (2011). *The Law of Journalism & Mass Communication.* New York: McGraw-Hill.

Notes

chapter 12

ETHICS AND SOCIAL CRITICISM

Public relations is all about conveying information between organizations and target audiences. Its practitioners are zealous about setting and implementing strategies. Creativity and imagination are boundless when devising plans to help clients meet goals. Are there, however, limits to what should be done to reach a goal? How far does one push the boundaries? When does the desire to win become "winning at all costs?"

In Chapter 11, the focus was on some of the legal issues that PR practitioners grapple with every day. The focus of this chapter is on **ethics**, professional responsibility and the role that individual practitioners play in elevating the status and reputation of the profession.

P. T. Barnum used flashy showmanship to entice and attract attention. Sometimes his promotions achieved success through extreme exaggeration. Success came at the expense of truth. He was a masterful publicist, but his behavior has forever tainted public relations with questions about its ethics.

When the public sees manipulation or management of the truth, particularly in politics, international relations or business matters, they tend to question the ethics of the public relations profession. Most public relations practitioners do not resort to half-truths or lies to do their jobs. These professionals apply ethical codes to guide their conduct.

What is the value of an ethical code? In her book, "Ethics in Public Relations: A Guide to Best Practices," Patricia J. Parsons defined public relations ethics as "the application of knowledge, understanding and reasoning to questions of right or wrong behavior in the professional practice of public relations." Parsons writes that the public relations field has a strong need for honesty because PR history has shown that "honesty has not always been part of that image."

An examination of ethics also involves understanding morality—doing the right thing, making the right choice. To whom should practitioners feel obliged to practice this morality?

In "Media Ethics: Cases and Moral Reasoning," the authors outline five categories of obligation:

1. Duty to ourselves;
2. Duty to clients/subscribers/supporters;
3. Duty to our organization;
4. Duty to professional colleagues; and
5. Duty to society

These duties may seem self-evident, but the most difficult ethical dilemmas usually include a conflict between them. For example, suppose a client instructs a PR practitioner to release information he or she knows is untruthful. The practitioner can argue that such a directive would violate all of the duties, but refusing to carry out the client's instruction may at the very least threaten his or her job or the retention of the client, the duty to self and the duty to a client. Assuming the most strident commands, a public relations practitioner likely would refuse to carry out the directive. Such a decision might cost an individual a job or a PR firm an entire client. Yet, the individual and the PR firm would have upheld its ethical standards and those of a profession.

Public Relations Society of America ▼

The need to promote professional and ethical standards for public relations led to the creation of the Public Relations Society of America in 1947. Soon, thereafter,

◄ *P. T. Barnum, 1810–1881*

Member Statement of Professional Values
Public Relations Society of America

This statement presents the core values of PRSA members and, more broadly, of the public relations profession. These values provide the foundation for the Member Code of Ethics and set the industry standard for the professional practice of public relations. These values are the fundamental beliefs that guide our behaviors and decision-making process. We believe our professional values are vital to the integrity of the profession as a whole.

ADVOCACY

We serve the public interest by acting as responsible advocates for those we represent. We provide a voice in the marketplace of ideas, facts, and viewpoints to aid informed public debate.

HONESTY

We adhere to the highest standards of accuracy and truth in advancing the interests of those we represent and in communicating with the public.

EXPERTISE

We acquire and responsibly use specialized knowledge and experience. We advance the profession through continued professional development, research, and education. We build mutual understanding, credibility, and relationships among a wide array of institutions and audiences.

INDEPENDENCE

We provide objective counsel to those we represent. We are accountable for our actions.

LOYALTY

We are faithful to those we represent, while honoring our obligation to serve the public interest.

FAIRNESS

We deal fairly with clients, employers, competitors, peers, vendors, the media, and the general public. We respect all opinions and support the right of free expression.

prsa.org

PRSA adopted a code of ethics that it has periodically updated and revised, most recently in 2000.

The PRSA Code Provisions of Conduct outlines six core principles, including the intent behind each of the principles (www.prsa.org/AboutPRSA/Ethics/CodeEnglish/). There are also guidelines for members to follow and examples of violations. The six principles are:

1. Free flow of information
2. Competition
3. Disclosure of information
4. Safeguarding confidences
5. Conflicts of interest
6. Enhancing the profession

> *Protecting and advancing the free flow of accurate and truthful information is essential to serving the public interest and contributing to informed decision making in a democratic society.*

Free flow of information

Potecting and advancing the free flow of accurate and truthful information is essential to serving the public interest and contributing to informed decision making in a democratic society.

Intent

- ► To maintain the integrity of relationships with the media, government officials and the public.
- ► To aid informed decision making.

Guidelines

A member shall:

- ► Preserve the integrity of the process of communication.
- ► Be honest and accurate in all communications.
- ► Act promptly to correct erroneous communications for which the practitioner is responsible.
- ► Preserve the free flow of unprejudiced information when giving or receiving gifts by ensuring that gifts are nominal, legal, and infrequent.

> **Be honest and accurate in all communications.**

Examples of Improper Conduct Under this Provision

- ► A member representing a ski manufacturer gives a pair of expensive racing skis to a sports magazine columnist, to influence the columnist to write favorable articles about the product.

    A member entertains a government official beyond legal limits and/or in violation of government reporting requirements.

Competition

Promoting healthy and fair competition among professionals preserves an ethical climate while fostering a robust business environment.

Intent

- ► To promote respect and fair competition among public relations professionals.
- ► To serve the public interest by providing the widest choice of practitioner options.

Guidelines

A member shall:

- ► Follow ethical hiring practices designed to respect free and open competition without deliberately undermining a competitor.
- ► Preserve intellectual property rights in the marketplace.

Examples of Improper Conduct Under This Provision

- ► A member employed by a "client organization" shares helpful information with a counseling firm that is competing with others for the organization's business.
- ► A member spreads malicious and unfounded rumors about a competitor in order to alienate the competitor's clients and employees in a ploy to recruit people and business.

Disclosure of information

Open communication fosters informed decision making in a democratic society.

Intent

- ► To build trust with the public by revealing all information needed for responsible decision making.

Guidelines

A member shall:

- ► Be honest and accurate in all communications.
- ► Act promptly to correct erroneous communications for which the member is responsible.
- ► Investigate the truthfulness and accuracy of information released on behalf of those represented.
- ► Reveal the sponsors for causes and interests represented.
- ► Disclose financial interest (such as stock ownership) in a client's organization.
- ► Avoid deceptive practices.

> **Avoid deceptive practices. PRSA Code**

Examples of Improper Conduct Under this Provision

▶ Front groups: A member implements "grass roots" campaigns or letter-writing campaigns to legislators on behalf of undisclosed or temporary interest groups.

▶ Lying by omission: A practitioner for a corporation knowingly fails to release financial information, giving a misleading impression of the corporation's performance.

▶ A member discovers inaccurate information disseminated via a Web site or media kit and does not correct the information.

▶ A member deceives the public by employing people to pose as volunteers to speak at public hearings and participate in "grass roots" campaigns.

Safeguarding confidences

Client trust requires appropriate protection of confidential and private information.

Intent

▶ To protect the privacy rights of clients, organizations and individuals by safeguarding confidential information.

Guidelines

A member shall:

▶ Safeguard the confidences and privacy rights of present, former, and prospective clients and employees.

▶ Protect privileged, confidential, or insider information gained from a client or organization.

▶ Immediately advise an appropriate authority if a member discovers that confidential information is being divulged by an employee of a client company or organization.

Examples of Improper Conduct Under This Provision

▶ A member changes jobs, takes confidential information and uses that information in the new position to the detriment of the former employer.

▶ A member intentionally leaks proprietary information to the detriment of some other party

Conflicts of interest

Avoiding real, potential or perceived conflicts of interest builds the trust of clients, employers and the publics.

Intent

▶ To earn trust and mutual respect with clients or employers.

▶ To build trust with the public by avoiding or ending situations that put one's personal or professional interests in conflict with society's interests.

Guidelines

A member shall:

▶ Act in the best interests of the client or employer, even subordinating the member's personal interests.

▶ Avoid actions and circumstances that may appear to compromise good business judgment or create a conflict between personal and professional interests.

▶ Disclose promptly any existing or potential conflict of interest to affected clients or organizations.

▶ Encourage clients and customers to determine if a conflict exists after notifying all affected parties.

Examples of Improper Conduct Under This Provision

▶ The member fails to disclose that he or she has a strong financial interest in a client's chief competitor.

▶ The member represents a "competitor company" or a "conflicting interest" without informing a prospective client.

Enhancing the profession

Public relations professionals work constantly to strengthen the public's trust in the profession.

Intent

▶ To build respect and credibility with the public for the profession of public relations.

▶ To improve, adapt and expand professional practices.

Guidelines

A member shall:

▶ Acknowledge that there is an obligation to protect and enhance the profession.

▶ Keep informed and educated about practices in the profession to ensure ethical conduct.

▶ Actively pursue personal professional development.
▶ Decline representation of clients or organizations that urge or require actions contrary to this Code.
▶ Accurately define what public relations activities can accomplish.
▶ Counsel subordinates in proper ethical decision making.
▶ Require that subordinates adhere to the ethical requirements of the Code.
▶ Report ethical violations, whether committed by PRSA members or not, to the appropriate authority

> *Decline representation of clients or organizations that urge or require actions contrary to this Code.*

Examples of Improper Conduct Under This Provision

▶ A PRSA member declares publicly that a product the client sells is safe, without disclosing evidence to the contrary.
▶ A member initially assigns some questionable client work to a non-member practitioner to avoid the ethical obligation of PRSA membership.

Violation of the PRSA Code

The organization may expel violators of the PRSA code, but PRSA has no legal authority and virtually no one has ever been disciplined. Further, PRSA can only discipline its own members, who represent less than 10 percent of PR practitioners. The Bureau of Labor Statistics estimated that there were 320,000 full-time PR practitioners in 2010, some 21,000 of whom are members of PRSA. The enforcement of the Code is so weak that when the PRSA revised the Code in 2000 it de-emphasized enforcement in favor of promoting education and understanding the provisions.

Licensing

PR pioneer Edward Bernays campaigned throughout his long life for the state licensing of public relations professionals. He believed that the only way to elevate the status of PR practitioners to the recognized status of "professionals," like doctors and lawyers, was to have a comparable system for licensing them. Licensing, he thought, would guarantee that professionals had a minimal level of education. It would also force them to behave in an ethical manner or face expulsion from the profession.

No state today requires licensure of PR professionals, nor has any ever required it. Interestingly, Puerto Rico introduced licensure for PR professionals in 2010. The requirements include a university degree related to public relations, two years of experience and accreditation from the Public Relations Society of America.

PRSA Code of Ethics Pledge

I pledge:

To conduct myself professionally, with truth, accuracy, fairness, and responsibility to the public; To improve my individual competence and advance the knowledge and proficiency of the profession through continuing research and education; and to adhere to the articles of the Member Code of Ethics 2000 for the practice of public relations as adopted by the governing Assembly of the Public Relations Society of America.

I understand and accept that there is a consequence for misconduct, up to and including membership revocation.

And, I understand that those who have been or are sanctioned by a government agency or convicted in a court of law of an action that is in violation of this Code may be barred from membership or expelled from the Society.

> *No state today requires licensure of PR professionals, nor has any ever required it.*

Accreditation (APR) ▼

An alternative method of promoting professionalism in public relations is accreditation. The PRSA began accrediting professionals in 1965. Earning the Accredited in Public Relations (APR) certification requires five years of full-time experience in PR and either a bachelor's degree in a communication field or equivalent work experience. Three APRs must then interview applicants face to face to ascertain whether the candidates have a grasp of the knowledge and skills of the profession. Finally, candidates must pass a four-hour comprehensive written examination.

About one fourth of PRSA's 21,000-plus members are accredited, which represents only about 2 percent of all full-time practicing PR professionals. APRs must complete ongoing training every three years to maintain their accreditation.

Accreditation is a voluntary program administered by the Universal Accreditation Board, a consortium of nine public relations industry organizations, including PRSA. Accreditation identifies PR professionals who have broad knowledge and experience. The program seeks to improve professional practice in public relations. Once certified, professionals can use the APR designation after their names: "John Doe, APR." It is intended to signify the highest professional level of experience and competence. An added benefit is that national job opening postings for PR professionals increasingly list "APR preferred."

Society of Professional Journalists ▼

Because public relations professionals interact with journalists, it is helpful to examine ethical codes that journalists aspire to follow. One that is typical of journalism societies is the Code of Ethics from the Society of Professional Journalists (spj.org). Journalists adopted it at the 1996 SPJ National Convention.

The Code provides four guiding principles:

COURTESY OF SOCIETY OF PROFESSIONAL JOURNALISTS

► Seek truth and report it
► Minimize harm
► Act independently
► Be accountable

Seek truth and report it

Journalists should be honest, fair and courageous in gathering, reporting and interpreting information.

Minimize harm

Ethical journalists treat sources, subjects and colleagues as human beings deserving of respect.

Act independently

Journalists should be free of obligation to any interest other than the public's right to know.

Be accountable

Journalists are accountable to their readers, listeners, viewers and each other.

Online News Association ▼

As innovations with the Internet and mobile technology continue to expand, it is important to consider a relatively new organization, the Online News

Association, and what it offers for the ethical behavior of digital journalists (www.journalists.org/).

Founded in 1999, ONA is a nonprofit organization dedicated to digital journalism, and identifies five main values:

▶ Editorial Integrity
▶ Editorial Independence
▶ Journalistic Excellence
▶ Freedom of Expression
▶ Freedom of Access

Editorial Integrity

Because it can be difficult to determine the source of online information, ONA encourages responsible journalism that clearly differentiates between editorial content and paid promotional material.

Editorial Independence

Online journalists should endeavor to be fair, accurate, objective, responsible and independent in their reporting.

Journalist Excellence

Online journalists should strive for the highest quality in delivering news online.

Freedom of Expression

Access to information online is an important component of free expression—the right to express but also the right to receive information.

Freedom of Access

Online news organizations and journalists should have the same access to information and events as traditional news organizations.

Comparing the Codes

At first glance, there are a number of similarities in the codes of ethics and values for public relations professionals and journalists. There are also, however, some guidelines that offer the potential for conflict, such as:

▶ Distinguish news from advertising and shun hybrids that blur the lines between the two.
▶ Avoid conflicts of interest, real or perceived.
▶ Remain free of associations and activities that may compromise integrity or damage credibility.
▶ Refuse gifts, favors, fees, free travel and special treatment, and shun secondary employment, political involvement, public office and service in community organizations if they compromise journalist integrity.
▶ Deny favored treatment to advertisers and special interests and resist their pressure to influence news coverage.

Public relations professionals should abide by the PRSA Code while also honoring the ethical codes of other professionals with whom they interact. Advancing one profession by encouraging practitioners in another profession to violate their ethics is a recipe for a downward spiral of professional practice for all concerned. It is useful to be aware of the ethical guidelines for other associated professions to avoid coming into conflict with them accidentally.

Code of Ethics

Society of Professional Journalists

Preamble

Members of the Society of Professional Journalists believe that public enlightenment is the forerunner of justice and the foundation of democracy. The duty of the journalist is to further those ends by seeking truth and providing a fair and comprehensive account of events and issues. Conscientious journalists from all media and specialties strive to serve the public with thoroughness and honesty. Professional integrity is the cornerstone of a journalist's credibility. Members of the Society share a dedication to ethical behavior and adopt this code to declare the Society's principles and standards of practice.

Overzealous public relations professionals have offered enticements as part of the invitation to report on a certain topic or to write a certain story. These have come in the form of travel junkets, extravagant parties, gifts and personal favors. Most journalists refuse freebies and explain their newspaper's policy toward such things. There are also situations that are less clear-cut attempts to sway a reporter than the above-mentioned examples. All sorts of conventions and professional sporting events organize "media rooms," "hospitality suites" or other areas that offer everything from beverages and snacks to full-blown buffets. Reporters enjoy the benefits of such offerings and freely scorn organizations for failing to provide such services. Should public relations workers offer nothing and let media fend for themselves? Should members of the media fend for themselves? Probably not.

Business reporters often find themselves dining with people who customarily "buy lunch" for one another. It is a practice regarded as a courtesy, not so much an attempt to buy influence. Nonetheless, this is a sensitive area for business reporters. Many, if not most, business executives understand the independence of the media. They may offer to "pick up the tab." In many cases, reporters will politely refuse, and everyone understands. Increasingly, business editors understand the value of lunches in cultivating sources and want to foster relationships. Reporters, then, receive the discretion and budgets in certain situations to allow such lunches so long as the reporter reciprocates the next time. This scenario tends to work in certain situations when everyone understands that a reporter's work won't be compromised.

Music writers, movie reviewers, and sports beat writers typically receive free tickets or credentials to cover events. It is as much a custom as it is a courtesy. The public relations officials who handle such requests understand that writers and reviewers are free to write what they want. No one is compromised. Some publications, however, routinely refuse all free tickets and purchase them to avoid any appearance of a conflict of interest.

Seasoned reporters also know that many good stories have come to light over a meal or a pitcher of beer for which they pay. Unethical? Or is this friendly act the cost of getting a crucial source to corroborate information. People have a sense of right and wrong. Editors and public relations executives should discuss issues early and often. Many editors routinely say, "If you are

not sure about a situation, ask me." Violations can compromise the ethical codes and standing of both journalists and public relations professionals.

Social criticisms ▼

The public has directed many criticisms at public relations. Some say that much of what professionals call public relations is really propaganda. Others argue that public relations practitioners manipulate language into doublespeak which disguides, distorts or even reverses the meaning of words. In fairness, virtually every profession has unethical practitioners whose behavior is not representative of the vast majority of people in the profession. Another concern is the use of front groups that deceive the public by appearing to be one thing while in truth serving a completely contrary purpose.

The most egregious behaviors are contrary to the PRSA Code, and most public relations professionals do not practice them. The fact that the behaviors do occur, however, points to a danger of public relations when practiced by unethical people.

Propaganda

The American Heritage Dictionary defines propaganda as "the systematic propagation of a given doctrine." The Random House Dictionary defines it as "information or ideas methodically spread to promote or injure a cause, group, nation, etc."

As Chapter 2 mentioned, the word comes from the Latin verb "*propagare,*" which means to reproduce, propagate or enlarge. Pope Gregory XV created an Office for the Propagation of the Faith in 1622 to counter the global spread of Protestantism with missionary efforts of the Catholic Church.

The word was not in common use until World War I. Its original use in modern times was to describe persuasive techniques employed by evil or totalitarian governments, notably Nazi Germany and Adolf Hitler, who assigned Joseph Goebbels as his Minister of Public Enlightenment and Propaganda. Today, however, the meaning has evolved to include attempts to engage in mass influence through skillful use of images, slogans, symbols, and other persuasive devices that play on prejudices and emotions.

One definition of public relations is the "deliberate and planned effort to influence public opinion and policies." How does that differ from propaganda? Often the answer is just a matter of perspective. If an enemy engages in mass persuasion we label it propaganda. If a friendly government engages in the same practices we call it public relations or public information

It can be a matter of point of view. Anthony Pratkanis and Elliot Aronson (2001) observe that the question of whether something is propaganda or just information is often "in the eye of the beholder."

> *When persuasive communication tries to sell a belief system or political dogma we call it propaganda. We classify other persuasive communication more benignly as public relations.*

Sometimes we delineate public relations and propaganda on the basis of subject matter. When persuasive communication tries to sell a belief system or political dogma we call it propaganda. We classify other persuasive communication more benignly as public relations.

Pratkanis and Aronson do not accept that classification system. They argue in their book, "Age of Propaganda" (2001), that "every day we are bombarded with one persuasive communication after another. These appeals persuade not through the give-and-take of argument and debate, but through the manipulation of symbols and of our most basic human emotions. For better or worse, ours is an age of propaganda."

Pratkanis and Aronson believe that persuasion that is devoid of reason and logic is propaganda, and most advertising and many other mass media messages in our post-industrial society involve psychological manipulation that fits the definition of propaganda.

Media literacy advocates encourage media consumers to analyze and understand messages by asking questions. For example, before accepting a message as credible it is advisable to know who created the message and what their agenda or motives might have been. It is particularly advisable to critically examine messages that bombard the audience with exciting visual images that elicit an emotional response but lack real substance.

Doublespeak

Euphemisms are inoffensive words that are less direct and distasteful. We substitute mild words or phrases

for harsh or blunt ones. They make a bad event seem less bad. Instead of saying "die," we substitute the euphemism "pass away."

George Orwell in his book "1984" introduced the words "doublethink" and "newspeak." The totalitarian government of "1984" manipulated language to manipulate thought. They later combined doublethink and newspeak into a new word: **doublespeak**, which is another term for euphemism.

The Cato Institute, a Washington-based public policy research foundation, has criticized the U.S. government for its use of doublespeak. For example, in a report about hunger in the United States, the government found that there was no hunger; instead, it reported "food insecurity."

Euphemisms are conscious obfuscation of language to conceal the real meaning of words. Acronyms and jargon confuse audiences, too, but their use is most often innocent. Euphemisms are more intentionally manipulative. The Cato Institute noted that euphemisms like these corrupt language and allow those in power "to fool others about their activities and evade responsibility and accountability."

Janet Napolitano, the head of the Department of Homeland Security under the administration of President Barack Obama decided "terrorist attack" was perhaps too edgy. She referred to such attacks as "man-caused disasters." Some newsmen grapple with words associated with such groups. Some news organizations refer to terrorists as "gunmen"; others call them "militants."

Public relations professionals have an obligation to communicate in a straightforward and credible way. Journalists and the public both know when a

◄ *George Orwell*

AP/WORLD WIDE PHOTOS

Media literacy questions

Ask these questions about persuasive messages to understand their purpose:

▶ Who produced the message?

▶ What was their purpose or agenda?

▶ Who is the intended audience?

▶ Is the message credible?

▶ Are there other sources of information that verify the information?

▶ Are the other sources of information more reliable?

▶ What technique does the producer use to make the message attractive or believable?

▶ Who makes money or benefits from the message?

▶ Is there more than one way to interpret the message?

Euphemisms or Doublespeak

Euphemism	Meaning
aerial ordnance	bombs and missiles
biosolids	sewage
collateral damage	civilian casualties
ethnic cleansing	murder of other nationalities
downsizing or right-sizing	layoffs
realignment	layoffs
smartsizing	layoffs
pre-owned	used
friendly fire	shooting at your own troops
predawn vertical insertion	invasion of Grenada with early morning paradrop of troops and equipment
negative growth	a decline
routine drug testing	mandatory drug testing
honesty testing devices	lie detectors
fare modifications	airline fare increases
suboptimal	failed
temporarily displaced inventory	stolen goods
substantive negative outcome	death
negative patient care outcome	death
pain compliance	torture

SOURCES INCLUDE: sourcewatch.org and wordspy.com/words/smartsizing.asp

manipulation of language has occurred that obscures the real meaning.

Front groups

Grassroots lobbying refers to efforts to mobilize individuals and groups to support or oppose legislation. The National Rifle Association is famously successful at mobilizing gun owners in opposition to gun control legislation at the national and state levels. Environmentalists, labor unions, extremist religious groups, teachers, senior citizens, and arts groups all mount large-scale grassroots efforts when legislation is under discussion that affects their interests. Grassroots lobbying is both legal and ethical. The First Amendment of the U.S. Constitution guarantees citizens the right to free speech and peaceable assembly, and the right to petition the government.

Sometimes, however, what appears to be a grassroots effort is really **stealth lobbying** by *Astroturf* groups. These campaigns are called Astroturf because the "grass" is artificial. The groups do not really represent genuine public (grassroots) interests. They are **front groups** that appear to do one thing but are set up to do something else. They commonly receive funding by corporations or other large organizations that want to influence the political process without having their names directly associated with the effort.

Front groups represent themselves as large, influential entities. Unnamed individuals can form them, and special interests can fund them. They make a lot of noise and gain a lot of media attention, but they often have a short life. They come into existence to advocate for a particular point of view on an issue and go out of existence when the issue becomes resolved or the election occurs. The groups often have long and impressive sounding names.

The problem is that less-than-honest advocacy only adds to the cynicism in society and further contributes to criticism of the public relations field. Consider Carl Byoir, a public relations pioneer who was said to have created fake grassroots groups such as the National Consumers' Tax Commission that lobbied against particular taxes for chain stores. A&P, a grocery chain that had a vested interest in the cause, guided the effort, but they used the front group as a ruse.

Front groups are legal. They are also protected speech under the First Amendment. However, public relations professionals do not regard them as an ethical practice. The PRSA code specifically forbids this public relations tactic (prsa.org):

> "Front groups: A member implements 'grass roots' campaigns or letter-writing campaigns to legislators on behalf of undisclosed interest groups. . . .
>
> PRSA members should recognize that assisting front groups and individuals that represent undisclosed sponsorships and/or deceptive or misleading descriptions of goals, causes, tactics, sponsors or participants constitutes improper conduct under

Stealth lobbying

Front group	Sponsor
Clean and Safe Energy Coalition	Nuclear Energy Institute
Working Families for Wal-Mart	Wal-Mart
WakeupWalmart.com	Opposition Citizen Group
Global Climate Coalition	American Petroleum Institute
Forest Alliance of British Columbia	Canadian timber industry
Friends of Eagle Mountain	Company seeking to create landfill
Workplace Health and Safety Council	Employers seeking to avoid regulations
Americans Against Unfair Gas Taxes	American Petroleum Institute
Americans for Better Food	Promotion of genetically modified food
Greening Earth Society	Western Fuels Association
Non-smoker Protection Committee	R.J. Reynolds Tobacco Co.
Citizens for Better Medicare	Drug companies

the PRSA Member Code of Ethics and should be avoided."

Most public relations practitioners behave ethically. They work hard at getting out news about their organizations, raising funds, organizing events, and doing all the other things that PR people do. The nature of their clients and the type of messages they communicate do not even easily lend themselves to manipulative or deceitful practices. The PR person for a library, for example, knows that neither she nor the library have much to gain by behaving unethically. Where a lot of money or power is at stake, however, people face greater temptation to bend rules for personal or institutional gain.

PR practitioners have families, mortgages, college tuition to pay, and other commitments. When an employer instructs them to behave unethically, they may have to choose between doing what they are told and doing what they know to be right. That is a difficult position. The PRSA Code says that they should choose the ethical course, even if it puts their employment at risk. Ideally, when pressed to behave unethically, an experienced practitioner may suggest an alternative strategy that is both ethical and persuasive. Sometimes a practitioner will have a conflict of interest in tackling a particular assignment. He or she should make this conflict known to a supervisor so someone else can receive the task.

Tension between PR and journalism

Public relations and journalism have a lot in common—including similar ethical codes. These two professions depend on one another to get information to the public. Public relations professionals rely on media outlets to deliver their messages to mass audiences. Journalists rely on PR practitioners to supply story ideas, background information, and spokespersons for interviews.

Despite the symbiotic nature of the relationship between journalists and public relations practitioners, there exists a tension between the two professions. Journalists operate with the ideal of objectivity; public relations practitioners take a partisan stance in promoting something. Journalists ideally seek the truth based on an understanding of many, if not all, sides of an issue; public relations practitioners work to have their point of view prominently presented. It is common to hear journalists chastise a former colleague who has gone over to "the dark side," i.e., a former journalist who has changed careers to become a PR practitioner. Where does this animosity come from?

The tension stems from how the two professions define news, according to Philip Patterson and Lee Wilkins, authors of "Media Ethics: Issues and Cases." For example, PR practitioners want to see more positive stories about their clients. Journalists, on the other hand, are not interested in writing stories about what they perceive as the status quo. Rather, journalists are drawn toward disruptions in the normal routine. The disruptions are new—or news. Unfortunately, disruptions can mean a crisis for a company that leads to a circling of the wagons and a refusal to comment, just at a time when journalists are seeking information.

It is important to be aware that journalists and public relations practitioners must work together and do need each other. Following the PRSA Code of Ethics, and being aware of the SPJ Code of Ethics and ONA's values also will help practitioners be more effective and more ethical.

Review questions

1. To whom do we have a duty to act ethically?
2. What are the PRSA's six core professional values?
3. Suppose your client orders you to release information with which you personally disagree strongly. What guidance does the PRSA Code of Ethics offer to resolve this?
4. What are the consequences for violating the PRSA Code of Ethics?
5. What are the advantages of seeking APR certification?

6. What are the four guiding principles in the Society of Professional Journalists' Code of Ethics?
7. When should public relations practitioners avoid in their interactions with journalists?
8. How is public relations like propaganda? How are they different?
9. What are front groups and what does the PRSA Code of Ethics say about them?

Supplemental resources online

http://www.sourcewatch.org
http://www.corpwatch.org
http://www.journalists.org
http://www.prwatch.org
http://www.pac.org
http://www.prsa.org
http://www.spj.org

Center for Media and Democracy
Corporate Watch
Online News Association
PR Watch
Public Affairs Council
Public Relations Society of America
Society of Professional Journalists

Chapter references

Black, Jay, Steele, Bob, & Barney, Ralph. (1995). *Doing ethics in journalism: A handbook with case studies.* Boston: Allyn & Bacon.

Christians, Clifford G., Rotzoll, Kim B., Fackler, Mark, McKee, Kathy Brittain, & Woods, Jr., Robert H. (2005). *Media ethics: Cases and moral reasoning.* Boston: Pearson.

Ewen, Stuart. (1996). *PR! A social history of spin.* New York: Basic Books.

Gower, Karla K. (2003). *Legal and ethical restraints on public relations.* Long Grove, IL: Waveland Press.

Guth, David W., & Marsh, Charles. (2006). *Public relations: A values-driven approach.* Boston: Allyn & Bacon.

Lattimore, Dan, Baskin, Otis, Heiman, Suzette T., Toth, Elizabeth L., & Van Leuven, James K. (2004). *Public relations: The profession and the practice.* New York: McGraw-Hill.

Lutz, William. (1996). *The new doublespeak.* New York, NY: HarperCollins.

Parsons, Patricia J. (2004). *Ethics in public relations: A guide to best practice.*

Patterson, Philip, & Wilkins, Lee (Eds.). (2008). *Media ethics: Issues & cases.* New York: McGraw-Hill.

Pratkanis, Anthony, & Aronson, Elliot. (2001). *Age of propaganda: The everyday use and abuse of persuasion.* New York: W. H. Freeman and Company.

Serrin, Judith, & Serrin, William (Eds.) (2002). *Muckraking! The journalism that changed America.* New York: The New Press.

Smith, Bruce L. (2007). *Engaging public relations.* Dubuque, Iowa: Kendall/Hunt.

Stauber, John, & Rampton, Sheldon. (1995). *Toxic sludge is good for you! Lies, damn lies and the public relations industry.* Monroe, Maine: Common Courage Press.

Tye, Larry. (1998). *The father of spin: Edward L. Bernays & the birth of public relations.* New York: Crown Publishers.

Wilcox, Dennis L., Cameron, Glen T., Ault, Phillip H., & Agee, Warren K. (2003). *Public relations: Strategies and tactics.* Boston: Allyn and Bacon.

Woodward, Calvin. (2006, Dec. 3). "Language of politics often tough to comprehend." *Austin American-Statesman*, G1.

Notes

Notes

GLOSSARY OF TERMS

Account executive—In a public relations firm, the liaison between the client and the firm. Coordinates services on behalf of a client.

Acronym—Using the first letter of words in name or phrase. The United Nations shortens to UN, for example. Mothers Against Drunk Driving becomes MADD.

Actual damages—The type of damages that a plaintiff wins based on provable harm. Includes compensation for embarrassment and loss of reputation. Also called general damages.

Agenda setting—A theory of communication that says media set the agenda for what the public talks about by choosing stories to include in the news. Stories important enough to make the news are part of the agenda for public discourse.

Alert—A search engine action that allows readers on the Internet to have news items for a designated topic automatically sent to their e-mails.

Annual report—The SEC requires corporations to do an annual report with information about their finances and operations. Most annual reports contain additional information that is promotional.

Audience—The people who receive a message or to whom public relations targets a message.

Backgrounder—Provides in-depth, objective, and historical information concerning any given topic. It is a useful product for reporters, executives, political leaders, advisers, strategists, and others who would have to spend their own time researching a topic.

Baseline data—A measure of the starting point for purposes of comparing with a future outcome. Also called a benchmark. It is important to have a baseline for the purpose of evaluating outcomes.

Benchmark data—A measure of the starting point for purposes of comparing with a future outcome. Also called a benchmark. It is important to have a baseline for purpose of evaluating outcomes.

Bleed—An image, a photograph or an advertisement that runs to the edge of a page.

Blog—A term shortened from "Web log." It is a single written expression or collection of entries about a wide variety of topics.

Boilerplate paragraph—A paragraph at the end of a company news release that contains information about the history, purpose, and performance of a company or organization.

Boundary spanning—Public relations connects public relations clients with their publics. It spans the gap between clients and publics. Also referred to as linking.

Brainstorming—A technique for quickly gathering many ideas from a group of two or more people for solving a problem.

Central route to persuasion—Part of the Elaboration Likelihood Model. The central route is a direct approach that emphasizes benefits that are more functional. It is more an appeal to logic.

Channel—A medium of communication, such as television, print, voice, e-mail.

Closed-ended question—A question that restricts the answers a respondent can give, such as true or false, multiple-choice responses or numeric responses on a scale.

Confidentiality agreements—An understanding, usually signed, between the PR practitioner and client that prohibits the signer from revealing secret information, such as proprietary information or strategic planning.

Consent—Giving permission or approval.

Controlled media—Media vehicles owned by the organization that publishes them. For example, a university alumni magazine or a corporate annual report.

Controls access—Editors and reporters are news media gatekeepers, deciding whether, when and how they will report a story.

Convergence—A news gathering process that incorporates video online with traditional note-taking and information gathering techniques, giving the consumer a multimedia experience.

Convergent thinking—The second stage of a creative problem-solving process that moves thinking from consideration of many different ideas to focus on a single solution.

Copyright—Legal protection that allows a creator to profit from his or her creative work. Usually noted with this symbol: ©.

Corporate advertising—Advertising that has as its purpose to build image and reputation rather than to sell products. This public relations oriented advertising is also called institutional advertising.

Courtesy bias—Research subjects are inclined to say what they think researchers want to hear. If they know who is sponsoring research, subjects will have a greater inclination to favor the sponsor in their responses. The sponsor of research often remains unidentified to avoid this bias.

Creative Problem Solving (CPS)—A creative problem solving process originated by Sidney Parnes that includes six steps beginning with mess finding and ending with acceptance finding.

Creative process—Any system or process designed to encourage creative thinking.

Creative product—The end result of a creative process. It could be an object, an idea or an image.

Crisis management—A plan for managing crises, usually including the identification of people who will be in charge of the effort and the spokesperson who will interact with media. It sometimes involves a process of reacting to an unexpected event. At other times, it is a proactive plan created before a crisis that tries to anticipate as much as possible the people who will be involved and the steps that will be taken.

Cutlines—Also known as captions, cutlines are descriptions that identify or explain the contents of a photograph.

Daily briefing—A summary of news of interest to a particular individual or group. The intention of the briefing is to give the reader a basic understanding of the day's news events.

Data—Facts, statistics, tables of numbers.

Declaration of principles—The first set of guiding principles for public relations, created by Ivy Lee.

Decorative fonts—also known as art fonts, these fonts are an artist or designer's embellishments of letters, numerals or other characters.

Defamation—Harming someone or something's reputation in the public eye.

Demographic segmentation—Segmenting a population according to demographic categories such as age, sex, race, ethnicity, language spoken, geographic location, religion, sexual orientation.

Disclaimer paragraphs—a paragraph at the bottom of an e-mail that generally states that the e-mail is intended strictly for the receiver of the communication. It appears at the bottom of the e-mail to indicate the confidentiality of its contents.

Disclosure of private facts—Revealing private information not intended for public consumption, especially when the information has no news value and is not a matter of public concern.

Divergent thinking—The first type of thinking in a creative problem-solving process. The emphasis is on generating as many ideas as possible.

Dominant coalition—The key people in the leadership circle of an organization. The handful of people in a position to make important decisions.

Dpi—Dots per inch. A term used to define the resolution of a printed photograph. It actually enumerates the number of dots per square inch of a photograph.

Elaborated likelihood model—A communication theory that identifies two paths to persuasion: the central and the peripheral routes. The first uses direct logical messages. The second uses more indirect, entertaining and emotional messages.

Emoticons—the stringing together of punctuation and other symbols used to depict emotions like happy, shocked, angry, and sad: (:-) :-O >:(:-(They are cute perhaps but not professional or suitable for business communication.

Engineering of consent—A phrase associated with Edward Bernays, who argued that effective public relations could engineer or change public opinion.

Equal Time Rule—Federal regulation that requires broadcasters to provide equal time to candidates in a political election.

Ethos—One of three of the three methods of persuasion identified by Aristotle. It focuses on importance of source credibility.

Exclusives—Story ideas that news organizations would compete against each other to report first. It is a strategy used by media relation specialists in an attempt to secure news coverage.

Executive summary—The first page of a PR plan. It provides a persuasive overview of the strategy and tactics of the plan.

Experimental research—Use of experimental research methods. It involves subjects who are exposed to some treatment or stimulus. Researchers compare the results to those of control subjects that did not receive the treatment or stimulus.

Fact sheet—The fact sheet is a useful tool for both the public relations practitioner and the media. It gives reporters and editors a snapshot of an organization, event, product brand, or political candidacy. It gives reporters, editors, and the public an overview of a particular subject. PR people typically produce a fact sheet to announce an event, a new product or an issue.

Fair comment—A major defense to libel claims that allows media outlets to criticize and comment on the public performances of public figures and public officials.

Fairness Doctrine—A federal regulation that required broadcasters to provide balanced coverage of public interest issues. It was abolished in 1987.

Feedback—Messages from the receivers of communication back to the source of communication.

Flack or flak—Derogatory term for public relations professionals, often used by journalists. It originally was an acronym for a type of German anti-aircraft gun used during World War II. That type of flack attempted to intercept or divert aircraft. In a PR context, it usually refers to a PR person who deflects criticism.

Flesch-Kincaid—One of several methods of calculating the ease with someone can read a document and the amount of education required to read the document easily.

Flexibility of ideas—The ability of a brainstorming or other ideation group to produce a wide range of different kinds of ideas.

Fluency of ideas—The ability of a brainstorming or other ideation group to produce many ideas. The emphasis is on quantity.

Focus group—A research method usually involving eight to 12 subjects who are asked open-ended questions. A trained facilitator guides the discussions, which are usually videotaped.

Formal research—Primary research using either quantitative or qualitative methodologies.

Formative evaluation—Research conducted during the execution of a PR plan to determine how much progress is occurring and whether a change in strategy or tactics is necessary to achieve objectives.

Fourth Estate—Refers to the press as a check on the three branches, or estates, of government.

Free media—Media that is the result of a successfully pitched news release. Unlike advertising, the space in a publication or on air is unpaid or free. The group making the pitch relinquishes control over the use of the information.

Frozen behavior—Changing the behavior of an institution or individual usually involves motivating people to overcome behaviors that are comfortable or habitual—called frozen. People have to be willing to let go of frozen behaviors before change can occur.

Functions of PR—The many different tasks performed by PR practitioners, such as writing news releases, organizing news conferences, writing speeches, and so forth.

Gantt chart—A graphic chart that illustrates the timeline for tactics in a public relations plan.

Gatekeeper—Individuals who control access. Journalists and their editors are media gatekeepers who decide whether, when, and how to use stories generated by public relations.

Guerrilla marketing—Marketing activities that require little expense and that smaller, low budget organizations commonly use. Examples include fliers, low-cost staged events, giving away advertising specialty items, and increasing low cost use of the Internet, blogs, and social marketing sites.

Halftone—A black-and-white photo screened at different levels of resolution. Halftones actually consist of a series of dots of various intensities.

Heuristics—Routine behavior. Automatic responses that enable us to make routine decisions with little thought. Many of the decisions made in a grocery store, for example, have a basis in heuristics. It saves a lot of time when decisions are routine and do not require extended problem solving behaviors.

Horizontal design—Page layouts dominated by multicolumn elements that extend beyond half of the page's width, often the full width of a page.

Hype—Excessive promotion, sometimes involving exaggeration.

Hypodermic needle theory—A now discredited theory of communication that once assumed that media had extraordinary power to persuade audiences. The fear was that media could inject ideas into audiences, who would be powerless to resist them. It is also called the Magic Bullet Theory.

Ideation—A process for generating many ideas. Brainstorming is a common technique.

IMC—Acronym for integrated marketing communication

Informal research—The review of secondary research information and interviewing a few key people to gain some insights about a topic.

Information—Data becomes information when analyzed and understood. The process of making meaning of data produces information.

Informational objective—An objective that focuses on awareness and education but is not action-oriented. Informational objectives contrast with motivational objectives that focus on behavior such as sales, contributions, attendance, e-mail responses, Web site clicks, and return of postcards soliciting additional information.

In-house—Using one's own staff to do something. The organization's own public relations staff does PR in-house.

Inoculating sentence or paragraph—This sentence or paragraph, typically read in a column, letter to the editor or op-ed piece, presents an opposing view, and then refutes it. This tactic aims to inoculate and weaken the other side's best argument, thus strengthening the proponent's position. It is an excellent strategy for writing persuasively.

Integrated marketing communication—Abbreviated as IMC. Companies coordinate all types of marketing communication to achieve maximum impact. This includes integrating advertising, public relations, sales promotion, and other messages.

Intellectual property—A broad area of law that covers creative works, such as books, music, and art. IP law includes copyright and trademark.

Intercept interview—Research interviews that involve intercepting research subjects in a busy location and asking them some questions. It occurs commonly in shopping malls.

Italics—Letters, numerals, and other characters tilted or slanted from the usual upright or Roman position.

Jargon—Words and phrases that belong to a particular activity, profession or group. Most professions have their own terminology or jargon. Insiders well understand the words, but others may not.

Kerning—the space between characters of text. Also called character spacing.

Leading—a measurement of space between lines of type. Also called line spacing.

Libel per quod—A statement that, on the surface, is not defamatory unless the viewer or listener has additional information to understand that the statement harms a person's reputation. Compare with libel per se.

Libel per se—A statement that harms someone's reputation without the need for additional information. Just referring to the person with the words is enough to cause harm.

Lines only—A story told in a cutline only. A small headline also accompanies the caption.

Linking function—Public relations serves the function of linking an organization with its publics. It is similar to the idea of boundary spanning.

Listserv—a list compiled electronically for distributing information through the Internet.

Logos—One of three of the three methods of persuasion identified by Aristotle. It focuses on the importance of logic and evidence to support an argument.

Loop—Public relations is a two-way process. Organizations communicate with their publics. The publics provide feedback. This forms a communication loop. Ludlow massacre

Margin of error—No research is error free. Depending on the size of a sample and the quality of the rest of the research methodology, the results will reflect some amount of error. A small sample typically has a large margin of error. Large samples usually yield small margins of error.

Marketing mix—Marketing involves decisions about product, price, place (distribution), and promotion. These are called the four P's of the marketing mix. Advertising and public relations are part of the promotion component of the marketing mix.

Mea culpa—A Latin term that means, "It's my fault."

Media—Plural of medium.

Media advisory—A notice announcing a schedule to the media when new information concerning an event will become available.

Media kits—A compilation of materials sent to the media that deal with a particular individual, group, product, issue or idea. The contents may include, but are not limited to, fact sheets, backgrounders or position papers, pitches, news releases, features, speeches, editorials and op-ed articles, letters to the editor, memos, brochures, newsletters, advertising, photographs, and other artwork. Also called a press kit.

Media vehicle—A specific television program, magazine or newspaper. For example, television is a medium. The Oprah show is a specific media vehicle.

Medium—A channel of communication, such as radio, television, newspapers, books, and the Internet. The plural of medium is media.

Message—The content of communication. What the source hopes to communicate to the receiver of the communication process.

Modular design—Page layout that combines horizontal and vertical elements in a format squared off with other elements on a page, such as a photograph, a boxed item or an advertisement.

Motivational objective—An objective that focuses on behavioral outcomes. For example, sales, contributions, attendance, e-mail responses, Web site clicks, and return of postcards soliciting additional information. This contrasts with informational objectives that focus on awareness and education but are not action-oriented.

Muckraking—President Teddy Roosevelt coined this pejorative term to describe reporters who do investigative journalism. The term originally referred to a character in John Bunyan's book, "Pilgrim's Progress."

Mug shot—Shows a head and shoulders image of an individual. The mug shot is sometimes called a head shot.

Multitasking—The art of doing many tasks at virtually the same time. People popularly use the term to describe activity carried out while using a personal computer or a sophisticated telephone.

News conference— An announced gathering of media organized to facilitate the dissemination of information to a large group of reporters. Also called a press conference.

News release—A story written in news style that announces information that a source wishes to make available to the public. The news release typically is time-sensitive.

Newsletters—Publications that have limited circulations and more narrowly-defined content than magazines or trade publications

Newsworthy—The impact information has on a community often determines what news organizations judge as newsworthy. The newness or novelty of something also may determine that impact as well as how different it is from the ordinary; how it affects a large number of people; or the definition of an event in quantifiable terms (people, dollars, losses, gains).

Noise—In the SMCR model of communication, noise is anything that interferes with a message. In public relations, the concern is with semantic noise, which results from poorly worded or thought-out messages that audiences cannot easily understand.

Objective—The desired future outcome of a public relations plan. What will it accomplish? Objectives are usually of two types: informational and motivational.

Op-ed—Short for "opposite the editorial page." The editorial page of a newspaper generally contains the opinions of that newspaper. The page typically opposite the editorial page also presents opposing or supporting views.

Open design—Page layout that features few elements that command the reader's attention. Such layout is common to magazines or newsletters.

Opened-ended question—An essay-type of question that asks respondents to answer a question in their own words.

Outsourcing—Hiring people outside an organization to do work. Organizations often outsource public relations activities to PR firms who may handle all or just some of their PR needs.

Pantone—A numbering system used to identify a broad palette of colors. Used with spot color printing.

Pathos—One of three of the three methods of persuasion identified by Aristotle. It focuses on importance of appeals to emotion.

PDF—Portable document format, or pdf, is a file format that allows users to send documents incorporating existing, fonts, photos, and paginated documents.

Peripheral route to persuasion—Part of the Elaboration Likelihood Model. The peripheral route is an indirect approach that targets passive audiences with information that is entertaining, visual, and emotional.

Personal Attack Rule—A federal regulation that required broadcasters to provide a reasonable opportunity for people to respond to attacks on a person's character on the air. Abolished in 2000.

Picas—A measurement that measures one-sixth of an inch. Six picas, then, equal an inch. It is used to identify the width of a column, a photograph or an entire page.

Piggyback survey—A survey that asks questions for several organizations. Organizations save money by sharing the cost of the survey. Each organization pays based on the number of questions asked for it.

Podcasts—A recorded event made available on the Internet for public "downloading."

Points—A measurement used to measure the size of type. Seventy-two points equal an inch.

Post-test—Measuring the results of a message. The goal is to determine, after the fact, the effectiveness of a message.

Press agent—Also called a publicist. This PR practitioner's purpose is to get a client as much media coverage as possible.

Press kit—A compilation of materials sent to the media that deal with a particular individual, group, product, issue or idea. The contents may include, but are not limited to, fact sheets, backgrounders or position papers, pitches, news releases, features, speeches, editorials and op-ed articles, letters to the editor, memos, brochures, newsletters, advertising, photographs, and other artwork. Also called a media kit.

Press party—An organization invites media representatives to a gathering where a PR person usually makes an announcement. There are often refreshments and entertainment. This is unlike a news conference because it is less formal and more social.

Press release—A story written in news style that announces information that a source wishes to make available to the public. The press release typically is time-sensitive. Most commonly called a news release today.

Press tour—There are two types of press tours: 1) A group of journalists is invited to tour a facility together; and 2) A newsmaker may tour the country conducting interviews with the media, usually to promote a book, movie or television program.

Pre-test—Testing a message before it gets used. The goal is to see if the message is effective in accomplishing its objectives before spending substantial money distributing it in print or electronic media. The pretest seeks to answer this question: Does the message work as intended?

Primary audience—The most important target audience(s) for a public relations plan. What groups of people the plan absolutely must reach.

Primary research—Original research created to answer the specific questions of an organization. Surveys, focus groups, experimental studies, and content analysis generally accomplish this.

Privacy—A reasonable expectation to be let alone from government intrusion and from others.

Privilege—A legal term that means immunity from a court order that allows certain communications to remain private. Absolute privileges are rare, but examples include attorney-client and doctor-patient privileges.

Proactive PR—Public relations plans that try to anticipate future circumstances. Rather than reacting to events, proactive PR tries to develop strategies and tactics that best manage an organization's image and reputation.

Process color—Color that uses a combination of four colors, cyan, magenta, yellow, and black.

Product placement—Placing products clearly in view in movies and television programs. The products pay a fee to appear. The Coke cups clearly visible on the desk of the judges for "American Idol" are an example.

Propaganda—Originally, propaganda had to do with the propagation of ideas, values, and beliefs. The Catholic Church, for example, used the Latin word for propaganda in connection with the propagation of the faith. In the 20th century, the term became associated with falsehoods or half-truths used to harm or disparage individuals, groups or nations. The public generally associates it with political communication today.

PSA—Public service announcement. A short radio or television announcement for a nonprofit organization. A PSA is similar to a broadcast commercial, but they are free.

Psychographic segmentation—Segmenting a population based on their values, attitudes, and personality.

Public media—Media for sale on newsstands or broadcast to everyone over the air or on cable or satellite. It contrasts with controlled media that are a media voice for an organization and are distributed in a more controlled manner to that organization's publics.

Public opinion research—Measuring public opinion using research techniques such as in-person interviews and telephone surveys. Polling is a popular form of public opinion research during election seasons.

Public relations firms—Companies that specialize in providing public relations services. Similar to advertising agencies but with a focus on PR.

Puffery—Legal exaggeration in advertising and public relations. No factual claims are made. For example, saying a product is "the best." Audiences understand that there is no specific factual claim being made. It is hyperbole, not to be taken literally.

Pull quotes—Also known as readouts, pull quotes are enlarged and repeated to add emphasis to a significant point or colorful quote in an article or to fill space and "break up the gray."

Punitive Damages—A type of damage award added to actual and special damages in a civil lawsuit. The purpose is to send a message to the defendant for egregious behavior that harmed the plaintiff.

Qualitative research—Research methods that yield unquantifiable information about people's attitudes, beliefs, and lifestyle. PR practitioners use focus groups to produce qualitative research. They call the results soft data and unreliable from a statistical point of view.

Quantitative research—Research that produces hard statistics that are reliable, using probability samples. Public opinion polls use quantitative methods.

Quiet registration period—Refers to the time period after a company offers new securities, but before the registration with SEC has approved.

Quota sampling—A research sample that attempts to include certain categories of respondents. Also called proportional sampling, the researcher might seek to have a certain percentage of men, women, minorities, and other categories. This approach compromises some reliability, but the researcher wants to be certain that the results represent certain voices.

Random sample—Each member of a population should have an equal chance of being selected to be in the sample. The basis of most reliable research is random samples.

Reactive PR—Public relations that mostly reacts to events as they occur. News releases go out when needed. Crises are managed. Rather than using public relations to manage image and reputation through a strategy and tactics, PR practitioners deal with what comes up on a day-to-day basis.

Readability—Body copy that one can easily read is said to be readable. This is a function of font styles and sizes and various other typographical decisions.

Readouts—Also known as pull quotes; readouts are enlarged and repeated to add emphasis to a significant point or colorful quote in an article or to fill space, "break up the gray."

Receiver—The person(s) to whom a source directs a message. They are the intended recipients of messages.

Reliability—One can reproduce reliable research with the same results. Results are consistent.

Remedial need—In public relations planning, a remedial need is generally a crisis that has damaged the image and reputation of an individual or institution. The focus of PR efforts is on restoring or remediating reputation.

Reputation—The general opinion of an individual or institution, usually formed over a period.

Reverse type—Type produced over and that contrasts with a darkened field. In terms of black and white, professionals consider reversed type "white on black."

Roman type—upright type, the opposite of italic type.

Sample—A group of people selected by researchers to represent the opinions of a larger population.

Secondary audience—Public relations plans sometimes target secondary audiences if resources permit. These people are less important to the success of a plan than the primary audiences that the plans must reach.

Secondary research—Information previously collected for another purpose but that is useful and relevant as background for a PR plan. Examples include an organization's own records, library reference documents, Internet research, and trade journals.

Securities and Exchange Commission—A federal agency charged with regulating and protecting the securities markets.

Selective filters—People have the ability to filter out messages that are not relevant to them. These include selective attention, exposure, perception, and recall.

Self-censoring—An unwillingness to share ideas during brainstorming out of fear of being criticized or made the object of ridicule.

Serifs—Endings of a type face—tails and stems—that are thinner than the rest of the letter's formation. Times and Garamond are common serif faces.

Situation analysis—A section of a public relations plan that describes the current situation, with relevant facts about the organization's history, growth, products, sales, market share, strengths, weaknesses, opportunities, and threats.

SMCR model—A model of communication that includes source, message, channel, and receiver. Noise and feedback are also usually discussed as part of the model.

Solution finding—the convergence stage of creative problem solving. Alternatives are evaluated and the best solution(s) are chosen for execution.

Source—the creator of a message. Discussed in the SMCR model of communication.

Spam—Unwanted and promotional e-mail messages.

Spin—The filter through which professionals send information, often negative, to create a positive impression.

Spin doctor—a reference to PR people who attempt to use spin to create a positive impression.

Spot color—Specifies the use of one color to complement black and white. The color may come from a photograph or that which is used, for example, to identify school or corporate colors. It draws attention to an otherwise ordinary document.

Staged events—Events designed to be newsworthy to attract media who will do free news stories about the event and the organization.

Strategy—The overall arrangement for a PR plan. A broad, nonspecific statement about the approach to take. Strategy usually makes clear the theme or underlying message of the plan.

Summative evaluation—Conducted at the end of a public relations campaign a summative evaluation answers the question: Did the plan achieve its objectives?

Surveillance function of media—One of the functions of media according to Uses and Gratifications Theory. This function focuses on monitoring the environment and includes news and weather.

SWOT analysis—Part of a situation analysis in a public relations plan. It outlines an organization's strengths, weaknesses, opportunities, and threats.

Tactics—The action steps to take to implement a strategy and accomplish the objectives of a PR plan. They can include news releases, fact sheets, special events, and other activities.

Target audience—The specific group of individuals to whom public relations specialists will direct messages. They are also termed primary and secondary audiences.

Trade publications—publications that reach an audience within a particular industry.

Trademark—An identifying mark that shows that a product is authentic and protected by a company or corporation. Usually noted with this symbol: ® or ™.

Two-step flow—A theory that PR plans should target opinion leaders, whose opinions will flow down to those they influence in the broader audience.

Uses and gratifications—A theory that says people use media for a variety of reasons, including surveillance of their environment, entertainment, reinforcement of opinions and values, and companionship.

Validity—A characteristic of research. Validity requires that research results reflect the real status of what the research is measuring. It is often a function of asking good, unbiased questions.

Vertical design—Page layout dominated by one- or two-column elements in a multicolumn format. The design generally guides the eye from the top of the page to the bottom of a page.

Viral marketing—A practice using the Internet that forwards information from one source to at least one other source who, in turn, stands to forward the information to other readers, Web sites, blogs or elsewhere electronically

VNR—video news release.

VOA—Voice of America

Voice of America—An organization of the U.S. government that broadcasts radio and television propaganda to other countries around the world. Also called VOA.

White space—Space purposely left blank to allow the other elements on a page to attract the eye of the reader.

INDEX